Nameless Towns

NAMELESS TOWNS

Texas Sawmill Communities, 1880–1942

By Thad Sitton and
James H. Conrad

University of Texas Press
Austin

Requests for permission to reproduce material from this work should be
sent to Permissions, University of Texas Press, Box 7819, Austin, TX
78713-7819.

∞ The paper used in this publication meets the minimum requirements
of American National Standard for Information Sciences—Permanence
of Paper for Printed Library Materials, ANSI z39.48-1984.

Library of Congress Cataloging-in-Publication Data
Sitton, Thad, 1941–
    Nameless towns : Texas sawmill communities, 1880–1942 /
by Thad Sitton and James H. Conrad. — 1st ed.
        p.   cm.
    Includes bibliographical references and index.
    ISBN 0-292-77725-6 (alk. paper). — ISBN 0-292-77726-4 (pbk. : alk.
paper)
    1. Texas—History, Local.   2. Texas—Social life and customs.
3. City and town life—Texas—History.   4. Sawmills—Texas—History.
5. Lumbering—Texas—History.   I. Conrad, James H.   II. Title.
F391.S6254   1998   97-15563
976.4'06—dc21

No wonder the hotel was empty, the bank closed, the stores out of business: for on the other side of the railroad, down by the wide pond that once held beautiful, fine-grained logs of longleaf pine, the big sawmill that for twenty years had been the pulsing heart of this town was already sagging on its foundations, its boilers dead, its deck stripped of all removable machinery. Within the town grass was beginning to grow in the middle of every street, and broken window lights bespoke deserted houses. In county after county across the South the pinewoods have passed away. Their villages are Nameless Towns, their monuments huge piles of saw dust, their epitaph: "The mill cut out."

R. D. Forbes, 1923

For Vastine Polk
and all those
who shared
his fate.

Contents

Preface and Acknowledgments

Southern "company towns" began with Jamestown, Virginia, in 1607, so the sawmill communities of East Texas followed in a long tradition. During the late nineteenth and early twentieth centuries, textile mills, mining companies, cotton plantations, sawmills, and other large enterprises all found it expedient to create and operate proprietary communities to house, support, and control their employees.

Despite their economic importance, the hundreds of East Texas sawmill towns, large and small, that came and went between 1880 and the beginning of World War II have received scant attention from historians. The Texas "Paul Bunyans," and the big woods and sawmill towns in which they plied their trades, have played little part in the state's popular historiography, which has been so preoccupied with cowboys, cattle kings, oil barons, and the wide open spaces that it sometimes even omitted the cotton farmers.

Nonetheless, Texas's first industrial revolution began in the virgin pine and hardwood forests of East Texas, and for decades before and after 1900 the timber companies drew tens of thousands of Texans into their sawmill towns and woods camps. It was a rare family that remained entirely untouched, and sometimes industrial contacts were rude indeed. One author's grandfather was eviscerated by a fragment from an exploding saw blade around 1900 (while trying to make enough money to escape the mill to attend pharmacy school), survived his injury, became an independent druggist, then—somewhat to his disgust—spent his declining years as pharmacist in the commissary of the Angelina County Lumber Company at Keltys. Lumber-industry work might be dangerous and poorly paid, but often the sawmills were the only game in town.

Little has been written about the Texas timber towns, and the authors of this book concentrated on the social historian's first directive, "tell what life was like." To that purpose, oral histories, written memoirs, and company records have been sawtimber for our mill. This book is a social history of life in the company towns of East Texas during the bonanza era of "cut and get out." We are not economists, and this is not intended to be an economic history of the timber industry. But everyday life in the sawmill towns derived from the economic realities that led scholar Ruth Allen to label the East Texas timber counties as a "Land of Deep Poverty." Much of this book does deal with the economics of the lumber industry in Texas—as ordinary people experienced those economic realities.

Some historians have described East Texas mill workers as dull, docile, and colorless company men, very different from the romantic loggers of the northeast. However, we found this view of the East Texas sawmill employee rather difficult to reconcile with some of our data—with the accounts of fistfights on the mill floor, stomp-and-gouge combats in the mill-town street, industrial sabotage, "railroad ladies," pistol-packing woods crew men, and other things, including monthly job turnover rates sometimes exceeding 15 percent. By their own testimony (and by evidence in the voluminous Kirby Lumber Company papers and other company records), Texas sawmill hands seem not to have been so dull and docile after all.

Hundreds of Texas sawmill towns came into existence, thrived for a time, and passed away during the sixty years between 1880 and World War II. All were of equal interest, but readers will notice an emphasis in our book on Wiergate in Newton County, Diboll and Manning in Angelina County, and the ten or so Kirby Lumber Company towns in southeastern Texas. We simply followed the data where it led and focused on the towns for which we found the most. The Newton History Center holdings, the oral history transcripts in the Diboll Public Library, and the Kirby Lumber Company papers in Nacogdoches and Houston provided especially rich veins of evidence.

Secondary sources for the Texas lumber industry form a rather short list, but all proved invaluable to our research. Ruth Allen's *East Texas Lumber Workers* (1961) and Robert S. Maxwell and Robert D. Baker's *Sawdust Empire* (1983) (as well as Maxwell's earlier writings) provided essential information and interpretations. Hamilton Pratt Easton's pioneering dissertation, "A History of the Texas Lumbering Industry" (1947), offered early interview data and a wonderful eyewitness account of operations at Wiergate during that mill's last days. And among more recent publications, Megan Biesele's oral history of Diboll, *The Cornbread Whistle* (1986), and W. T. Block's monumental three-volume reference work, *East Texas Mill Towns and Ghost Towns* (1994), also proved indispensable.

Besides these earlier scholars, living and dead, the authors wish to thank several individuals who helped us during the research phase of our book. Bonnie Smith, chairman of the Newton County Historical Commission, unlocked the remarkable resources of the Newton History Center. Pauline Hines shared her memories of Wiergate and guided us to other sources of information. Doyle Smith, former postmaster at Wiergate, graciously allowed us to make use of his personal photo collection. For unfailing help and courtesy, we thank the staffs of the East Texas History Center of Stephen F. Austin State University and the Houston Metropolitan Research Center of the Houston Public Library. Mark E. Martin of the T. L. L. Temple Memorial Archives in Diboll and Carol Riggs of the Texas Forestry Museum in Lufkin assisted us in locating photographs of the sawmill towns, and Carol supplied us with important information from the museum's East Texas Sawmill Data Base Project. Finally, we offer our thanks to the University of Texas Press's manuscript readers, Henry C. Dethloff of Texas A&M University and Robert L. Schaadt of the Sam Houston Regional Library and Research Center, for their helpful suggestions.

Thad Sitton and James H. Conrad
Austin, Texas

Chapter One

INTRODUCTION

D URING October of 1899, R. M. Keith, a land agent for the Central
Coal and Coke Company of Kansas City, Missouri, arrived at the
backwoods community of Ratcliff, Texas, in eastern Houston County,
and began to buy tens of thousands of acres of virgin pine timber. The
community had been established ten years before by J. H. Ratcliff, who
built a small sawmill and opened up a post office at the site. Word of the
rich Yankee stranger spread quickly among the hardscrabble farmers and
free-range stockmen of the vicinity, and many rushed to strike deals with
Keith, selling "stumpage," the right to cut all marketable timber on their
properties. Many local people still regarded their pine forests as an im-
pediment to agriculture, more a curse than a blessing, and happily sold
them to the outsider for less than two dollars an acre.[1]

Throughout 1900, Keith quietly went about his business of buying
120,000 acres of land and stumpage, but then on January 10, 1901, he purchased Ratcliff's "peckerwood" sawmill, and things began to move
swiftly. Immediately, the mill started cutting lumber with which to build
a big mill and sawmill town. By June of 1902, a 486-foot sawmill, a 450-
foot planer mill, a commissary store, company offices, and hundreds of
employee houses had been constructed, and three screaming band saws
powered by a mighty Corliss steam engine swung into action, converting
local sawtimber to yellow-pine lumber at the rate of 300,000 board feet
each eleven-hour work day. Mill hands loaded the lumber on boxcars and
shipped it to the main line at Lufkin on the new company railroad, the
Eastern Texas. Conductors on the main line coming into Lufkin, exag-
gerating only slightly, now encouraged passengers to take a side trip to

Ratcliff on the Eastern Texas Railroad to see "the largest sawmill in the world." The owners organized their new enterprise as the Texas and Louisiana Lumber Company, a wholly owned subsidiary of the Central Coal and Coke Company, but everyone called the mill the "4-C."[2]

By summer of 1902, Houston County farmers looked out with wonder and disquiet at a lumber boomtown suddenly arrived in their midst. Every evening at dusk, at the flip of a company switch, steam-powered generators instantly illuminated every structure in the new "company town," from the company offices to the employees' smallest shotgun house, creating an island of bright electric light in a dark sea of "coal-oil" countryside. Yankee engineers and mill managers, imported black mill hands, and exotic Italian yard workers that locals called "Dagos" now walked the dusty streets of a transformed Ratcliff, conversing in alien accents and foreign tongues. By 1910, the 4-C's Ratcliff had a thousand-man work force in woods and mill, a total population approaching ten thousand, a telephone company, a newspaper, several cafes and stores, and a variety of saloons and other businesses. Harvey Steed, one-time owner of a Ratcliff store, recalled that during the boom years Ratcliff grew so crowded on Saturdays that "you couldn't hardly squeeze your way down the sidewalk."[3]

Local people once had ordered their daily lives to the casual rhythms of season and sun and had worked from "can see to can't," but now mill whistles blew reveille in the dark and regulated lives by the clock. In 1901, the manager at a new mill town had directed his Houston agents to purchase the most basic operating gear for the heavy-industry workplace, newly arrived in the East Texas backwoods. "You had better buy them a large steam whistle with a 2" outlet," he wrote, "something that will wake the natives up and get them to the mill in time to start up and also a suitable clock for the mill."[4]

By the turn of the century, many "natives" in the Texas pineywoods counties already had learned to live with the sound of clock-driven mill whistles ringing in their ears. C. B. Spivey of Cherokee County recalled that around 1905 he could stand on his front porch in the morning and hear, from near and far, the wake-up whistles of twenty sawmills.[5] By 1905, lumbering and sawmilling had become the state's most important industry, and two years later over six hundred Texas mills sawed an all-time high of 2.25 billion board feet of pine lumber that made Texas the nation's third-largest lumber producer. The period from 1907 to 1916 was the "golden decade" of Texas lumbering, with production averaging over

1.75 billion board feet a year. During this boom era, timber was king, and sawmill companies could do little wrong.[6] Many Texans agreed with the *Jasper Newsboy*, which editorialized in 1911, "in Texas a smokestack is as sacred as a church steeple."[7]

Between 1880 and 1890, the first generation of rural East Texans made the decision to leave the farm for company employments in lumber camp and sawmill town, and many of them soon got "pine resin in their blood," as one man told, and they stayed—along with their children and in-laws and grandchildren—until the companies "cut out and got out" and the timber boom busted.[8] Vivian Warner's report of how her father left the farm to go to work for Southern Pine Lumber Company at Diboll was told in one version or another by thousands of families. Warner recalled: "My father left home when he was 14 years old. He was plowing one day, and when he plowed to the end of the row, he laid his plow over, un-hitched the mule, and said, 'I plowed my last row.'" Then, he took a job in the Southern Pine woods crew, remaining in company employment the rest of his working life.[9]

Why he remained was a question that Warner's father sometimes asked himself, and many other mill employees doubtless did the same. Working and living conditions in the sawmill towns were less than perfect. While generally sympathetic to the bonanza-era companies, lumber-industry historians Robert Maxwell and Robert Baker nonetheless observed of the early Texas sawmill:

> It devoured the men, father and son; it ate up the forest; it transformed the countryside into a desert of sawdust dunes; it destroyed the tranquillity of rural life; and finally, more often than not, it destroyed itself—by fire. Sawmill work offered long hours, low pay, little chance of advancement, an uncertain future, and, by the law of averages, a good chance of at least one serious injury.[10]

In truth, although it may have been more interesting than following a plow, timber-industry work was risky. Lumbering was the most dangerous industrial operation at the beginning of the twentieth century, seven times the national average, and sawmilling ranked third, immediately after coal mining.[11] For example, during 1925 alone, 582 of the Kirby Lumber Company's total 4,762-person work force suffered a significant injury, and at one Kirby mill town 26.3 percent of the workers sustained injury.[12] As Brown Wiggins of Hardin County grimly observed, "everything that could happen to a man happened to us." Summing up a lifetime spent in mill towns and logging camps, Wiggins seemed a little uncertain about

Flatheads with a crosscut saw stand over a log. East Texas backwoodsmen like these tree cutters adapted rather quickly to the demands of the timber industry.
Courtesy of Texas Forestry Museum, Lufkin, Texas.

why he had laid down the plow or had never returned to it. A half century of working for the big companies had left him with mixed feelings.

> I spent most of my life in the woods, working in sawmills, around the edge of the Thicket. Most of the mills were small, but I liked to work in the bigger ones, those that ran about a hundred thousand feet per day. There were about fifty houses, the white people would be on one side of the mill and the Negro quarters on the other. They just stuck the houses here, there, and yonder, no order to it, and it didn't look too good, but we made lots of lumber. They gobbled up most of the finest timber in our country, and the sawmills didn't make too much out of it, and we didn't do too well either.[13]

In Wiggins's father's boyhood, twenty years before the great 4-C mill came to Ratcliff, a bird's-eye view of southeastern Texas would have revealed a vast, almost unbroken forest, cleared for cotton, corn, and sugarcane fields at scattered sites along alluvial valleys and around Nacogdoches, Newton, Jasper, Livingston, and other small communities of a few hundred souls. An ancient hardwood forest of oaks, gums, and cypresses dominated the river valleys of the Sabine, Angelina, Neches, and Trinity rivers and their many tributaries. Moisture-loving loblolly pine thrived on slightly higher ground along the bottoms, and the sandy uplands grew mixed groves of loblolly, shortleaf pine, and various hardwoods. The great East Texas forest was thinner and more open to the north and west, where small prairies occasionally broke its expanse, especially in the "Redlands" around Nacogdoches. East and south of Nacogdoches toward the Sabine, rainfall increased, the forest grew thicker and more luxuriant, and the "openings" gradually disappeared. Sweeping across the Sabine into southeastern Texas and reaching beyond the Trinity River was the westernmost wedge of a huge, 230,000-square-mile Southern forest of longleaf pine, *Pinus palustris,* the most valuable of all Southern pine species.[14] Periodic fires set by man and lightning swept through the thin grasses and leaf debris under the longleafs, killing other species but leaving the fire-resistant pines unharmed. The result was a vast forest of open parklike stands, where travel was easy and a person could see a long way. The reddish brown longleaf trunks were huge, often exceeding three feet in diameter and soaring fifty feet to the first limb. In 1992, 103-year-old Walter Cole of Jasper County recalled the ancient longleaf forest from his boyhood.

> It'll never come back like it was when I's a boy. When I was a boy I could ride a horse a hundred miles cross country through Louisiana and Texas in virgin

timber, pine timber. And it was longstraw, we called it longhaired pine—longleaf pine. It was two-thirds heart, fine timber, wasn't a limb on it for fifty feet. You could see a deer a half mile across the pineywoods. I've cut a-many a one. I've sawed trees I had to ring saw; I'd walk around em to saw em down—saw em all around and wedge em over. And when they hit the ground, you'd hear em three, four mile.[15]

Several generations of Southerners gradually had spread across the longleaf "pine barrens" from Virginia, through Georgia, Mississippi, Alabama, and Louisiana, until they reached the end of the great forest west of the Trinity River.[16] By 1870, the scattered settlers of southeastern Texas had become accustomed to the great Southern forest and practiced a form of agriculture and a method of stock raising well adapted to the big woods. Nearly all were "backwoodsmen," skilled in techniques for pioneering the forested environment.[17] Folklorist William A. Owens, who interviewed the children and grandchildren of the southeastern Texas settlers, described a typical arrival of the Southern backwoodsmen.

Camping out under trees while they worked, they built log houses, covered them with hand-split boards, and chinked and daubed them with red clay. They built stick-and-daub chimneys. Fireplaces were for heat and cooking, and for light at night, the only light except for the red, smoky glare of a lightwood knot. They cleared only as much land as they could work with one horse hooked to a Georgia stock or Kelly turning plow, enough land for a little cotton, a little corn—for a patch of sweet potatoes and blackeyed peas. Their cattle grazed on the open range. So did the razorback hogs. There was elbowroom to spare. They had no wish to obliterate the wilderness.[18]

Southeastern Texas backwoodsmen were cotton entrepreneurs, as well, especially before the Civil War, and where soil and circumstances encouraged this they raised a good bit of the white staple. Even the longleaf counties of Newton, Jasper, and Sabine produced two thousand to eight thousand bales a year during the decade of the 1850s, this at a time when the biggest Texas cotton counties produced over twenty thousand bales.[19]

The sandy pine uplands, the so-called pine barrens, proved poor cotton soil, however, and many southeastern Texans depended more on running "rooter hogs and woods cattle" on the surrounding free range than they did on farming cotton and corn. Southern woods-adapted stock-raising practices were at least two centuries old by 1870.[20] Most stockmen ran both cattle and hogs on the open range, letting them go semiferal and fend for themselves most of the year, locating, penning, and butchering

A stand of mature, virgin longleaf pine near Wiergate, early 1920s. The longleaf-pine forests that dominated upland areas of southeastern Texas had a parklike quality, with little undergrowth. *Courtesy of the Newton History Center, Newton, Texas.*

them as needed. Periodically, the stockmen gathered some up and drove them to market—often eastward through the longleaf to the plantations of Louisiana or even to New Orleans. People worked hogs and cattle with dogs in much the same way and even seemed to think about them much the same; even the adjectives used to describe stock seemed interchangeable—"rooter hogs and woods cattle," "woods hogs and rooter cattle." These forest-adapted hogs and cattle wandered into the pine uplands in spring and summer, then moved into creek and river bottoms in the winter—the cattle feeding on switch cane and the hogs on acorns. In the lean days of midsummer, hogs ate almost everything, including last year's soured acorns, berries, grass, earthworms, carrion, freshwater mussels on creek sandbars, and river fish trapped in drying pools. Meanwhile, cattle foraged for sparse grass on the pine hills under the virgin longleafs.[21]

"Good range" in this Southern stock tradition could be an entirely wooded environment, and how much land a family owned made little difference; the Southern stockman's landholding was his home base, only. Solomon Alexander Wright's family settled during the 1830s in what would become Jasper and Newton counties, and after Grandfather Wright died around the time of the Civil War his labor of land on the Sabine went to Solomon's father. Solomon wrote of his 180-acre homeplace between Nichol's Creek on the north and Big Cypress Bayou and Boggy Branch on the South: "It was the most ideal location for a ranch imaginable. It was a wilderness country even after my time. Our range—not all owned, but what we had use of—comprised about 80,000 acres, the west half slightly-rolling, longleaf pine woods, the east half marshes, alternating with strips of level pine woods and numerous small swamps."[22]

Solomon Wright viewed the land from the perspective of a typical Southern stockman, and his "ideal ranch" was all big woods. The Wrights's small landholding mattered little, since everything was open range, and the only fences were "fence-them-out" fences around rare cultivated fields. Every family had the customary right to range their stock on the lands of everybody else, and this tradition would continue for a century. So, why own more land than you needed? Basic to the way of life of many East Texans in 1870 was the Southern custom of the "free range" or "open range," which gave every family a variety of usufruct rights on other families' land. Besides the right to range stock, people could trespass, hunt, fish, rob bee trees, gather hickory nuts, build stock pens, and—when the time was right to encourage grass growth under the pines—set the woods on fire.[23]

As historian Thomas Clark noted, Southern backwoodsmen of the nineteenth century often lived subsistence-farming and hunting-and-gathering lifestyles, employing knowledge and techniques learned from the southeastern Indians, but they also tried to make money.[24] They had no wish to "obliterate the wilderness" in their economic exploitation of it, as William Owens noted, but—lost in the great forest—this scarcely seemed possible. As they had farther east and in earlier generations, in East Texas Southern backwoodsmen girdled trees to clear "new ground" for cotton, trapped furbearers, shot deer for their skins, killed wild cattle for their hides and tallow, and nibbled away at the awesome forest resources, transporting these wilderness products by water to Harrisburg and Houston on Buffalo Bayou, Beaumont on the Neches, and Orange on the Sabine. Beginning during the 1840s, fine bottomland white oaks were laboriously axed, sawed, and split for barrel staves and hoop poles, and riverside cypresses were felled and rived for shingles; these products then were floated downriver beside bales of cotton on flatboats, keelboats, and steamboats. Soon after the founding of Beaumont and Orange, part-time loggers and raftsmen began floating cypress logs directly to the new shingle mills and (by the 1850s) small steam sawmills operating in these towns. Many of the cypress-shingle logs and whiteoak-stave trees had "free range" origins like the pineywoods hogs and cattle.[25] Log raftsman Louis Bingham explained: "A lot of people in the olden days, they cut them old cypress, they just run em out of there and carried em to the mill. They didn't belong to nobody—belonged to them, if they got em."[26]

Before the Civil War, most up-country sawmills were small, water-powered, sash-saw affairs that combined the slow production of lumber with ginning cotton and grinding corn. In such a mill, a sash-saw blade fixed within an upright wooden frame was moved up and down by a crank attached to a large, over-shot water wheel. The log moved against the saw, which cut only on the downstroke, either pushed by hand (often on a wagon) or drawn by a paul-and-ratchet gear worked off the water wheel. A water-powered sash saw cut no more than two or three thousand board feet a day and went so slowly that the sawyer could read the Bible while he operated it.[27]

Gradually, primitive steam engines (some salvaged from wrecked steamboats) began to replace water power on the sash-saw rigs, lumber production went up, and Bible reading in the mill ceased. Few such sawmills operated before the Civil War in the East Texas up-country, but even before Texas won its independence from Mexico, certain operations on the edge of the coastal plain presaged the big mills and mill towns to come. The cutting, transport, and sawing of timber required a considerable work force, even for a small mill, and that work force had to be housed and provided for. William Zuber visited the Harris brothers' operation at the head of navigation on Buffalo Bayou in 1831 and offered this description.

> The Harrises had built a sawmill and grist mill, combined as one. It was propelled by steam and drove two saws, which worked perpendicularly, like whipsaws worked by hand. This was the first steam mill I ever saw—the first built west of the Sabine River, and, in 1831, the only one in Texas. Most of the land owned by the Harris brothers was a forest of noble pines growing within two hundred yards of Bray's Bayou. These were cut down for saw stocks, hauled to the bayou, floated to the mill, and sawed into lumber. The Harrises boarded their employees, the number of whom, including choppers, haulers, floaters, sawyers, and cooks, were generally twenty men.[28]

Such mills remained rarities until the Civil War and were limited to the coastal counties, such as Orange and Harris. The Census of 1850 listed no sawmills, water powered or steam powered, in Tyler County and few elsewhere, and the Census of 1860 noted no Hardin County sawmills.[29] Part of the problem was technology; sash-saw mills cut slowly, and the primitive steam engines of the time often broke down or blew up. Circular saws had reached the South, but before the Civil War they could not handle logs much larger than sixteen inches in diameter and so were entirely inadequate for the massive pine timber. As a consequence, as late as the 1850s, Texas newspaper editors constantly bemoaned the fact that—despite the state's great inland forests—most Texas construction lumber still had to be imported by sea at very high rates.[30]

Beginning around 1875, everything began to change very quickly, as Yankee lumbermen, railroads, and improved sawmill technologies came to the pineywoods. Far to the north and east, timber companies were cutting out in the white pineries of Pennsylvania, Wisconsin, and Minnesota, and the timbermen—casting about for new virgin forests to exploit—swiftly overcame their old prejudices against resin-filled Southern "yellow pine." Pennsylvania lumbermen Henry J. Lutcher and G. Bedell Moore were the first of many northerners to come south. Traveling across southeastern Texas in 1877, they surveyed with growing excitement the virgin longleaf forest, where stumpage might be had for as little as fifty cents an acre, and estimated the log-floating capacity of every stream they passed. Lutcher and Moore chose Orange on the Sabine River as the site of their first sawmill, which soon cut 80,000 to 100,000 board feet a day, roughly quadrupling the daily production of the next largest Texas mill.[31]

Other northerners quickly followed the pioneers in establishing big mills, and there were other good reasons to come south after 1876. With the repeal of the U.S. Homestead Act of 1866 at the end of Reconstruction, Southern legislatures threw open their states' public lands for unrestricted purchasing, and homegrown investors and the men Southern historian Thomas Clark called "the carpetbaggers of the woods" rushed to purchase them. Clark noted:

> In most of the wooded South in 1876 it was possible for speculators and mill men to manipulate the land laws to acquire large tracts of pine and hardwood lands at ridiculously minimal cash outlay. [After the 1866 Homestead Act was repealed] to permit unrestricted cash entry, the door to the Southern timberland was thrust wide open. Land speculators of every stripe rushed into the region in search of virgin tracts of timber to lay low. After 1880, speculators and lumbermen gobbled up millions of acres of virgin timberlands at the standard century-old price of $1.25 an acre.[32]

Profits from such land purchases could be very great, and it was not uncommon for a northern company to find that no sooner had its trusted land agent reached the Southern pineries than he had turned disloyal, buying land for himself or for some other company that had offered him a better commission. During the 1870s, investors often found that they could buy an acre of virgin pine forest carrying as much as 20,000 board feet of timber for only $1.25—timber that sold as processed lumber for $200! No wonder, then, that the speculators sometimes preceded the lumbermen, who were then obliged to buy back stumpage at inflated prices, and that by 1885, a scant nine years after the new Homestead Act of 1876, Texas had sold or given away about 32 million acres of state land, most of it heavily forested.[33]

Texas railroads were primary recipients of the free public timberlands. The state awarded sixteen sections of land, 10,240 acres, for every mile of track constructed, and this could be track of any gauge and in any location. The first mile of Texas railroad track had been built near Houston in 1853, but the great era of state railroad construction came between 1880 and 1902, at which time the state's ten-thousand-mile rail system was virtually completed.[34]

Also by 1902, and not coincidentally, most of the large blocks of East Texas timberland had been purchased by a relatively small number of

Texas and out-of-state lumber companies. From first to last, East Texas bonanza-era lumbering and railroading went hand in hand. Backed by financier Paul Bremond, the narrow-gauge Houston, East, and West Texas Railroad built north from Houston to Shreveport from 1875 to 1886, and by the time the line reached Cleveland five sawmills with the combined capacity of 100,000 board feet a day cut timber behind its construction crews. Other lines followed, with the same effects on new sawmills and bonanza lumbering operations. The Texas and New Orleans built from Beaumont to Dallas, crossing Bremond's line at Nacogdoches. As in the cases of the HE & WT ("Hell Either Way Taken") and the T & NO ("Time No Object," or "Turnips and New Onions"), the new railroads invited witticisms with their initials, but they engaged in serious business. Every new track gobbled up vast quantities of nearby timber for ties, trestles, and fuel, opened the virgin forest along its right-of-way to swift exploitation, spawned lines of sawmill towns (and county-seat towns) as it built north, and shifted East Texas in one decade from an economy based on cotton to one based chiefly on sawtimber. Already by 1904, 62 sawmills operated along the tracks of the Gulf, Colorado, and Santa Fe Railroad; and by 1906, 230 sawmills with a potential annual capacity of 2.4 billion board feet cut timber along the tracks of the Santa Fe, the Houston, East, and West Texas, the Texas and New Orleans, and the International and Great Northern.[35]

Throughout the process of opening up the great East Texas forest, railroad builders and timbermen often were closely linked and sometimes were one and the same. Such was the case with a third major railroad, the Atcheson, Topeka, and Santa Fe. In association with lumberman John Henry Kirby, the AT & SF bought Kirby's Gulf, Beaumont, and Kansas City Railroad (which went nowhere near Kansas City) and extended the line up the easternmost tier of East Texas counties to Jasper in 1902 and to San Augustine in 1903. This line played a large role in helping Kirby Lumber Company become the biggest producer of yellow-pine timber in the South.[36] Mainly strung out along the Santa Fe, by 1907 the fourteen Kirby sawmills and sawmill towns cut a combined total of 950,000 board feet of timber every eleven-hour working day.

"Sawmilling is logging, logging is railroading," one Kirby mill superintendent liked to say; "learn logging and railroading, and the rest is easy."[37] This was true in more than one sense. No sooner did the advancing main line spawn a new company mill town than the mill town spawned a company railroad system, eventually reaching far out into the surrounding

Main-line locomotive and crew. *Courtesy of the Texas Forestry Museum, Lufkin, Texas.*

forest and usually—even if run for only a few miles or so—organized as a commercial carrier.[38]

By 1880, improvements in sawmill technology necessitated railway delivery systems to feed the increasingly voracious saws. Big Allis sixty-inch and seventy-two-inch circular saws were the early standard, capable of making short work of the largest logs, and during the 1880s steam log-carriage machinery appeared, along with the first single-cutting band saws, continuous blades rotating on eight- or nine-foot "dogs," or wheels. A decade later the band saws had become double-cutting, toothed on both edges, slicing a log from alternate ends on each swift to-and-fro of the steam carriage. The new saws were powered by Corliss steam engines of several hundred horsepower that turned massive flywheels of over twenty feet in diameter, which in turn ran belts to energize the saws and other mill machinery. The Sabine, Neches, and Trinity rivers, as well as lesser East Texas streams, had proved too shallow, lacking in gradient, and seasonally variable in flow to consistently supply such sawmills with floated timber, so after 1880 virtually every new operation included a tramway system to transport its timber to the mill. "Sawmilling is logging, logging is railroading," and at new mills large and small companies built tramway systems at the same time that they constructed millponds, commissary stores, employee housing, and the mills themselves.

Each sawmill town was a railroad town, as well, and Manning in the Angelina County longleaf forest typified many. The company railroad, the Shreveport, Houston, & Gulf ("Shove Hard and Grunt"), despite its official name, ran only a few miles to connect with the nearby Texas & New Orleans at Huntington. From the mill, a tramway system stretched into the company's timberland, its rails frequented by five steam locomotives and a Shay woods engine, which normally stayed in the woods with the steam skidder and steam loader. The locomotives were equipped with "cabbage-head" smokestacks—huge, round, bowl-like screens designed

A Shay locomotive and log train on the way to the sawmill. *Courtesy of the East Texas Research Center, Stephen F. Austin State University, Nacogdoches, Texas.*

to prevent sparks from setting woods fires. The engines, like the rest of the woods machinery, ran on "fat pine" fuel gathered from the pine-knot debris on the floor of the longleaf forest. The resinous pine burned "hot but dirty," with many sparks, necessitating this precaution.[39]

The Shay engine was specialized, a slow, hard-pulling, bevil-gear-driven machine designed for woods work. Railroad men said that the Shays pulled five times as much, went one-fifth as fast, and made five times as much noise as regular locomotives. The various engines, and the men who ran them, were well known by inhabitants of Manning, and they easily identified the individual locomotives by sight and the operators by their peculiar "signature" whistle patterns. A former Manning resident recalled of one such engineer: "Bledsaw Duncan was the 'Casey Jones' of the SH & G Railroad. His old Number 3 engine, with him at the throttle, could bring out more logs over the steep grade from the Neches River bottom than any man alive. He had his own brass whistle that he could play a tune of pure rhythm so sorrowful that you couldn't believe it."[40]

The big steam locomotives of the logging-bonanza era fascinated many, and railroad jargon permeated mill-town language. "The steam engine was the most majestic, throbbing, fascinating, and inefficient machine ever conceived by mortal man," one former sawmill machinist wrote.[41] And most male Manningites would have understood every word of this engineer's official court deposition of a tram engine's too-speedy approach to the railyard, emergency braking, derailment, and wreck: "I seen her coming through the cut, and she was working steam and putting up a feather. Hogger cut her off at the limit board, and she come in greasing at about 25. When she passed the target, the ponies split the switch and took down the siding. The hogger bigholed her, but she jumped the rabbit and took to the country."[42]

Sawmill-railroad empires had a long reach, involving many people who never drew a formal company paycheck. Along the edge of the nearby Neches bottoms, clans of backwoodsmen, like the numerous Havards, still lived a pioneer lifestyle of free-range stockraising, cotton farming, gardening, hunting, and fishing during the heyday of Manning, but even these free spirits served the SH & G as tie choppers and pine-knot gatherers. Young Charlie Havard added these activities to the others in his complicated subsistence round of farming, syrup making, trapping, hunting, fishing, and running hogs and cattle in the Neches bottoms.[43] Carter-Kelly Lumber Company bought hewn ties at ten to twenty cents each, and fat pine by the cord, the latter stacked beside the tramways in easy reach of train-crew firemen. Tramway requirements were prodigious—an average of 2,640 ties per mile of track constructed and 140 cords of fuel wood per mile of track a year.[44]

As Manning grew, it also became a marketplace for products from the surrounding countryside, and Charlie Havard and other country people went into town to peddle vegetables, fresh beef, dairy products, and other goods to the company commissary or door-to-door. Charlie and his brother also found a lively market for river fish and skinned-out possum and coon carcasses left over from their trapping operations, though their African American customers insisted that the Havards leave at least one foot on each carcass so they could tell for certain what the creature had been in life.[45]

Manning had its origins around 1903, when Texas sawmill man W. T. Carter joined forces with emigree Yankee lumberman G. A. Kelly to form the Carter-Kelly Lumber Company, bought stumpage in southern Angelina County, and set about building a typical sawmill town. The location had everything they needed—tens of thousands of acres of virgin longleaf at a good price, a creek big enough to dam for a millpond, and an easy access to the main-line railroad at Huntington. In a sequence repeated at many other places, the company first built the millpond, then a small mill to cut lumber for the big mill and mill town, then the black commissary and "quarters" (which temporarily served and housed the white construction workers while the remainder of the construction work was being completed), then the mill and railroad, then the white commissary and housing. Sometime during 1907, the steam carriage in the main mill rushed the first big longleaf log into the screaming band saw, and the Carter-Kelly Lumber Company went into full operation.[46]

The several-hundred-man work force that came to the new town of Manning was drawn partly from the farmers and stockmen of the surrounding countryside but mostly from other mill towns. By 1907 many sawmill people had been in lumber work for a generation or more and had adopted it as a way of life. The larger mills like Manning, which cut at 100,000 board feet a day at its peak, often were much the same, offering similar wages, opportunities, conveniences in town, and dangers on the job. Except for the top echelon of company employees—the sawyers, saw filers, foreman, and managers—who received high wages to discourage their migration to other Texas mill towns or the mills of the Pacific Northwest, sawmill wages were low, often under two dollars a day, so it made little difference at which mill town one made one's daily wage.[47] Many sawmill families shifted often from mill to mill and town to town, so much so that one company foreman remarked that he had "three sets of workmen; one at work, one going, one coming."[48] Typical of many, young Guy Croom of Angelina County grew up in several mill towns, and by the time he left home in 1916 at age twenty-three he had lived in fourteen different houses.[49] Self-taught engineer Claude Barr Kennedy, skilled boiler man and mechanical jack-of-all-trades, became even more of a sawmill gypsy. Kennedy's family for a third of a century lived in so many different mill towns that they could not remember them all, rarely staying anywhere more than a year. A touchy, argumentative man much better at repairing machinery than at getting along with his supervisors, Kennedy typically would come home one day and give the order, "Pack up," offering no further explanation. His family then did as they were told, having moved so many times before that they had the process down to a science. A son recalled:

Papa had a little old contraption called a spring wagon. Lots of people had em. Most people hitched up just one horse to a spring wagon. Papa piled our beds in the wagon and what clothes we had. He didn't take the cookstove or the tin heater—I think he gave them to one of the neighbors. He knocked the table apart and put the legs in the wagon. All we ever moved of our table was the legs. When we'd get to a new place, Papa would just get some boards and make us a new table. But he always moved the legs.[50]

Spring wagon packed, wife and two little girls perched on the spring seat, boys lying on mattresses in the back, off went the Kennedy family to Manning, or Groveton, or Ratcliff, or somewhere else; it mattered little where. Claude Kennedy always could get another job at another town, and a new cookstove and tin heater could be picked up from the items recently discarded by sawmill families leaving that place.

Claude Kennedy was a sawmill gypsy by choice, but many moves from mill town to mill town were forced marches, triggered by job layoffs or some sort of company disaster. Economic downturns haunted the lumber industry long before the Great Depression sent the remaining residents of John Henry Kirby's sawmill town of Call to scavenging their neighbors' abandoned gardens for dried butterbeans, poaching deer, and gigging frogs in the company millpond.[51] Lumber prices depended on the construction trade, and that depended on the national economy, so every downturn in the economy had magnified effects on the mill towns, which quickly cut production and wage hours in response. The lumber industry ran boom and bust. Cherokee County millowner C. B. Spivey recalled of his lumbering career: "I hit it lean and I hit it fat. I sold dry-kilned B & B in the rough for $5 per thousand feet in the 90s and $55 during the boom during 1905–06."[52] However, Spivey's workers, hired and laid off as needed, doubtless never "hit it fat."

Local disasters caused most mill-town exoduses—company misman-agements, destructive fires, and exhaustions of timber resources. "Cut and get out" was an old story throughout the bonanza era of East Texas lum-bering. Most companies bought a certain amount of timber along the railroad and cut it as fast as they could (or as fast as the economy justi-fied). Then, when the timber ran out, the company moved its machinery to another location and began again, or, perhaps more commonly, it sold mill and company town, lock-stock-and-barrel, to anyone willing to pur-chase it. Timber companies sometimes tried to accelerate the date of their rivals' cut-out by beating them to land or stumpage purchases and by blocking them in. According to some accounts, this is what happened to the 4-C mill, which cut out in 1917, after only fifteen years of operation. At the same time that a new mill began operating, other mills in the area usually neared cut-out under palls of doom, and, like sailors deserting sinking ships, sawmill families often moved to the new town for a new lease on life. Manning, for example, drew workers from the Angelina County mill town of Michelli, then in its final days.

Cut-out could be seen approaching and to a degree planned for, but destruction of the mill by fire cast every sawmill family adrift at once. It was a rare and lucky mill town that did not suffer at least one sawmill or planer-mill fire during its history, and each major fire launched an exodus of families on their way to somewhere else. Even if the mill was to be built back, as normally was the case, a long period would ensue in which only the construction crew would draw wages, and most sawmill men could not afford to wait. No less than five of lumberman Alexander Gil-mer's Orange sawmills burned over the decades, and about that many of the mills of W. T. Carter, each time casting most of their mill workers to the four winds. The Carter-Kelly Lumber Company's luck proved about average at Manning, since the planer mill burned in 1911 and the sawmill in 1916. Twenty years later, as the company approached cut-out, the entire Manning mill burned and was never replaced.[53] In truth, so many mills burned just before cut-out that the matter aroused people's suspicions about arson and insurance coverage.

Manning was an average large sawmill town in other ways, cutting at 80,000 to 100,000 board feet a day during most of its existence. At any one time during the bonanza-era decades after the turn of the century, East Texas had around six hundred sawmills, with just under one hundred of them classifiable as big mills. Two to three hundred additional mills cut at moderate capacities of 20,000 to 80,000 board feet, and the rest—sometimes as many as three or four hundred in good lumber years—were small "peckerwood" mills cutting rough lumber for sale to local farmers or for resale to nearby big mills. The peckerwood mills waxed and waned with the rise and fall of the timber economy; many were seasonal operations of rural stockmen and farmers, like the small mill of Oscar Allen's family in the Hudson community of Angelina County that cut about 10,000 board feet a day. Such mills often went uncounted by the U.S. Census, even though incipient sawmill towns tended to grow up around them. Peckerwood operations like that of the Allens might operate a tiny commissary to service the needs of the few employees who were not family members, and thus were numerous tiny towns begun.[54]

Sawmill towns of moderate size or larger were of varied origins and character, though at the same time there was a great sameness about the sawmill way of life. Some were big, northern-based, absentee-owned operations like the Texas and Louisiana Lumber Company's town of Ratcliff (managed from Kansas City, Missouri) and the Trinity Lumber Company's town of Groveton (managed from Chicago). Industry historians Maxwell and Baker estimated that of the thirty-three largest timber companies during the Texas boom era, only five were locally owned and home grown.[55]

Two of the largest Texas-based companies, however, exemplified the shape of the lumber industry's future in their massive landholdings and multiple mill towns. Beginning with a small sash-saw mill near Kilgore in 1852, John Martin Thompson and other Thompson family members entered a long career in Texas sawmilling that by 1907 had seen eight ever-larger sawmills and sawmill towns come and go. In 1908, the year after J. M. Thompson's death, the Thompson-Tucker Lumber Company owned 1,628,000 acres of virgin timber in southeastern Texas, most of it yellow pine, and operated mills at Trinity, Doucette, and Greyburg.[56] The Thompson timber empire, however, was dwarfed by that of native Texan John Henry Kirby in that year. With the aid of northern capital, the Kirby Lumber Company had amassed 320,000 acres of timberland and stumpage rights to 900,000 more acres owned by the Houston Oil Company. In these two acreages, Kirby controlled somewhere between 40 percent and 60 percent of all the longleaf pine in Texas. Fourteen major sawmills (and sawmill towns), thirteen logging camps, and more than a hundred miles of tram road connecting with the Santa Fe Railroad exploited the vast holdings of John Henry Kirby, the "Prince of the Pines." At its peak, the Kirby Lumber Company's work force approached five thousand and its mills produced 950,000 board feet of lumber each day.[57]

Most of Kirby's sawmill towns had been founded and operated by other companies before he began to buy them out in 1901, and life in the Kirby towns differed little from life in other company towns. The company-town idea had come south with northern capital and the railroads after the Civil War, and the concept had been well described by George Pullman, who created a model town emulated by many. "A man who can bring his mind to understand the simplest business proposition can fathom the Pullman scheme very easily," the industrialist told. "It is simplicity itself. We are landlord and employers. That is all there is of it."[58] In Southern cotton-mill towns, coal-mining towns, and big cotton plantations on the Mississippi Delta, the Arkansas Delta, and the Texas coastal plains north of Corpus Christi, the same idea had been applied, and for the same economic reasons. Being both "landlord and employer" was necessary to house and feed one's workers, it could be profitable, and it certainly increased the company's control of its work force.[59] Each boom-era timber company established itself as both landlord and employer, and, as at Ratcliff, town and company were virtually the same thing. An *American Lumberman* editorial pontificated in 1908: "The manufacturer of lumber is not a manufacturer only. Store, dwellings, offices, and other necessary facilities must be provided. [The sawmill owner] is a railroad builder and operator, a storekeeper, and the ruler of an estate equal in area and complexity of difficulties encountered in many countries."[60]

Company towns belonged to the companies that created them, but some of them began small and grew, helter-skelter, over several decades, as did the Angelina County Lumber Company's town of Keltys just out of Lufkin. Towns like Ratcliff were different—built all at once and more clearly revealing of the company's intentions. Beginning in 1901, construction crews worked around the clock transforming little Ratcliff into a typical company town. It had a huge commissary store, where workers purchased food, clothing, and household supplies with the tokens, or "bo-

John Martin Thompson, founder of the Thomp-
son Lumber Company, ca. 1907. *Courtesy of the
East Texas Research Center, Stephen F. Austin
State University, Nacogdoches, Texas.*

zos," the company paid them with instead of United States currency. A
mile-long, sixteen-foot-high board-and-batten fence blocked employees
off from private merchants in the village of Ratcliff and made it incon-
venient for them to buy supplies outside the commissary or to exchange
company tokens for real money at the usual rate of "six bits on the dollar."
Every family man who worked for the 4-C had his company house, and
the location and size of the house were closely calibrated with his race
and position in the pecking order of the mill. The non-English-speaking
Europeans that locals called "Dagos" got the smallest houses, even inferior to those of the blacks, who like the Europeans were strictly segregated to their part of town. The location and quality of the housing for
Anglo-Americans depended on their jobs at the mill. However, even the
poorest of the company houses glowed with electricity from the 4-C's
huge steam-powered generator—this at a time when the rest of eastern
Houston County languished in the age of kerosene.[61]

Fifty miles or so northeast of Ratcliff, across the Neches River in Cherokee County, lay the disorderly community of Kilraven, a fitting representative for the hundreds of small East Texas sawmill towns that grew, flourished after a fashion, peaked out at production levels well below 100,000 board feet a day, cut out, and passed away with scarcely a memory.[62]

The community began when Bill Spinks moved his peckerwood sawmill from the old river community of Shooks Bluff on the Neches to a location on the new Cottonbelt Railroad. In the early 1890s, Spinks's mill cut at 3,000 to 4,000 board feet a day, and timber crews delivered logs directly to the mill in ox wagons. At times it became so boggy around the mill that only one load of logs could be hauled in a day, the oxen groaning and heaving as they pulled the log wagon axle-deep through the mud. Spinks roofed his mill but otherwise left it open to the elements, a design that facilitated employee escape when, as often happened, a belt broke on the machinery. Whoever saw this occur gave a cry to sound the alarm, and all hands immediately sprinted out from under the mill shed to escape injury.

In 1900 Bill Spinks sold his mill to the Arkansas Lumber Company, and the mill community, until then known as Spinks's Switch, promptly renamed itself Morton in honor of the new owner, D. T. Morton. Under Morton's leadership the company upgraded the existing mill-town infrastructure of company housing, commissary, and post office, and installed a new boardinghouse, electric-light plant, and tramway system. At first, mules pulled logging cars down wooden tracks, then the company replaced them with a small "dinky" engine. Tramlines pushed west down Devil's Bayou toward the Neches bottoms and east toward the Angelina River. In 1909 Morton sold out to the Killy-Craven Lumber Company, and the town received its third and final name, Kilraven. Soon, production peaked at 50,000 board feet a day—although, for some reason, transport technology had slipped back a notch. Mule wagons now furnished the mill with saw logs.

Kilraven witnessed dances at the boardinghouse, fights in the street, occasional fatal accidents in both woods and mill, and confrontations at the pay window—the usual interesting incidents that punctuated the daily life of an average mill town. It also had something of a moral problem. Gambling was common, winked at by the resident constable, and prostitution was a daily phenomenon. Although only one known prostitute ever stayed in the boardinghouse for any length of time—according to one informant—this mattered little, since a sufficiency of whores arrived daily on the four passenger trains that came to call. Workmen would make some excuse for leaving the job and walk out in the nearby woods to meet them. The respectable wives of Kilraven referred to these professional visitors as "woods rats." The Kilraven mill cut out in 1921, and the town disappeared in a few weeks—one of hundreds of "nameless towns" that came and went during the boom era of East Texas lumbering—places fully as representative of the sawmill-town experience as the big mill towns of Ratcliff, Groveton, or Wiergate.[63]

Wiergate, company town of the Wier Long Leaf Lumber Company, became the last and largest operation of East Texas bonanza-era lumbering. Experienced lumberman R. W. Wier of Beaumont formed a company with his brother and in 1917 struck a deal with Lutcher-Moore Lumber Company to timber off 90,000 acres of that company's pine forest, mostly in Newton County, one of the last large blocks of virgin longleaf remaining in the American South.

Matters moved swiftly after the signatures were on the contract. A company town called "Wiergate" (modesty in sawmill town namings was not the norm) quickly came under construction at a remote site on Cow Creek, a few miles out of Burkeville. As at Manning, the company constructed a new dirt highway and a company railroad, the fifteen-mile Gulf and Great Northern, to link up with the nearest main-line railroad and market town. Swiftly, Wier built a small mill to saw timber for the big mill and the town. As at Manning, the company first constructed the black commissary and crude, board-and-batten shotgun houses for black workers. The white construction crew lived in these while they built the sawmill, planer mill, white commissary, company offices, Anglo-American and Mexican housing, and all the characteristic infrastructure of the now-standardized sawmill town. So swiftly did Wier build mill and town that the company sent the first log to one of its two state-of-the-art, double-cutting band saws in December of 1918 and within a year sawed 250,000 board feet a day.[64]

As teen-aged boys, Howard Montgomery, Harry Eaves, and Earl Hines all witnessed the transformation of the Cow Creek Community and took part in the construction of R. W. Wier's new town. The area had been a near-wilderness before the coming of the mill. Farming, stockraising, and a few water mills and cotton gins had offered some jobs, but a diversified, Southern backwoods lifestyle had been the norm. Montgomery recalled: "Most of the people in the area earned a living by farming cotton,

Survey crew for the Wiergate mill, 1916. The company first constructed a small
sawmill on the site to saw lumber for the big mill and town.
Courtesy of the U.S. Post Office, Wiergate, Texas.

corn, sugar cane, watermelons, and vegetables. There was some trapping
of animals for their hides, a bit of snake-root digging and syrup-making,"
but nothing to prepare them for the arrival of the big company.[65]

Montgomery first entered company employment in 1917 at age eleven,
making $1.50 a day as waterboy on the new road building out from New-
ton, the county seat. Earl Hines and Harry Eaves became part of the crew
building the "little mill" that subsequently built the big one. Hines would
go on to employment in the Wiergate drugstore and commissary, remaining until the day the commissary finally closed its doors.[66] Harry
Eaves recalled that his father knew the Wier brothers, had a high opinion
of them, and had high hopes for the new mill town.

> The Wiers, who founded the mill, had strong feelings about labor efficiency.
> They said they were going to hire men and pay them more than anybody else,
> but they must be efficient. And they were because the mill was built efficient-
> ly, and the people were supervised efficiently. I can remember before we got
> the big mill going hearing my Daddy talk about how it was going to be set up.
> "We won't hire no losers, and no drunks, because we're going to get a certain
> number of these anyway. We're going to hire high-class men, good moral
> men, men that you can induce to do something better. That will be the whole
> idea of this operation—so we can be proud to be a part in it.[67]

Partly because of their quest for greater operating efficiency, the Wiers evidenced an unusual and immediate concern for employee health. The company hired a trained nurse to instruct mill families about healthful diets, and "they built the ice plant even before they built houses, and the reason they did this was that at the average mill it usually took three crews because people stayed sick all the time."[68] "Opera house" and community center, segregated baseball diamonds, and black and white swimming pools swiftly followed construction of the ice house, as this model mill town in the longleaf wilderness rushed to completion.

Mixed with hardwoods only in the creek valleys, the open cathedral-like longleaf forest stretched away from Wiergate for miles in every direction. Young Jake Cole often rode through the longleaf groves in 1918 checking on his family's hogs and cattle, and he recalled the peculiar noise the 150-foot pines made in a high wind—a deep, resonant, "thrumming" sound, quite unlike the soughing of wind in a modern pine forest.[69] Former residents of Wiergate well recalled the pristine beauty of the longleaf forest immediately around their town, since the company left those groves intact until the very end.

By 1918, the steam technologies of classic tramway logging—skidders, loaders, locomotives, and mill engines—had reached a terrible efficiency, powered by combustion of the forest itself. Civil engineers, right-of-way crews, steel gangs, and logging crews all entered each part of the forest in turn, and at the end of the process railroad crews dumped twenty flatcars of logs at a time, twice a day, into the Wiergate millpond.

First, however, came the turpentiners, using techniques dating from the seventeenth century. Employed by naval products companies that shared their profits with Wier, turpentine crews moved out every day from their isolated camps to work longleaf groves two to three years ahead of the cutting edge of the logging "front." From March to November, the turpentine crews went into new woods for "chipping," scarifying the virgin pines in a herringbone pattern with an instrument known as a "hack." As one observer explained, "the number of 'streaks' or 'chippings' put on during the season is usually 32."[70] The "gum" from the streaks on each "face" ran into a collecting receptacle, or "cup," suspended on a wooden peg in a notch cut in the base of the tree. Above the cut, a galvanized apron set in another notch in the tree guided the resinous sap into the cup. Every other day or so, "dipper" crews came through the woods pouring the sap into big buckets and pouring the buckets into galvanized barrels, set some distance apart in the woods.[71] Then, every few days, a wagon crew came through the forest, picked up the barrels, and hauled them to the turpentine still at the workers' camp for crude distilling into turpentine and its byproduct, resin. A certain amount of the crude gum hardened on the tree face before reaching the cup, and at the end of the chipping season this "scrape"— white flakes of resin—was scraped off, packed in barrels, and hauled off to the still for processing. The last operation of the year was "raking," using big rakes to rake away pine needles and other debris around the base of a tree to a distance of about three feet, this to protect the resin-covered trunk from roaming woods fires.[72]

At the end of the process, turpentiners left each pine tree scarred with several white, resin-coated faces extending up as high as the chipping tool could reach. Terribly injured already, the trees awaited the coming of the Wier logging crew. One man recalled that the doomed longleaf forest already "looked like a graveyard, those pineywoods did—trees skinned up that high on both sides."[73]

Then, employees of the Wier Long Leaf Lumber Company arrived in that part of the forest. First, two years in advance of the front, came the civil engineer and his helpers. They had to "locate the country" to determine the best places to put spur tracks, which had to be about 450 yards apart, since the company's skidder cables were 225 yards long. The engineer tried to plan the route to avoid bad hills and ravines, reduce curves, and reduce track distance—hence, to reduce steel and construction costs. Then came the right-of-way and grading crews, who cut trees, blew stumps, built bridges, and built tram roadbed along the line marked by the engineer. Then came the steel gang, laying tracks for the tramline, and finally the logging crew itself.

All these stages coexisted in the woods. When journalist Max Bentley visited the Wiergate front in 1921, he ate his lunch with the right-of-way crew building main-line tram, but while he did he heard the distant "chocks" of axes as felling crews V-notched trunks of doomed pines at the logging front—a few hundred yards away in distance, a few months away in time, but on the way.[74]

One morning in 1921, "at the crack of dawn," Bentley left on the morning train with the woods crew to observe the Wiergate front. The cars resembled cabooses, with wooden, trolley-car-like benches placed crossways for the men to sit on. No sooner had the engine pulled away than many of the men opened their syrup-bucket lunch containers and gobbled their dinners, spilling food scraps to the floor of the aptly named "crummy."

Turpentine worker chipping the pine in a herringbone pattern to extract resin for naval stores. *Courtesy of Doyle Smith.*

The crew would work right through the lunch hour to "make their day," cut or load their quota of logs. The train traveled at what seemed to Bentley a high rate of speed through the hilly terrain, picking up momentum on the downhills to make it up the grades on the other side. The "track was an engineering marvel: up one hill and down another, spanning canyons and rounding sharp curves—our speed was hair-raising."[75]

The route lay across land that had been logged out months before, which to Bentley seemed a desolate wilderness of stumps reminding him

Black workers loading barrels of raw pine resin for processing at a turpentine
still near Wiergate. *Courtesy of Doyle Smith.*

of the "no-man's-land of the Great War." At the end of the main tramline,
the crew got off the train and the visitors rode horses to the front itself.

> Single file we started off, away from the cut-over land, away from the grave-
> yard of hopes. From a veritable no-man's-land we eagerly turned our faces to
> the deep woods crowding up to meet us. I for one had the feeling of a worn
> soldier who, after weeks in the trenches, goes to the rear for rest. Ahead of us,
> as yet untouched, the great trees gave us welcome. Waving and rustling, nod-
> ding and bending, they seemed to be beckoning us on. Any forest is always
> beautiful, and the pine forest is the most beautiful of all, but to catch the real
> majesty of big trees one should see them against contrast of fallen trees—a
> background of destruction.[76]

At the front, Wiergate's twenty two-man felling teams, "flatheads,"
quickly moved into action. Each team carried an ax to "bed," or notch, the
tree trunk before felling, a six-foot Simon crosscut saw, a bottle of kero-

sene with a rag stuffed in the top (the kerosene to be used to lubricate the saw), and steel wedges to drive behind the saw as it cut through the trunk. The lead flathead in each team swiftly picked out a tree and calculated where he wished it to fall based on the tree's lean, the configuration of branches at its top, the direction of the wind, and the planned sequence for felling nearby trees. Then he bedded—V-notched—the trunk in the direction of fall, and he and his partner bent over their saw, whizzing it back and forth through the trunk at amazing speed, while spurts of sawdust shot out on alternate sides with each pull of the saw. The flatheads were the champion athletes of the woods crew, and their rate of work set the speed for everyone else. The fellers Bentley observed were physically awesome men, most of them blacks. He thought they would have been better termed "broadbacks" than flatheads.

I saw one giant pine, thirty-eight inches through, come crashing down two minutes after the flatheads inserted their saw. The noise of its falling crashed and reverberated through the forest like the crack of doom. One instant upright, gloriously alive. The next instant down—dead. A slight shudder, a lurch, a sudden pause as though the stricken giant was attempting to recover,

Wiergate woods crew of black fellers (flatheads) and their white foreman, 1942.
Courtesy of the U.S. Post Office, Wiergate, Texas.

then the long deliberate, graceful, the echoing roar—it was all over in the brief span of two minutes. It is appalling the speed with which the saw boss and his flatheads cut out their day's task. Five teams will be working in a small area. The crash of falling trees is incessant. Whichever way one turns there is a tree beginning its downward swoop. The effect is magic—the whole area is leveled flat as though a machine gun were pouring death into an oncoming enemy host advancing in dense formation. The forest is simply swept clean. The skyline suddenly broadens and tiny trees left standing show themselves for the first time. Oft-times they are crushed by falling trunks. Oft-times a falling trunk shatters itself to bits from the shock and distance of its fall. Once in a great while a flathead loses his customary sense of caution, makes his V-notch wrong, the tree falls in the wrong direction—and then it's all very sad. On the heels of the tree sawyers come the skidder crew. A perspiring horse came galloping over fallen stumps. Astride him was a yelling negro dragging a set of long tongs attached to a long wire cable. The tongs were flung into the log, the steam skidder a hundred and fifty yards away gave a deliberate "shoooo," the cable was jerked taut—away went the log, bounding and leaping to the railroad track.[77]

After the steam skidder came the steam loader, self-propelled like the skidder and running on the tramway tracks, then the logging engine and flatcars, then the long, slow, twice-daily trip to the Wiergate millpond. Of all these operations, the steam skidder most typified the danger, violence, and ruthless efficiency of cut-and-get-out logging in the longleaf. Virtually every company operating in the open longleaf woods used the skidder—despite its dangers and destructiveness, despite the condemnations of professional foresters. The Wier skidder was a monstrous machine, as large and tall as a two-story building, manned by a crew of twenty-six, and running four steam-powered drums that pulled logs on cables from four directions. On the day Bentley visited the woods, he heard nervous speculations on the train about the "new drum man" who would be operating one of the four skidder cables—and the speculation was nervous with good reason. A drum man played a delicate game managing two levers that alternately powered and braked the skidder cable, and his mistakes could kill the "tong setter" on the end of the cable or even turn the skidder over.[78]

Communication between the drum man and the tong setter two hundred yards away in the woods sometimes proved less than perfect. Sawmill men classified tong setting as "nigger work," one of that group of hard and dangerous jobs management usually assigned to blacks. African American tong setter Horace Warren recalled that the setters had to de-

Wiergate steam skidder and crew. Mounted on railroad tracks, skidders were
equipped with booms and power-driven drums that rapidly reeled in
logs from several hundred yards away. *Courtesy of the
Newton History Center, Newton, Texas.*

velop distinctive yells to ensure that their white skidder-men partners
would power their drums at only the right times. Mistakes were made,
however, and skidder horses and tong setters pulling cables sometimes returned toward the skidders at the same breakneck speed as the logs.
Warren quickly learned to leap off his horse when the drum puller pulled
while it was still attached. He explained: "You couldn't holler like the
other feller, had to have a different holler or you and the horse would go
right back to that skidder. That horse would be grunting just like he
would be trying to talk."[79]

   As steam shovels attacked coal in open-pit mines, steam skidders attacked the virgin longleaf forest, which was viewed like the coal as a non-
renewable resource to be mined until exhausted. That the coal was dead

Steam loader in action, Wier Long Leaf Lumber Company.
Courtesy of the Newton History Center, Newton, Texas.

and the forest was alive made little difference. Cost effectiveness required use of the skidder, the companies thought. Wier Long Leaf Lumber Company's contract with Lutcher-Moore typified most in requiring Wier to cut all merchantable pine timber of a diameter ten inches or larger. Smaller trees were left standing, but after the steam skidder had pulled many big logs at high speed, smashing and gouging their way across the forest floor, not many of them survived. As forester W. G. Jones of the Texas Forest Service observed in 1920, trees grappled by the skidder, "an octopus of steel, become enormous battering rams and lay low everything in their way. Standing trees that are not pulled down are skinned so badly as to be worthless. The remains of the forest are like the shell torn areas of France."[80]

Veteran woods crew men fearing nothing else in the hazardous logging operation feared the steam skidder and were ready to say so. Roy Smith of Trinity County noted: "Them logs would hit the ground ever once in a while in them woods! They tore the woods up. They'd jerk them trees, sometimes be pretty little old pine that was left there, they'd just tear em all to pieces—knock em down, knock the tops out of em, everthing. Course, they knowed they wasn't coming back there no more."[81] Walter Cole of Jasper County said, "I stayed away from em, I never did work around em. A limb could fall two hundred yards [away from the skidder] and kill an elephant. They'd drag that big log and it'd come across the little ones, and you'd just see the timber falling ahead of it. Oh, God, yes, they were powerful—turn the train over!"[82] The steam skidder decimated the Texas longleaf forest until the last longleaf had been cut—by Wier Lumber Company in 1942. Companies justified this practice with purely economic arguments during the heyday of East Texas bonanza lumbering. In truth, the companies knew that (as Roy Smith said) "they wasn't coming back there no more."

Chapter Two

PANORAMAS

———

S AWMILL communities like Wiergate were all company towns, but they varied in how well planned, elaborate, and well kept they were. Sometimes, as at Wiergate in Newton County, Manning in Angelina County, and Ratcliff in Houston County, a big company came in and built an entire planned community from scratch, in one fell swoop. Not surprisingly, these places were more organized and less chaotic than other mill towns that took shape over decades, as their companies evolved and grew.

What mill towns looked like also depended upon the eyes of their beholders. New workers fresh from tenant shacks in the farming countryside tended to see nothing amiss in the towns' unpainted board-and-batten houses, dirt streets, and primitive amenities. In fact, crude pit toilets might seem luxurious to families accustomed to the use of porcelain "thunderpots" by night and the brush by day. To townsmen's eyes, however, sawmill towns often seemed rough, primitive, and shabby places, eternally steeping in palls of their own wood smoke, with hogs, cattle, chickens, and other domestic animals wandering about.

Doubtless, mill towns varied a great deal. The company office, mill superintendent's home, and perhaps "union church" often were the only painted structures, but at Elmina the Walker County Lumber Company painted its buildings in all the colors of the rainbow, and at Groveton, as if racial segregation was not plain enough, homes of Trinity County Lumber Company's Anglo-American employees were painted white and homes of African American employees in the quarter were painted "chocolate brown."[1]

The Thompson sawmill town of Doucette, showing commissary, hotel, mill office, and workers' houses, 1907. *Courtesy of the East Texas Research Center, Stephen F. Austin State University, Nacogdoches, Texas.*

The underlying principle of the sawmill town might be fairly stated as, "The company does as it wishes, employees must accept circumstances or move on." Towns were expressions of company policies, and workers—who often had lived in several sawmill towns—developed strong preferences. The persons historian Bob Bowman interviewed regarding the John Henry Kirby mill town of Browndell and the Alexander Gilmer mill town of Remlig certainly recalled them as being different. Some remembered Remlig as a model community of "white bungalows" and swimming pools, where the manager of the commissary store walked out into the countryside every Sunday with a bag of groceries to give away to the poor, returning with a collection of wild plants to beautify his town. Conversely, former residents of nearby Browndell recalled it as a poorly constructed, badly maintained establishment of unpainted shacks and rough-talking, fistfighting sawmill men. One visitor described this town as "a collection of rotten shacks, rotten commissary, rotten doctors, rotten insurance."[2]

To a modern eye, the many historic photographs of East Texas mill towns clearly reveal one reality: the huge industrial workplace invariably dominates the scene, and everything else looks almost vestigial—a human-service area dedicated to mill operations. A constant haze of wood smoke from boiler fires, burning slab-pit wastes, and household wood stoves hung over the town. Sometimes, the air became so dirty that housewives could not even hang out their clothes, and when they shut their front doors cinders showered down from the rafters. Mill sounds also dominated the town: the periodic rumble of logs rolling off flatcars and crashing into the millpond, the mill whistles, and the scream of mill machinery. Powered by multiple boilers, at the heart of the mill, at the heart of the sawmill town lay the great Corliss steam engine, with its twenty-foot flywheel, powering the belts that drove the saws. Wiergate visitor Max Bentley wrote in 1921: "The center of the universe is the mill. In the grim business of denuding the forests for lumber the mill is the place where

Wiergate mill site, with millpond, planer mill, sawmill, and lumberyard, all overcast with smoke. *Courtesy of the U.S. Post Office, Wiergate, Texas.*

all trails meet. From seven in the morning until six in the evening, the great thing pulsates. The sound of the saw is incessant. Enough logs pass through the grist daily to fill eleven freight cars. Though it does not grind slowly, it grinds exceeding small."[3]

Of course, one's perspective on the grimy sawmill town, with Milton's "dark Satanic mill" at its core, depended on how familiar it all was. Dwayne Overstreet recalled of his Hardin County mill town, Honey Island: "As a youngster on the school yard, I used to play in the black cinders that came down all over town and the school yard. Dunc Brackin used to say that when the Honey Island sawmill whistle used to blow at noon, he thought it was twelve o'clock all over the world."[4] To real sawmill people, the cinders, smoke, and noise were nothing more than the friendly sights, sounds, and smells of everyday life.

Mill-town children grew up using their heavy-industry surroundings as a playscape. They walked the rails, visited the depot to meet passenger trains, clambered about on the elevated dollyways after quitting time, rode the big draft horses in the corral, tobogganed down sawdust piles, chased each other leaping from stack to stack of lumber air-drying in the yard, walked logs floating in the millpond, stole handcars from the shop and pumped them about on the rails, went on moonlit courting walks down the railroad tracks and across the lumberyards, and otherwise enjoyed the mill town and its environs. For children and adults alike, the millpond did double duty as a center of recreational life, which included fishing, swimming, frog-gigging, and even dancing. The Trinity County Lumber Company at Groveton built a large board "dance pavilion" in the middle of its millpond, and this became the scene of many torch-lit romantic affairs.

Emphatically, the dark Satanic mill often looked different to natives of the place. Robert L. Poland recalled of Manning:

One of the most beautiful sights I remember was the view of the sawmill from Pumpkin Hill as you look over the trestle across the Mill Pond. You could see the many steam exhaust stacks protruding from the roof of the sawmill, spitting white steam. The steam was discharged in spurts, then it would die down to a trickle and then spurt again. The odor of the sawmill is another thing to behold. The smell of freshly-cut pine logs and lumber and the aroma of steam is something one doesn't forget.[5]

Robert Poland had been born in Manning and had grown up there, but the first generation of rural East Texans to go to work for the big

Yellow-pine sawmill, pond, and railroad track.
Courtesy of the U.S. Post Office, Wiergate, Texas.

companies usually found adapting to mill-town life more difficult. Some people moved to town all at once; others phased in more gradually to the sawmill life, visiting nearby towns on recreational excursions, to peddle farm produce door-to-door, to shop in the towns' well-stocked commissaries, to see the company doctors, or to attend company schools, which usually offered higher grade levels and better instruction than the rural common school districts. Other people first resided in the tents and box-car houses of the companies' movable timber camps, only later going "in to town" to work at their sawmills.

Although some country people chose to steer clear of the larger saw-mill towns, they offered many fascinations. The towns had movie theaters and baseball teams, and they attracted minstrel shows, medicine shows, circuses, political speakers, and rural visitors. As a teen-ager, farm boy Earl Hines first went in to the nearby mill town to attend a political rally for Joe Bailey, candidate for governor. Fearful of possible conflicts with "big and tough sawmill workers," Hines borrowed a Colt .45 revolver to carry in his pocket, but the unfamiliar weight of the heavy pistol "almost pulled my britches off," forcing him to embarrassedly hitch up his pants, over and over again, all during the long speech.[6] Another farm boy, known as "L. B.," began a life spent in company employments helping his mother to peddle turnip greens, buttermilk, and ribbon-cane syrup in the nearby woods camps and sawmill communities of Southern Pine Lumber Company. His family of twelve raised bottomland sugar cane and made syrup, saving a hundred gallons each season for home consumption and selling the rest to company commissaries—in one season, 1,182 gallons.[7] As in the case of many other people, young Icie Waltman's first contact with the sawmill town was a visit to the commissary in search of something unobtainable in the countryside—in this case, in 1913, for a suitable "spring hat." A young woman in the ladies' department made these up from a plain straw hat form and furbished them to suit the purchaser's taste, adding ribbons, feathers, and other decorative elements as the customer desired. Larger sawmill commissaries offered resources far beyond those of country mercantile stores, and some of the desirable items on sale, such as spring hats, were viewed as essential even by country girls. "Back then, you didn't go into church without a hat on your head," Waltman explained.[8] Pearl Havard, years before she came into the mill town to live with her husband, walked into Diboll to attend school, having gone as far as she could go in the one-room classroom of the backwoods Beulah community. Havard well recalled her first impressions of Diboll.

> Not many of the houses were painted. Mr. Strauss and all the people that ran the office, theirs' were all painted, but the others were not. There were dirt streets, and the chickens and hogs and things like that in the street and on the school campus, almost everywhere. They didn't have any bathrooms or running water. They had electric light, but that came from the sawmill. You could see all the outdoor toilets. It was just like anywhere else. Diboll was just as clean as anywhere else.[9]

Cows, chickens, and hogs in the streets came as no shock to Havard, since most pineywoods counties were "free range" well into the twentieth century. Even the courthouse towns of Kountz, Livingston, Newton, and Jasper had free-range hogs roaming their streets into the 1950s. As in the countryside, houses invariably had picket fences around them to keep the larger animals out of the yards. Hogs roamed everywhere in the towns— a few kept by sawmill families, most wandering in from the surrounding open range—and they could be terrible pests. Guy Croom recalled that in the mill town of Warren, "these devilish hogs would get under the house, keep you awake at night and shed off fleas that eventually got into the house."[10]

The companies often encouraged the keeping of milk cows and chickens and in other ways contributed to the free-range menagerie wandering the streets of their towns. Southern Pine at Diboll offered free credit to families wishing to buy a milk cow, and owner T. L. L. Temple imported a blooded Guernsey bull to improve local stock.[11] Diboll milk cows roamed far and wide into local woods and cut-over lands during the day, then returned for milking at night. At the Kirby mill town of Honey Island, the company pensioned worn-out work mules into the streets of the town to join the roaming hogs and cattle. A former resident recalled: "At night, cattle and other animals bedded down in front of the store and post office, and naturally they left their droppings in the street. Every morning, the Kirby store sent a man into the street to scoop up and dispose of the manure."[12]

With their picket-fenced, bare-dirt yards and standard board-and-batten construction, most company houses in the mill towns approximated "country rent-house standard," though they sometimes offered amenities that went beyond that—water faucets instead of well buckets, electric lights instead of kerosene lamps. Wanda Gipson DuBose lived in a Big Sandy company rent house little better than housing in the nearby African American quarters, though it did have piped-in water near the back door. She described it as built "clapboard-style, of rough lumber, it was one big room, with a bed and a heater, like you put wood in to burn, an old iron heater. And it had two beds; it had my little bed, and mother and daddy had an iron bedstead. And then the kitchen had a big dining room table and a cook stove." A porch ran across the front, and a door from the kitchen opened out into a little "entrance," or porch, "where mother washed."[13] Young mechanic Claude Kennedy moved his new wife into a similar house at Groveton sometime during the 1890s. Larger than the Gipson's home, the Kennedy's company house had four rooms and front and back porches. Claude furnished this with a "four-eye kitchen cook stove," a "tin heater" set in a sandbox in the front room, a homemade dining table built of rough lumber with a piece of oilcloth to cover it, two wooden chairs, and an iron bedstead and mattress. A few pots and pans and a kitchen larder stocked with coffee, sugar, meal, bacon, syrup, and dried butterbeans completed the outfitting.[14]

Residence of C. H. Bateman, assistant foreman, Diboll, 1907. Sawmill housing varied greatly from town to town and from house to house in the same town. Fences were a necessity for keeping out hogs, cows, and other livestock during this open-range era.
Courtesy of the Temple Archives, Diboll, Texas.

Claude Kennedy and Wanda DuBose's father, Herman Gipson, both recently come into town, had grown up in cotton-renter families, and their mill-town diets and new homeplaces seemed familiar. Sawmill work was hard, but these men were country farmers, stockmen, and tie-choppers used to hard, unrelenting work. Other than that, some aspects of their jobs took more getting used to. Farmers worked at their own speed and under their own direction, but sawmill men labored to a rigid whistle sequence that regulated their work day, and they had to take no-nonsense orders from supervisors. If a person disliked people telling him what to do, he had come to the wrong place. In addition, machines drove the rates of mill work, and men had to get used to working not at their own comfortable speeds, as they had in the farming and tie-chopping life, but at the speed of production. As in the case of the man who ran the "bear pit," "fighting the bear" to sort the stream of lumber and scrap coming at him down the moving belt from the saws, a sawmill worker had to learn to labor at the hard-driving speed of production or get covered up. Then, there was the tremendous noise of the mill, worse in some jobs than others, but often leaving workers with ears ringing and hearing that only slowly returned after the six o'clock shutdown. Mill work also was far more dangerous than life on the farm, as Herman Gipson found out when he broke his ankle.

Gipson soon returned to cotton farming, while Claude Kennedy stayed on in the mills for three decades, but Kennedy had his own problems with sawmill work. He disliked taking other men's orders and often started arguments or fistfights with his bosses when he disagreed with them—and thus was repeatedly forced to move to other jobs. In the East Texas countryside, a strong egalitarian tradition held sway, and this tradition often came into conflict with the social hierarchies of the mill towns. If one Anglo-American male was better off than another, it was often unwise of him to act that way. This fictive social equality entirely disappeared in the mill towns, where a man's occupational status determined his pay, housing, location in town, treatment by the company, and social status in society. Claude Kennedy disliked this aspect of sawmill-town life so much that on two occasions during a third of a century he briefly tried farming. Each time, however, "Mr. Claude" swiftly returned to company employment; he loved big steam engines and boilers too much to leave them for very long.

When first arrived from the countryside, the Kennedy family and others like them found themselves having to adjust to aspects of sawmill-town life other than working conditions. For people accustomed to living on widely spaced farmsteads, the poorer mill-town housing seemed terribly crowded. Neighbor families often lived so close together they could hear each other snoring or talking in their sleep at night.[15] "Taking care of the neighbors" was an old country custom, but now the neighbors seemed unsettlingly near; domestic squabbles over the fence became commonplace. At the Tyler-Car Lumber Company town of Michelli in Angelina County, shallow wells served several families, and accusations of "hogging water" soon escalated to physical violence.[16] At Groveton, housewife Liddie Kennedy found a neighbor woman to be obnoxious and argumentative, and finally the relationship deteriorated into open conflict. The woman's little girl came over one day, and Kennedy noticed she had no underpants on. Not liking this exposed child around her boys, Kennedy sent her home, making the neighbor furious. She went out into her yard and began yelling for Kennedy to come out and fight her, and this went on for days. Kennedy ignored her until one day when she was hanging out clothes close to the fence line, and the woman stuck her head right in Kennedy's face and cursed her. Furious, Kennedy grabbed the neighbor's hair with one hand and slapped her face with the other. The woman then called the mill-town constable, who came out only to tell Liddie Kennedy, "That woman's had that coming for a long time, I just wish I could of seen it."[17]

Mill-town crowding also contributed to an increased incidence of contagious disease, especially in the early decades of the boom era, when companies paid less attention to employees' health. Claude and Liddie Kennedy left several dead infants behind them in different mill-town graveyards. Around 1903, smallpox and typhoid became so bad at the new Kirby mill town of Silsbee that the company doctor ordered wives to keep their children inside, lest they be infected by germs shaken from the pine coffins of disease victims wagoned through town on their way to the cemetery.[18] Turn-of-the-century housing in Village Mills approximated countryside standards, but living conditions were so crowded that the shallow household wells, nearby pit toilets, roaming domestic stock, and screenless windows propped open by sticks caused health problems. In 1901, a bad smallpox epidemic broke out in the mill town and many residents died; then, in 1903, a typhoid epidemic struck. Village Mill's historian noted, "In spite of all the scrubbing and washing of floors and walls with strong soap and hot water, its health hazards were many."[19]

At times, outbreaks of disease threatened to shut down mill operations. Kirby Lumber company official C. P. Myer wrote in 1915, after the Galveston hurricane and accompanying torrential rains of that year had contributed to a huge mosquito outbreak: "It is hardly possible to realize the amount of sickness that there is throughout East Texas at this time. At some points work is very much handicapped on this account. The mill foreman, saw bosses, office forces, and shipping departments are all badly crippled."[20]

Of the turn-of-the-century mill town of Hyatt, owned by the Rice Brothers Lumber Company, a former resident recalled:

Sanitation was very bad. Houses had no screens. At times it was better to wait until after dark for the evening meal, on account of flies. In summer, typhoid fever, smallpox, and the ever-present TB took their toll. Pneumonia was a scourge in winter. Doctors of the day were poorly equipped to combat disease. In spring and summer it was a foregone conclusion that we had chills and fever (malaria). A malaria chill is not fatal, but I'll have you know it is a dreadful thing. You are so cold you simply shake every muscle in your body, and no amount of cover, hot brick, or anything else can bring relief.[21]

Many country people did not believe that mosquitoes caused "chills and fever," attributing it instead to the eating of "trash," warm-weather foods such as dewberries, watermelons, peaches, or muscadines, and they had other traditional rural beliefs and attitudes.[22] Consequently, when people moved into up-to-date sawmill towns with screened windows, "safe water," electricity, telephones, and other technological wonders, they sometimes found these modernities difficult to adjust to. In truth, the larger sawmill towns were a strong dose of the twentieth century for recent arrivals from the coal-oil- and mule-powered countryside.

Sometimes even painted buildings came as a shock. The union church in the Thompson-Tucker Lumber Company town of Willard was the first Trinity County structure to be so graced.[23] Houses in Willard had tap water and electric lights very early, as did those at the Carlisle Lumber Company town of Onalaska in adjacent Polk County, which by 1905 had an ice plant, a modern electrical generating plant, a telephone system, the first concrete sidewalk in the county (which ran from the mill superintendent's home to the mill office), and the first screens on rent-house doors and windows.[24] Some countrymen found it hard to believe that any man-made machinery could make ice blocks in torrid Texas midsummer, and theological conflicts over this matter exploded one rural congregation. A few church members had been to town and seen the ice plant in action, but other members refused to accept their words even with the evidence of a forty-pound block of ice wrapped in a cotton sack.[25] Electricity gave other persons pause, and when Southern Pine Lumber Company first threw the electrical switch around 1904 a Diboll woman recalled that a neighbor "was so scared she grabbed all of her children and ran outside."[26] Some people also worried that the electricity in early telephone systems might spread disease. Nor were company window and door screens at Onalaska in 1905 always well regarded, no matter how efficiently they kept out malarial mosquitoes from the nearby Trinity River bottoms. Screens did not come into general use in Polk County until around

1925, so mill-town families were unfamiliar with them. Some thought they blocked the free flow of air on stiflingly hot days and nights and the spontaneous movement of household pets, and thus allowed their children to tear holes in them. Anything that made the one-story, uninsulated—sometimes unceiled and unwalled—houses hotter was to be avoided, people believed. One Onalaska mill official found a company house with two ground-level holes torn in the front screen door. When questioned, the renter freely admitted that one was for his dog and one was for his cat. When he said, "Get out!," he wanted them to be able to exit the house immediately.[27] Even the safe company water, after 1910 often condensed from mill boilers and stored in cypress tanks for gravity feed to homes, drew complaints. In Diboll the water might be clean and safe, but it had a distinctive taste, turned foods green, and, in hot summertime at houses closest to the mill, sometimes exited faucets admixed with live steam. One man customarily added a piece of block ice to Diboll water to prepare his bath.[28]

If someone had climbed the Diboll water tower just after the turn of the century and looked around, he would have seen a typical East Texas mill town, grown up since 1894 along the tracks of the main-line Houston, East, and West Texas Railroad. The *Angelina County Weekly Tribune* remarked in 1902, "Diboll Junction and sawmill is another mill village, with its tall smoke stacks, big log lakes, and singing saws. There are several hundred people here and they all seem busy."[29] In 1908, the *American Lumberman* noted that Southern Pine now had 710 persons on its payroll, a thriving commissary store with a manager and 12-clerk staff, a post office, white and colored schools, and "a neat little yellow pine church, two stories in height, on the lower floor of which services are held by the Baptists, the Methodists, and one other denomination. On the upper floor is a secret society chamber in which the Odd Fellows and the Woodmen of the World hold regular convocations."[30]

Former residents of the sawmill towns rarely commented on the mill complex itself in their memoirs, but the observer on the Diboll water tower probably would have found his eyes drawn to the big sawmill and planer mill dominating the scene. Viewed from high above, commissary, company office, and employee houses shrank to insignificance beside the huge mill buildings, extensive wooden dollyways, dry kilns, acres of stacked lumber in the yards, lumber sheds along the railroad, millpond full of floating logs, and the big machine shop and roundhouse that serviced and repaired the company's railroad cars and locomotives. At Diboll and other sawmill towns, the mill complex physically dominated the town it had called into being. Although some companies paid more attention to the human side of their towns than did others—provided more services and painted more buildings—the needs of the mills always reigned supreme; towns served the mill and not the other way around. Diboll by most accounts resembled Manning a few miles away, an average, well-maintained, respectable, large mill town. Other towns were not as good. After visiting Diboll, Manning, Keltys, and other area mill towns, a researcher observed of a smaller Angelina County sawmill community: "Ewing is a small town with a population of about six hundred. It has a distinctive industrial atmosphere that makes one forget that it is a town. That is, the industrial features stand out."[31]

As mills shrank in size to the shabby average of around 40,000 board feet production a day, their supporting towns often diminished to the bare necessities of company offices, commissaries, hotels for single workers, rent houses, and perhaps a multipurpose "community center," or

Aerial view of the Kirby mill and town at Evadale, early 1930s. *Courtesy of the East Texas Research Center, Stephen F. Austin State University, Nacogdoches, Texas.*

"hall," which, as at early Village Mills and Deweyville, often served as
schoolhouse by day, meeting hall by night, and church on Sundays. Many
smaller company towns had no formal community hall, as at Ewing in
Angelina County, Kilraven in Cherokee County, and Carmona in Trinity
County. Commissary stores and boardinghouses served such functions
at these places—in as much as they were served at all. Sometimes, as at
Carmona and the similar mill town of Pollock in Angelina County, mill
hands and local farmers pitched in to build community centers without
company help. Carmona's "hall" was the only painted and well-maintained structure in the town when visited by geographer William Chambers during the late 1920s.[32] The Pollock community hall was thirty by
twenty feet in size and took two years to complete. Former Pollock postmaster Roy Sanders recalled: "It was worked on by everyone in the community. If the mill was down, the sawmill boys worked. If it was too wet
to plow, the farm boys worked. Brother Key [the preacher] worked tirelessly collecting money for lumber, nails, and screws. When we ran out of
lumber, he would make another round. He also worked on the building
along with the workers." When completed, the Pollock hall served as
nondenominational church, school, voting site, and host of the occasional
"singing school" or "traveling show."[33]

Wiergate, Manning, Ratcliff, and other larger company towns stood in
great contrast to the numerous shabby "Pollocks" and "Carmonas" of the
sawmill world. Not only did such towns have far more elaborate infra-
structures, but in an era of rigid racial segregation they often had multiples
of everything—schools, churches, hotels, baseball fields, barber shops,
swimming pools, and even commissaries. An anonymous former resident
of the Peavy Moore Lumber Company town of Deweyville, Newton
County, offered this excellent brief sketch of the place—a description virtually interchangeable with other accounts of the larger sawmill towns.

> There were three elements of the town clearly defined— white, Mexican, and
> Negro. The white section was located at what might be considered the lower
> part of Deweyville. This consisted of the commissary, which included the
> barber shop, pressing shop, meat market, ice house, grocery, and dry goods
> store; and the two-story L-shaped hotel with eating facilities inside and courts
> outside for baseball, softball, tennis, and croquet. Also here were the com-
> munity church building, constructed in 1919, a grammar school, high school,
> the clinic, business offices for the mill officials and most of the mill homes for
> both the workers and the management. The Mexican quarters, where about
> thirty families lived, was to the west of the white community and included the

hotel known as the "Yellow Dog." The Negro settlement lay in the general area to the north and behind the present post office. There were 180 houses in this section, with their hotel known as "Little Africa."[34]

If a company painted any part of its mill town, it painted the central structures of company office, commissary, and railroad depot, and perhaps the mill manager's residence. As many surviving photographs attest, company offices often were substantial two-story buildings designed and furnished to impress the commercial visitor. "The office building is the prettiest one in Manning," a high school student wrote in the early 1930s. "It is very attractive, resembling a home more than a public building and being painted white."[35] On the inside, however, most companies furnished their offices in keeping with the male-dominated work place— maps and deer antlers on the walls, oriental rugs on the wooden floors, ornamental wood stoves, and roll-top desks that grew ever larger and more elaborate as their users moved up the chain of command. Offices

Interior of the temporary office of the Thompson Lumber Company, 1907. The farther away from the corporate headquarters, the less lavish the offices.
Courtesy of the Texas Forestry Museum, Lufkin, Texas.

and their surroundings might reveal the unusual or eccentric tastes of mill managers or owners, as at the Knox Lumber Company's town of East Mayfield. A visitor from Diboll reported of this place: "We looked at everything and saw the ducks and geese and deer around the office, and flowers. The office was fixed up pretty, just like a picture. Everything was in order."[36]

Doubtless the Diboll visitors spent the night in the better of East Mayfield's two company hotels intended for Anglo-Americans. As at Diboll and Manning, companies often maintained separate hotels for "office men and managers" and for "working men." At both towns, the larger, more elaborate hotel was known as the "Star" and the other as the "Beanery."[37] The need for companies to provide room and board for their single workers began with the first sawmills, as at the Harris brothers' sash-saw operation on Buffalo Bayou in 1831, and the need to employ a multi-ethnic work force required a hotel for every ethnicity. Diboll had hotels for Anglos, blacks, and Italians; Deweyville and Wiergate had hotels for Anglos, blacks, and Mexicans. As at Deweyville, minority hotels often accrued derogatory nicknames—"Yellow Dog" and "Little Africa," among others.

Virtually every sawmill town had at least two hotels, one for blacks and one for whites, although in the smaller mill towns these places were more likely to be referred to as "boardinghouses." Ewing's two boardinghouses stood facing each other across the racial divider of the railroad tracks but were otherwise rather similar. Both were plain two-story buildings run by women with reputations as outstanding cooks. Meals in the white boardinghouse were served at a long table, able to take eighteen people on each side. The boarding-house staff worked a long day, since breakfast had to be ready at 6 A.M., as did the syrup-bucket lunches of the woods crew. Boarders often sat on the porch after supper to watch "what little activity there was on the road," contemplating their black counterparts across the tracks doing the same thing.[38]

In most towns, minority hotels left much to be desired. Southern Lumber Operators' Association inspector L. M. Wade traveled between Kirby Lumber Company sawmill towns and timber camps in 1914 and tactfully reported to company management that its black boardinghouses were dirtier, less well kept, and more unsanitary than the Anglo ones.[39] Many white hotels had bedbugs in this pre-insecticide time, but black hotels had them more often. Ervelia Jordan recalled weekly battles with the nocturnal bloodsuckers at the Anglo-American boardinghouse in the Southern Pine timber camp of Fastrill. Three bags of mothballs dissolved

Boardinghouse for white workers, Diboll. Known as the "Beanery," this establishment accommodated mostly single men who worked for the company.
Courtesy of the Temple Archives, Diboll, Texas.

in five gallons of gasoline formed the standard mix used to wash down
every mattress once a week, but, "back then, there was nothing that would
kill bedbugs."[40] The black hotel in Diboll had bugs even worse. Horace
Warren spent one night there and recalled: "I couldn't sleep that night,
them bedbugs ate me up all night. I walked all night, they didn't bother
you, then." Asked what furnishings had been in his room, Warren replied:
"Just the bed and a dresser, that's all—and the bugs, they was there. All
night I was hittin and slappin."[41]

Many Anglo boardinghouses were not much better. Fred Kennedy recalled a company hotel at Shamrock, Louisiana, that his family stayed in.
"We had two rooms. Wasn't nothin in them but a iron bedstand and a
washstand with a pitcher and a washpan. We had to go downstairs and
out behind the building to get to the privy. We ate our meals in the din-

ing room, where everybody ate at one long table, family style. We didn't
like the food."[42]

Food varied a great deal at the company hotels and boardinghouses
and was a major topic of conversation among the guests. Kilraven served
a monotonous menu emphasizing the country survival fare of cornbread,
biscuits, bacon, beans, potatoes, and syrup.[43] Conversely, Diboll's Antlers
Hotel, Wiergate's main hotel, and the elegant "Hotel des Pines" of the
Gulf Lumber Company at Fullerton, Louisiana, developed local reputations for epicurean delights. Lumberman John Henry Kirby often
stayed in special suites at the elite hotels of his principal company towns,
and he expected the food to be good. In the hierarchical society of the
mill towns, owners and superintendents were not persons to displease.
Kirby might never have been so abrupt, but at Haslam on one occasion
the mill manager dumped the contents of a particularly unappetizing
plate over the hotel manager's head.[44]

This probably never happened at the elite Antlers Hotel, which replaced Diboll's Star Hotel in the 1930s. Of native log construction ap-
proximating a "Northwoods lodge," the Antlers had a peaked roof, big
front porch, and rugged exterior. Mr. and Mrs. J. P. Cammack, who operated the Antlers, decorated its interior in an eccentric manner, with
stuffed animal trophies, Indian blankets, old coach-lamp light fixtures,
and various antiques. The Antlers became the center of off-duty activities
in Diboll, good and bad. The *Angelina County Free Press* noted, "It became the scene of many a nighttime fight, and the town got such a reputation that the late Henry Temple brought in a Texas ranger named Jay
Boren to put things in order."[45]

T. L. L. Temple, who had founded Diboll in 1894, strongly disapproved
of drinking, fistfighting, and other bad behaviors, and had constructed
church and school at company expense forty years before to help civilize
his mill town. Temple, John Martin Thompson, R. A. Long, and other
millowners were strongly moral men concerned that their mill towns had
such educational and uplifting institutions to encourage Sabbath obser-
vances, piety, and sobriety. Temple and Martin often inspected their
towns, but even when owners resided in far-away Chicago or Kansas City
and rarely visited, they usually provided full or partial support for community churches and schools.

There were exceptions, however, even among the major mill towns.
John Henry Kirby sometimes gave each mill family in his towns a Bible

for Christmas, but—often strapped for operating funds—his company offered inconsistent support for churches and schools. The voluminous Kirby Lumber Company papers at Nacogdoches and Houston contain many requests for the company to donate land, lumber, and supplemental preacher and teacher salaries to support churches, schools, and other community improvements, and a good many negative responses. In 1903, Kirby Lumber Company executive B. F. Bonner told one supplicant, "This company has been doing a great deal in the way of making donations for school buildings and we do not feel called upon to make donations for churches."[46] True to his word, two weeks later Bonner replied in the affirmative to a request that the company donate land for a new school at Buna, only ordering that the school should be located "where it would be advantageous to our store and on our property on the opposite side from where our competitors are located."[47]

Other companies also thought of churches and schools in their communities as closely related policy matters—perhaps because they both often occupied the same building during the early days or because both were deemed important for control of the work force. Around 1910, at the Sabine Tram Lumber Company town of Deweyville, several Protestant denominations, the public school, and the Masons, Odd Fellows, and other community groups all used the same, multipurpose community center. As former mill superintendent W. A. Smith told researcher Hamilton Pratt Easton, Sabine Tram's policy had been to hire ministers and teachers like any other employees, pay them at the pay window with all the rest, and make sure they "confined themselves to the duties for which they were paid." Sabine Tram expected its teachers to teach and its minister to preach, visit the sick, and administer the church sacraments, and all professionals were expected to watch what they said. Smith recalled: "If a minister proved unsatisfactory, or by stirring up dissatisfaction and labor trouble among the men, or by developing friction through preaching too hard against Sunday habits such as card playing, the superintendent discharged him as quickly as he would any other employee."[48]

As time went on, most companies provided separate community or "union" church buildings that were used in turn by the main denominations. A recurrent problem, however, was the repeated requests for separate churches from the more "apostolic" and "evangelical" Protestant denominations that wanted nothing to do with religious unionism. Owners varied in how much they personally encouraged religion, but few chose to operate on Sundays, even in boom times. J. M. Thompson once ordered workers to leave a derailed logging train lying on its side until the follow-ing Monday, telling them that things unaccomplished on Saturday were best postponed until after the Day of Rest.[49]

Women and children attended church far more regularly than did men and often were the stalwarts of community religious life. At Deweyville, Diboll, and everywhere else, charity was administered locally, and women usually played important roles in this. At Sabine Tram's Deweyville, "If a man died, accidentally or naturally, or was hurt while employed by the company, it often provided for his family, charging the expense to profit and loss at the end of the year." Deceased employees of Sabine Tram re-ceived a free company coffin.[50] Mill superintendent W. A. Smith's wife worked long hours at such philanthropies, handing out clothing to the needy with the Ladies' Aid Society and assisting the doctor with the sick. "She held a position in Deweyville somewhat similar to that of a min-ister's wife in a small town parish," Easton judged.[51] At Diboll, Mrs. Frank Farrenton, wife of the commissary manager and, like Tom Temple, a Christian Scientist, did the same. Farrenton began a PTA, promoted Wednesday-night prayer meetings, organized a mission church for fami-lies recently arrived from the company timber camps, promoted Prohibi-tion, helped the doctor tend the sick, and assisted in laying out the dead.[52] At Manning, the Women's Missionary Union (Baptist), the Women's Missionary Society (Methodist), and the interdenominational Young People's Union and Young Women's Association all stayed active.[53]

Ministers seldom lived in town in early times, often visiting one Sun-day each month to hold several services. Summer revivals, under brush arbors or in the churches, were common and often well attended; bap-tisms took place in the millponds. Men encouraged their wives and chil-dren to attend Sunday services and other religious affairs—even when they elected to play cards or go hunting and fishing. Over the years, com-panies and congregations constructed larger churches and hired full-time ministers, as at Wiergate and Manning. Wiergate Long Leaf Lumber Company paid $100 a month to a succession of young Methodists, just out of seminary, to serve the Wiergate community for one year at a time, and around 1917 the Carter-Kelly Lumber Company at Manning ob-tained a resident minister and, across the street from the company hotel, built a fine new five-room church with stained-glass windows. The com-pany paid the minister the same amount paid him by his congregation, a practice followed by many other companies.[54]

Black churches and black schools were far more likely to remain in the

Union Church at the Thompson Lumber Company town of Willard, 1911.
Courtesy of the Texas Forestry Museum, Lufkin, Texas.

same one-story, one- or two-room, unpainted frame structures built at the beginnings of the mill towns. Many companies constructed minimal black churches and schools in their towns and then more or less forgot about them. The buildings often grew more shabby over time, no matter the occasional fervor of the worship or intensity of the instruction going on within them.

Manning typified many such towns. In 1917, the same year the new church was built, Manning's Anglo school moved from the old church to a new, two-building campus on a hill one mile south of town, "where everything was quiet and out of way of the sawmill."[55] The location was scenic. One new building served as combined high school and grammar school, and had four large rooms and an auditorium. The other building functioned as kindergarten, library, and office. Manning remained a common school district, though it prided itself on its academic excellence and became accustomed to finishing just behind the courthouse town of Lufkin at the "county meets."[56]

Mill-town schools generally were better than the country schools but worse than those in the principal towns. Before World War I, Texas lagged behind the rest of the United States in literacy rate and average years of schooling, East Texas lagged behind the Texas average, and the timber counties were at the bottom of the East Texas list. In 1920, the state illiteracy rate was 9.6 percent, but in Newton County it was 14 percent and in San Augustine County, 16.9 percent. Many teachers in mill-town schools lacked certificates. Historians Robert Maxwell and Robert Baker observed of such schools: "Many schools were square boxes, largely unfurnished on the inside, and divided into two to four rooms. The courses were confined to the fundamentals. Orders for textbooks at the Angelina County Lumber Company commissary [at Keltys] included Swenton's *American History*, Monteith's *Geography*, McGuffey's *Revised Speller*, and McGuffey's *Readers*, first, second, third, and fourth. Pens, copybooks, crayons, and paper were also available at the company store."[57]

Manning's black school went undescribed in the various accounts of the town, though one person remarked in passing: "The colored quarters were equipped with the same conveniences as the whites. They had their school, churches, pool hall, barber shop, hotel, and cemetery, but they stayed on their side of town."[58] Apparently, African American education was no more a priority at Manning than it was in most other rural common school districts, sawmill communities, and county seat towns of early twentieth-century Texas. According to a survey of 1934, Manning oper-

The black school at the Southern Pine Lumber Company town of Diboll. At the
teacher's command, a student climbed the ladder to ring the school bell.
Courtesy of the Temple Archives, Diboll, Texas.

ated a two-room, two-teacher black school with eighty-seven students attending.[59] As they did nearly everywhere else, black students used worn-
out textbooks from the white institution. In Diboll at a slightly later date,
a newly employed black principal found all of his school's textbooks and
other instructional materials piled within a single large barrel.[60]

Drawn from memory, Robert Poland's map of Manning shows a characteristic downtown infrastructure of commissary, company office, railroad depot, post office, hotel, barber shop, and nearby "pressing shop,"
several of which were duplicated on a smaller scale in the quarters to keep
blacks as much as possible on their side of town. Manning's downtown
also featured a typical "picture show," built in 1913 and originally named
the New Lyric Theater for the famous Lyric Theater in New York. The
picture show doubled as a community center, since court sessions were

held there, and the Masons and other lodges met on the second floor. Sawmill towns absolutely had to have some type of two-story public building, since the Masons and others needed to meet above ground level to guard their secret rituals from the public gaze.

At the epicenter of company towns like Manning lay the big company commissary store, which usually included a grocery department, meat market, hardware department, men's and ladies' wear departments, and drugstore, and (as at Manning) often incorporated the post office, doctor's office, ice house, and a building for storage of animal feed and other bulk items. Before the turn of the century, the commissary complex sometimes included a company saloon, but by 1910, rising prohibition sentiments usually had banished alcohol to private establishments on the edge of company property.[61]

Commissaries normally stood two stories high, with a big porch across the front. Often, the upstairs served as display area for large items, such as wood stoves, furniture, and coffins, and also was used for storage and of-

The Wiergate commissary was an important center of activity for sawmill workers and their families. *Courtesy of the Newton History Center, Newton, Texas.*

fice space. Cashiers sat upstairs in cages at the centers of spiders' webs of wires radiating to every department in the stores below. With every transaction, company money and paperwork whizzed up to them along wires, then change and receipts whizzed back down.

Sawmill people remembered their commissaries as a wonderland of material delights, purveying "everything from lace to caskets"[62] Willie A. Burch recalled of the big Trinity County Lumber Company in Groveton: "It was crowded with practically everything a family would need—ready to wear, piece goods, shoes, groceries, notions, leather goods, hardware, butcher shop with fresh meat and various other things. I cannot recall all the activities going on there, or all the commodities that were on sale, but if ever there was a complete shopping center under one roof, that was it. The atmosphere, to me, was one of a big happy family."[63]

As elsewhere, the Groveton commissary served as an informal community social center. Men sat outside the front door in the numerous porch chairs, chewed tobacco, smoked, and conversed, and young people met after school each day in the commissary shoe department.

Lela G. Releford recalled the Village Mills commissary as a large, two-story structure with a wide front porch shaded by sycamore trees, their trunks protected by wooden frames from the horses and mules of country shoppers. In summertime, men gathered along the porch to chew tobacco, whittle, exchange opinions and spread gossip. The inside of the commissary had a peculiar odor that "penetrated every dark corner of the building." The separate odors that made it up could be detected as one approached them: pungent cheese, tobacco, smoked ham, smoked bacon, rancid butter in a big open wooden tub, and such bulk spices as peppercorns, allspice, cloves, and nutmeg. A side door opened into a small room with ready-to-wear clothing and pretty flowered hats. In this millinery shop, Miss Molly Allison: "assembled her hats for sale, beginning with a ready-made and shaped wire frame. She patiently sewed and adjusted fancy braid and lacy materials to cover the frame. Then she added ribbons and silk flowers in a profusion of colors, making beautiful headwear for ladies and little girls."[64] In the main part of the Village Mills commissary, open barrels dispensed sugar, lard, and other bulk items. Covers often were left off the barrels, and people made jokes about the "cats and rats playing in the lard and sugar." A barrel of syrup stood on its side in one corner. A clerk removed a wooden plug from a hole at the bottom edge of the barrel to fill the customer's jug. Some always dripped on the floor, attracting yellow jackets, and people had to watch out for these.

Sawyer's son James Griner worked at the large Wiergate commissary, and he recalled that some employees always showed up just as commissary doors opened at 6:30 A.M. to purchase "Brown Mule and work gloves." Tobacco-deprived users required nicotine before entering their "smoke-less" workplace, and most sawmill work absolutely required gloves. Saturday was the big day at the Wiergate commissary, as at all the rest. People shopped for the week, socialized, and took their time. Griner recounted: "All the people would come in with their wagons and go around behind the store where they had a blackjacket thicket. They'd unhook their teams and stick a branch of leaves in their harness so it would keep the flies off them. They'd hang around the stores, and at about 4 P.M. they'd get their week's supplies of groceries and go back home."[65] For mill families without transportation, two commissary wagon crews delivered groceries and animal feed all day Saturday.

Interior of the Wiergate commissary. Typical of commissaries in the largest mill towns, the Wiergate store sold groceries, hardware, furniture, clothing, and a wide variety of other merchandise. *Courtesy of the Newton History Center, Newton, Texas.*

Sawmill people's tendency to hang around and socialize at the commissary sometimes had to be discouraged, since space in the store was at a premium and others waited to be served. Clerks like Griner worked hard twelve-hour days, filling orders almost at a run under the eyes of managers. Commissary service could be intimidating, especially to rural people come to town to shop for what they could not obtain in their crossroads stores. For the "country trade," commissaries carried such rural hardware as plows, chains, crosscut saws, nails, hammers, froes, and similar items (as well as "spring hats"), but service might be brusque and formal. At Village Mills, "No words were wasted on selling. The commissary manager invariably wore a long-sleeved white shirt with a black vest and no coat. Pants were held up with shoulder suspenders. It was the custom for white-collared workmen to wear black calico sleeve protectors extending from the wrist to the elbow and held in place with elastic bands."⁶⁶ Aden ("Lefty") Vaughn, who went to work in the Diboll commissary during the 1920s, recalled that clerks waited on customers for every item; there was no self-service. Diboll residents came in with their color-coded cardboard "checks" to order a dime's worth of beans, rice, coffee, or dried blackeyed peas, often a pound of each, and Hunter, the store manager, served them himself with great speed. Vaughn told: "When he would get one waited on, he would holler, 'Get it and get out, ol' dude. Who'll be next, please?' He would take them one after another." Despite the service, people from miles around came in to shop at the Diboll commissary, whose excellent meat market and "fine Irish lace" even drew customers from the county seat of Lufkin.⁶⁷

Commissary managers often were no-nonsense, hard-driving individuals, expected by the companies to run their stores at good profits. However, even the formidable H. C. Hopkins, first manager of the Wiergate commissary, sometimes liked a good joke at the expense of his intimidated clerks. On one occasion he sent a dead rat in a cash cup up a wire to young Earl Hines, then working as a cashier. Hines, whose fear of rodents was well known, opened the cup and cried out, "God Almighty!," at which Hopkins laughed loudly—one of the few times his clerks observed this phenomenon.⁶⁸ Sometime during the 1920s, Calvin Smith's father followed Hopkins as commissary manager, having worked himself up through the ranks. Calvin Smith, Sr., "prided himself to really serve the people." He helped lay out and prepare the dead after families had bought coffins, and he courteously filled orders for blacks and Mexicans to set a high standard to his clerks. Smith Jr. recalled, "A lot of Mexicans and coloreds would run to my dad and wait for him, he was kind." However, the elder Smith worked from 6 A.M. to 9 P.M. six days a week, and his son complained: "I really didn't see much of my father when I was a little kid. I felt a kind of resentment because I didn't have much fellowship with my father."[69]

Earl Hines served as a druggist in the Wiergate commissary under Smith and his predecessors and successors until the doors closed for the last time in 1942, and he found this job an unrivaled vantage point from which to view Wiergate's passing show. "In the drugstore I could look out the front window and see the workmen going and coming to work—the woods crew and so on, the mill crew," he remembered. "And the other hands coming over the hill in front of the Booth's house, some running, if they wanted to get to the pay window first. I can see all of these men now in my mind, as I remember back to those days."[70] Hines sold candy to several generations of Wiergate children, who knew very well which clerks gave the best measures from the candy bins. He "jerked" tens-of-thousands of sodas at the soda counter, and he filled tens-of-thousands of prescriptions for such medical standbys of the Wiergate doctors as "Syrup of White Pine" and "Pink Powder Purgative." He also listened to decades of gossip about the "amusing and X-rated events" and "backyard fusses" of the town—for example, the lady who informed her pregnant neighbor that "she'd rather be knocked up by a hoot owl than old so-and-so," and the elderly woman who publicly remarked of a recently married local belle, "that was the first piece that gal ever had without pine straw sticking her behind."[71]

In time, Earl Hines became a keeper of Wiergate's secrets, closely allied with those other keepers of secrets, the Wiergate medical staff. Not a licensed druggist, Hines filled prescriptions ostensibly under the supervision of Wiergate doctors F. E. McAlister, T. M. Martin, and W. LeRoy Baird. He worked closely with them and helped them with minor medical procedures conducted in their clinic. As at Manning, Keltys, and many other sawmill towns, the company doctor had his clinic in a small room adjacent to the drugstore. Companies paid for this medical care with compulsory deductions from their employees' pay—usually $1.00 a month for unmarried men and $1.50 for married men. The company doctor went out on Wiergate house calls during the morning, then retired to his office to see walk-in patients and to handle the mill accidents of the day. People from outside the community often came in to see the doctor during the day at times when he had no company patients. After the workday and on weekends, company doctors traveled into the country-side to make house calls and extra income.

Sometimes these visits were adequately compensated, and sometimes they were not. Hines observed Dr. McAlister leave at first light and spend all one cold, dreary Christmas day delivering a baby at a remote farm-house. The doctor returned at dusk carrying the only things the man had with which to pay him—fresh "white perch" and just-pulled turnip greens.[72]

McAlister came to Wiergate at the start-up of the mill and stayed un-til it closed. He drew a salary of $375 a month, the highest pay in Wier-gate except for the company managers. McAlister grew crotchety and cantankerous over time, but after years of working with him Hines could "read his mind about what he thought and felt" and throw oil on the trou-bled waters after the doctor had passed through. "It took lots of diplo-macy and keeping my mouth shut to prevent a lot of bad feelings between the doctor, the store manager, the superintendent, different foremen—in fact a lot of other people, but he was a great friend of mine."[73]

Another good friend was young doctor W. LeRoy Baird, who arrived in Wiergate in 1930, fresh from internship at Bellvue Hospital in New York. Baird enjoyed practicing medicine at Wiergate after he got over his initial shock at the lack of resources of its clinic, which had no laboratory, no X-ray machine, and very little of the "accouterments of modern med-icine."[74] Baird recalled that Wiergate doctors had no regular hours and no time off, and that his door might be knocked on at any hour of the day or night. One night a man came on a "baby case." Baird had not seen this man before, but he followed him several miles back into the woods to a big tent where his wife was in labor. The couple already had thirteen chil-dren, and the delivery proceeded normally until, just as the baby began to emerge, the wind billowed the tent door and blew out the lantern. While the husband scrambled to light the lantern, Baird completed the delivery "entirely by feel in the dark." The couple named their new offspring "Fourteen," but a good number of Baird's estimated two-thousand Wier-gate babies were named LeRoy, in the doctor's honor.[75] At Manning, the common name was Linwood, for Dr. Linwood Denman, and at Diboll, Dale, for Dr. John Richard Dale.[76]

Wiergate doctors, druggists, and commissary clerks normally received U.S. currency from their customers, but this was not the case at many sawmill towns. The key to the operation of the company store (and the key to its profitability) was the "merchandise check," a form of company money. The check was not a check in the modern sense, but a pseudo-coin, base metal or cardboard, with the name of the company stamped on one side and the amount on the other. Hard-cardboard merchandise checks were most common, often color-coded for their respective denominations from five cents to five dollars. Color-coding made sense, because a significant fraction of the company's work force could not read or calculate. Instead of metal or cardboard "coins," some companies issued punch-out cards, coupon books, or merchandise books, but, whether these substitutes for cash were in the form of brass coins or coupon books, they had the same essential characteristic: they were good only for merchandise at the company store or for payments to the company.[77]

Companies did not redeem merchandise checks except on rare cash paydays: for a time, Kirby Lumber Company had only two of these a year. The Alexander Gilmer Lumber Company issued daily "pay slips" but had a formal payday, at which time the company redeemed pay slips for merchandise at face value, only once a month. An employee had to hold his daily pay slips for a month until they "matured" to receive full value for them—in merchandise, only. If used for merchandise at an earlier date they were discounted by the company, and if used for purchases from private merchants they lost 20 to 30 percent of their face value.[78]

Company money forced workers to trade at the commissary, where prices for most items ranged about 10 percent higher than in stores "on the outside." Kirby Lumber Company and others did everything in their power to keep private stores as far from their mills as they could, and, even when a worker trudged over to one of these stores, he usually found the merchant's cheaper goods did him little good. Private merchants discounted company money at 15 percent, 20 percent, or even "two bits on the dollar." Consequently, long walks to the free market made little sense, and most people traded at the commissary. Company money thus traveled a short loop from company pay offices to workers' pockets to company pay offices once again. Only the merchandise check explains the existence of full-scale commissaries at sawmills located within the corporate limits of major market towns, such as Long-Bell and Angelina County lumber companies in Lufkin and Texas Tram, Reliance, and Beaumont lumber companies in Beaumont; company money and company policies effectively insulated employees from the economic life of the largest towns.[79] Hence, as Harry Weaver aptly observed, "Since the checks had value only to the extent they would buy merchandise at the commissary, it can be seen that commissary practices were the major element in the true earnings of the worker."[80]

If an employee needed emergency cash for some crisis, such as a visit to a sick or dying relative, he had only two choices and both of them costly. He could draw a "time certificate" on his accumulated time at the company office and cash it in at the local bank at a 10 or 20 percent discount, or he could sell his accumulated merchandise checks to a private individual at a discount of 30 percent or more. Every company town had its "loan sharks," at Kilraven reputedly the commissary manager himself.[81] Asked by a federal investigator in 1914 if such transactions were common, a company official replied, "Oh, quite often. The people are ignorant."[82]

Lumber companies were defensive about their company commissary policies and their company money, which workers called "bozos," "chits," "bat-wings," "robissary money," and even ruder names. A major public-relations article about Kirby Lumber Company in the 1902 *American Lumberman* protested, "There is an impression prevalent among many that a company commissary is merely a polite name for 'hold-up.' Baseless stories regarding the prices demanded and the class of goods furnished by commissaries have been widely circulated."[83] However, a survey of comparative prices by the U.S. Department of Labor in 1914 found that commissary prices in Kirbyville were consistently over 10 percent higher than in nearby private stores—this despite the fact that Kirby Lumber Company's volume purchasing gave its commissaries a 10 to 15 percent wholesale price advantage over private competitors.[84]

Kirby Lumber Company papers reveal that so long as company merchandise checks forced employees to use their commissaries, company profits remained good. During 1915, for example, fourteen Kirby commissaries in company sawmill towns and timber camps netted $189,294.25.[85] Net earnings on sales in the stores ranged from a low of 3 percent to a high of 21.4 percent. Profitability of individual stores in 1916 depended mainly on the closeness of private-sector competitors and the frequency with which the stores drew cash customers from the surrounding countrysides. By the middle 1920s, however, commissary sales were down, partly because more workers had automobiles and could drive out of town to shop, but mainly because Kirby Lumber Company belatedly had decided to recognize the Texas law of 1914 requiring a cash payday in U.S. currency at least twice a month.[86] In 1923, the Kirby general manager mailed a revealing memo notifying his commissary managers that the "old method of forcing men to trade at the store has passed out, and the boys must meet the new conditions."

In the future, you are going to deal with people who have their own money, and can trade where they please. It is going to put each and all of you on your mettle, to show these people courtesy, and extend every accommodation, and demonstrate to them that you appreciate the trade they are giving you. You should see that your clerks are courteous and obliging to all patrons. We want this extended to every employee of the Kirby Lumber Company, and we believe that you will do as good business in a very short time, as you did under the old check system. You must not let your clerks act as though they did not care whether they sold a man or not, and treat the people who come in the store with indifference, because a man who had money in his pockets, can very easily go elsewhere and buy his goods, where he feels that his trade is appreciated. We are going to count on you to give our men goods at reasonable prices, and wait on them promptly and courteously. We buy our staples, groceries, etc., at a price at least 10% less than the ordinary country store, and our dry goods, shoes, and the like, we buy from 10 to 15% less than the country stores. Now, if you cannot take this advantage and get your part of the business, you are not measuring up to the requirements.[87]

The number and importance of private businesses in company sawmill towns seem quite variable, and this matter probably relates to critical decisions companies made at the origins of their towns. Very occasionally, companies like Lufkin-Land (later Long-Bell), Angelina County Lumber, and Thompson-Tucker chose to set up operations immediately adjacent to major market towns, such as Lufkin and Trinity. In these cases, private businesses lay just beyond the sawmill-town perimeters from the beginning, and there was nothing the companies could do about them except offer full-service towns, including commissaries, drugstores, schools, and boardinghouses, and pay only in merchandise checks. However, the merchandise check and company social pressure to trade at the commissary often did a remarkable job of keeping employees on the reservation, especially in the early days. Around 1910, for example, a Lufkin resident recalled that downtown merchants in the county-seat town catered mainly to the cotton-farming trade despite the presence of two, 100,000-board-feet-a-day mill operations immediately adjacent to the municipality. Company economic policies effectively insulated workers from the nearby "cotton town."[88]

Much more commonly, however, companies bought land and set up new towns in the remote countryside close to their timber holdings, and in this case they had the option of keeping all land in company ownership and leasing it out to private businesses on a case-by-case basis, or of selling off big blocks of property in their towns to whomever paid the price.

At Onalaska, Diboll, Manning, and other places the companies opted for maximum control (and long-term commissary profits) by retaining ownership; at Groveton and elsewhere, they chose to sell off adjacent lands at the creation of their towns—decisions that brought in more immediate revenues but caused increased long-term competition for their commissaries. The Trinity County Lumber Company bought land at a backwoods site along the new railroad, established a large mill town along one side of the tracks, sold off land to the public on the other side, and then used the combined vote of its employees to move the county seat to its new town. Possibly the company regretted this land sale in later years; as an omen of things to come, the first private business to open its doors on the private-sector side of the tracks was a saloon. Soon, perhaps to the absentee owners' dismay, a wild Texas town with whisky dives, gambling dins, fistfights, and shooting scrapes faced the company across the railroad, as the civilian side of Groveton became one of those places of which people said, "they kill a man there every Saturday night."

John Henry Kirby hated alcohol and saloons and would not allow them in his towns, but someone invariably established a saloon on private land at the closest approach to each Kirby mill town, and Saturday-night moonshiners and bootleggers often moved into Kirby's towns to conduct a brisk business. Kirby Lumber Company purchased most of its sawmills from pre-existing companies during 1901 and 1902, so it inherited a variety of town situations. In some places company commissaries had a near monopoly of workers' business; in others they faced fierce competition from private stores. Kirby Lumber Company showed variable attitudes toward private businesses in and around its towns. Where the company owned all the land, persons wishing to establish businesses had to ask its permission, and the company often gave it—so long as the enterprise in question seemed no threat to commissary profits. In 1919, for example, Kirby Lumber Company allowed a Browndell man to sell cigars and cigarettes on Sunday (when the store was closed), a Village Mills man to purchase and operate the company's unprofitable gas station and garage, and a Browndell woman to open a cold drink, sandwich, and oyster stand.[89] Often, as in the case of a proposed movie theater in Bessmay in 1919, Kirby Lumber Company weighed its options of building and operating the enterprise directly, as part of its company town, or leasing the operation out to a private operator. Anticipated profitability of the enterprise determined these decisions, and in this case Kirby chose to run a "company picture show."[90]

Major private mercantile stores were another matter, and the Kirby papers are full of discussions of measures or countermeasures to be taken against commissary rivals, which had to be combatted at all costs. Nevertheless, some private merchants proved clever at challenging the big company. One man worked for a Kirby mill-town store for three years, quit, played loan-shark for a time and purchased company money at seventy-five cents on the dollar, cashed in his chips to buy Kirby lumber, them built a rival store with it, one-half mile north of the commissary. A company spy reported that this man "Stated that his prices on everything are a little under those of the company store."[91]

Invariably, timber companies located their African American quarters at the greatest distance from the epicenters of their towns, the main commissary stores, thus setting up fertile grounds for private enterprise. Usually with company permission, the quarters developed their own private-sector establishments such as cafes, "food stands," billiard parlors, dance halls, and "barrel houses," the scenes of lively events on Saturday nights. Private merchants who took advantage of minority families' long walk to the commissary and set up competing stores were disapproved of, however—when the company had the power to disapprove them. Once they had become established, the common countermeasure was the construction of a "sub-commissary" in the quarters, such as the one proposed for the Kirby town of Merryville in 1925. Kirby's head of commissaries wrote: "I am going to put in a sub-store in the negro quarters. This is necessary for the reason that the quarters are almost a mile from the store and right in a bunch of our competitors and it is a hard matter for the negroes to come down to the store to buy from us, therefore, we are losing a good deal of this trade."[92] Sub-commissaries normally carried only limited stocks of the most common staples, and minorities continued to visit the main commissaries for other things; companies could not afford to allow racist sentiments to keep black, Mexican, and Italian customers away from their primary stores.

The private entrepreneurs serving the quarter were often white. Frank Ashby's father set up a small store to service the black and Italian quarters of Ratcliff, no matter the half-mile-long, sixteen-feet-high, board-and-batten fence the 4-C sawmill erected to try to keep its people away. Rebellious company employees repeatedly climbed over the fence, dug under it, and set it on fire. Mr. Ashby sold various staples in his store, cashed mercantile checks for currency at the usual discount of "two bits on the dollar," and often sent young Frank in the wagon to peddle pro-

Kirby workers at the Evadale mill, 1920. To promote racial harmony, companies
often built separate black sub-commissaries for their black workers.
Courtesy of the Texas Forestry Museum, Lufkin, Texas.

duce in the quarter. Frank learned to keep careful watch on the Italian
youths, who sometimes set up relay teams for pilfering apples; these
teams were capable of whisking a stolen fruit a hundred yards away
around a corner with three strong throws.[93]

Businessman John B. Oliver at Diboll played the same role as Frank
Ashby's father, though perhaps with even greater success. A farmer and
mercantile-store owner, Oliver moved to Diboll with his large family and
located in a settlement "behind the quarters" that came to be called "Olivertown." Being the black man's white man proved profitable. Oliver operated a private store with a black dance hall upstairs, sold liquor (until
Prohibition), rented houses, and took advantage of his peripheral location
to run a small cotton and subsistence farm, manned with cheap black labor. Besides these things, Oliver cashed checks for currency and loaned
money, often at the usual short-term loan rate of "two for one." Loaned a
dollar one Saturday, the debtor owed Oliver two dollars the next one.
Business proved especially brisk on the Sunday mornings following active
Saturday nights, as Jackie Oliver Morehead recalled:

Where we were over there, the black people were friends of ours. We loved them, and they loved us. Diboll was a haven for black people. My daddy got along with the black people very well. I can remember [that] many Sunday mornings black men would come to the front gate, and daddy would go out to meet them. They would want to borrow $5 or $2 or $3, and he would let them have it, and they would pay it back. Chester Willis, delivery boy for the commissary store, borrowed money from my daddy all the time. Daddy would just put it down in a book, and he would pay him a little interest along on it—he never did get the debt paid, he just kept paying interest on it. I remember that when my daddy died, my mother found a note in his books to tell Chester Willis that he did not owe any more money to any of us, that his debt had been paid, it had been cancelled.[94]

The high-interest loans with principal deferred in perpetuity may have had much to do with John Oliver becoming rich. During the Depression years of the 1930s, his daughters were shocked to learn that their father had so much money he was loaning it to Southern Pine Lumber Com-

The African American "quarter" at Sour Lake. Residential areas in sawmill towns were segregated by race and ethnicity, with (usually) separate neighborhoods for whites, blacks, Mexicans, Italians, and others. *Courtesy of the East Texas Research Center, Stephen F. Austin State University, Nacogdoches, Texas.*

pany in its hour of need. After thinking about this a while, the young Olivers began selecting free apples and other treats from the Diboll commissary on their way home to Olivertown after school each day, notifying the clerks each time not to worry because their father had loaned money to Southern Pine. One day, when "it was cold and rainy," the sisters chose handsome new blue raincoats to comfort them on their long trek back home through the quarter.[95]

The daughters of John Oliver did not comment on their family's position in the social pecking order of the mill town, but it must have been somewhat unique. In the sawmill towns, an occupational class system of great complexity was superimposed upon an underlying system of racial segregation to create an intricate social order. As one former native of Wiergate observed, "the caste system of India could have taken a short course from us."[96] Furthermore, a worker's race and his occupational niche at the mill determined the location and physical circumstances of his family's home in the mill town. As Wiergate mill superintendent's daughter Martha Bowers succinctly put it, "a certain job had a certain home that went with it."[97]

In the sawmill town, race and mill occupation determined residential location in a complex way. However, since company records say little about such matters and the last major East Texas mill town began operations in 1918, it is no longer possible to tell for certain what parts of this complexity were built into the towns by the companies and what parts simply evolved—matters of custom and voluntary association. No former resident of a mill town conveyed a better sense of the strangeness of a community's complicated social and residential system than did Manning native Miriam Havard Tatum in her memoir, *River Road*.

> Watching the men leave the caboose in the early winter evenings for the office, commissary and their homes is a scene not forgotten for the many years since; slickers shining in the drizzling rain, boots sloshing through the puddles, and the spurs of the mule skinners beating a rhythm with the whips flung over their shoulders. And that curious parting at the caboose door—the colored man to his quarters, the foreigner to his home down the tracks, and the white men to their separate streets, determined by the sawmill caste; the soft collar woods foreman to his isolated house, usually apart from the white collar office workers and mill and planer mill foremen. In Manning next to the boardwalk street where the office workers and local doctor lived, there was an unnamed street, where lived the barber, the carpenter boss, the planer mill boss, the sawyer, and the store manager. The streets next to this, and strange as

it seems, "Dirty Street," an extension of the Boardwalk, were respectable streets where the teamsters, grade workers, and slip gang lived. Farther out were "Sweet Gum Valley" and "Pumpkin Hill" where the log cutters and the rest of the woods gang lived.[98]

All sawmill work forces included Anglo- and African Americans, and most added at least one other race or ethnicity to the mix—often Mexicans, sometimes such exotic European nationalities as Italians, Bulgarians, Germans, and others. The non-native part of the work force grew over time, increasing from 7 percent in 1910 to 10 percent in 1920, and always was highest in the logging camps. Just over 23 percent of the East Texas logging force was non-native in 1919.[99] At times, local whites and blacks did not seem entirely certain just who they worked with; one man spoke of "Slobolians."[100] Carter Lumber Company towns for a time included Native Americans, probably Alabama-Coashattas, among their workers, thus necessitating an "Indian quarter" to go along with the more customary geographic divisions into Anglo, black, and Mexican precincts. Sometimes company towns and woods camps encountered local geographic traditions of "whites only," and sporadic trouble ensued. Around 1900, Sicilian workers came to the Polk County sawmill towns of Saron, Carmona, Asia, Bering, and Balda, but the rule in the nearby market town of Corrigan was, "no Italians in town after 6 P.M."[101] In 1914, an inspector of the Southern Lumber Operator's Association noted of the Kirby town of Bronson, "There are only a few negroes employed at this plant, in fact it is only recently that negroes were allowed in this community, there being a prejudice against them not on account of sawmill but on general principles."[102]

Companies seemed to have clear ideas about which group worked best at which jobs. Anglo-Americans dominated management and skilled blue-collar jobs at mill and logging camp, though many others worked as day laborers beside the minorities. Companies often put Mexicans and Irish nationals to work laying or repairing main-line track but usually preferred blacks for the woods camp "steel gang." Italians, usually termed Dagos, often worked as day laborers stacking lumber in the yard. African Americans labored in many lower-echelon jobs in woods and mill, some of them requiring a high level of skill, endurance, and nerve. As sawmill management unashamedly told master's-thesis researcher Effie Boon, they routinely assigned blacks to the hardest, most dangerous work in the mill—the "nigger work."[103]

Southern European immigrant family in front of their mill-town home.
Courtesy of the Texas Forestry Museum, Lufkin, Texas.

Race relations in the sawmill towns were characterized by close day-to-day working relationships and strict off-duty segregations, realities that led to ironies. Two doors opened into partitioned sides of the company meat market at the Southern Pine town of Diboll. The Anglo side of the meat market sold good cuts of pork like pork chops and pork sausage; the black side sold "scrap meat" like hog jowls and chittlins. But if a black man wanted pork chops or a white man chittlins, he just waited out front until someone he knew from the other race came along, gave him some money, then "swapped meat."[104]

The tenor of inter-racial relationships at a mill town often took its cues from the attitudes of the man at the top of the pecking order, the owner or superintendent. At Diboll, young African American mill hand Wilk Peters found that people did not customarily use the racist term for blacks so common in surrounding communities. Peters thought the reason was clear; millowner T. L. L. Temple did not want them to. According to Peters, Temple's philosophy was "to respect every man, whatever his station in life."[105] Generally, however, things were much worse for black people in nearby communities. Willie Massey recalled riding into Apple Springs, Trinity County, in the family cotton wagon and being told by his father at some point, "Boys, pull your hats off, we're getting into town now." African Americans could not wear their hats in Apple Springs; a black man had been shot dead a few years before for entering an Apple Springs store with his hat on.[106]

Not that Temple paid his African American employees higher salaries, however, or that Southern Pine really treated African Americans much differently than did other companies. The company classified most Diboll blacks as laborers, even those of many years' service working at skilled jobs, and paid them at the industry's standard base wage of $1.50 to $2.00 a day. Graveyards were segregated at Diboll like everything else, and the black graveyard unfortunately had suffered an indignity. Edwin Nelson told: "I remember that the trash pile of Diboll was all around it. There were rusty cans and trash scattered all around—in fact, it was in the midst of the trash pile."[107] Diboll housing for blacks approximated sawmill-town standard. Of these two- and three-room shotgun shacks, Horace Warren recalled: "Well, it was pretty good, we had to paper it up with newspapers—newspapers to put on the walls. And we had two bedrooms and a kitchen, the kitchen and dining room was all together. That was all we had in our house."[108] Wilk Peters recalled housing in the Diboll quarter as "very inferior" to housing on the white side of the tracks—at least what he could see of that housing. Except for the delivery man from the commissary, the man that limed the toilets, and a few maids, the white residential areas generally were off limits for African Americans, and, as in so many other towns, after a certain hour of the night, everything on the white side of the tracks became off limits. A special law-enforcement official called the "quarter boss" enforced this rule. However, no black residential area in Diboll ever deteriorated to the point that it acquired a nickname as pungent as the designation for the quarter of the Smith-Feagin mill town of Kountz—"Fly Blow."[109]

Superimposed upon the racial divisions, and especially complicated among the Anglo workers, was a class pecking order based upon workers' jobs in the mill. A man's job determined his position in the hierarchy of the mill, and this position determined the location, size, and amenities of his home, as well as many other things. As a man climbed the occupational ladder, his family moved to larger houses closer and closer to the social epicenter of the community at the commissary and mill office. Mill

Russ Muckleroy, longtime black employee of the Thompson
Lumber Company. *Courtesy of the Texas Forestry
Museum, Lufkin, Texas.*

towns' street names also improved as they approached the town center—
"Snuffy Road" and "Smokey Ridge" became "Silk Stocking Row" and
"Main Street."[110] With minor variation, the street names repeated themselves from town to town. The "Smokey Ridge" or "Smokey Lane" of
many towns related to another factor in the spatial pecking order, the position of workers' homes in the fallout pattern of cinders from the mill. As
a man climbed the company ladder, he moved farther from the zone of
smoke and ash fall. Mill-town quarters often were positioned northwest
of the mill, in the zone of maximum fallout from the prevailing south-
easterly wind. Conversely, superintendents often lived upwind, usually in
the southeastern quadrant, as in Appalachian coal-mining towns they
commonly resided "upslope," away from the coal dust.

As family homes improved, family water sources moved from down the street to a hydrant in the front yard or at the back door, then to a faucet in the kitchen. Other amenities improved as well, and the system could be extremely precise: for example, at one mill town only a few homes of the elite had electricity twenty-four hours a day, some (middle management, skilled blue-collar workers) had electricity twelve hours a day, and everybody else used coal oil.[111]

The best Anglo housing of the sawmill towns approximated the average owner-operated farmstead. The homes of James Griner and Cecil Smith at Wiergate, Ervelia Jordan at Fastrill, Guy Croom at Hyatt, and John Gee at Call all fit this pattern. They were well made, painted, roomy structures with large garden spots, sweet-potato beds, chicken houses, and cow sheds. Families effectively supplemented their diets with home-grown foods. The Gee children, for example, "worked that garden spot like as if our lives depended on it. We had about fifty chickens running loose on the yard, and we had three cows selected for their calving periods separated so that we would be milking at least two cows at all times."[112] Griner's father was an elite blue-collar worker, a sawyer, and the company built his family a special chicken house complete with chicken nests. The Griner's home had six rooms, a big sleeping porch, water in the kitchen, electricity, and an early kerosene stove. After a while, black maids did all the family's washing and ironing.[113]

Mill superintendents at Call, Wiergate, and other towns usually only socialized with white-collar workers and with sawyers, saw filers, foremen, and other elite blue-collar mill men, and the class system "even extended to the schoolhouse among the children."[114] As case in point, a former Manning student recalled a school incident in which the assistant superintendent's son was asked by the teacher, "Who makes the laws of our nation?" After a period of reflection, the boy replied, "I guess Daddy and Mr. Gibbs [the mill superintendent] do."[115] Harry Eaves explained: "Your father was a foreman or a laborer or he was somewhere in between. You could see it in the [Wiergate] dining room, for instance. Anyone could eat there, but only in certain places. Mill superintendents, sawyers, saw filers, millwrights, they had a special place to eat. If our mill manager had invited me to his house socially, I wouldn't have accepted. Not that I thought he was any better than me, but we were different kinds of people."[116]

Many of the engineers and higher management at Wiergate were German- and Swedish-Americans down from the white pineries of Wisconsin and Minnesota. Local Protestants like Eaves treated these Yankee

Home of company physician Dr. J. R. Towes at Willard, 1908. The company doctor was among the mill-town elite and thus had access to the best housing. *Courtesy of East Texas Research Center, Stephen F. Austin State University, Nacogdoches, Texas.*

Roman Catholics with a mixture of formal respect and social avoidance; for many, it was rather like working for foreigners.

Many social tensions lay embedded in the mill towns' caste and class systems. As incentives to stay with the company, sawyers, saw filers, and other skilled workers received a daily wage many times that of common laborers, whether black, Mexican, Italian, or Anglo. Workers at the bottom of the salary schedule, especially the blacks, tended to depart during good cotton-picking years, when they could double or triple their daily wage in the cotton fields. Mill hands of all races often moved restlessly from town to town.[117]

Use of this unstable, multiracial work force in a tightly articulated, isolated, industrial workplace at a time of strict racial segregation clearly gave the companies something to worry about. Wier Long Leaf Lumber Company was typical in geographically separating Anglos, blacks, and Mexicans into three separate sub-communities of the company town of

Wiergate—"White Town," "Darkey Town," and "Mexico"—each with its own homes, boardinghouses, commissary store, barber shops, community centers, schools, churches, swimming pools, and even baseball leagues. Races intermingled only at the sawmill, main commissary, company offices, and movie theater.

The last was a calculated exception to the general pattern of social segregation—a large barnlike building where races and occupational classes assembled three days a week to watch free movies provided by the company. Max Bentley attended the Wiergate theater, and he noted that in this isolated town travelogues seemed especially well received. "In this provincial community any film with a cosmopolitan touch is eagerly welcomed. There is a positive pathos in it. A picture of the New York skyline was flashed on the screen my first night at Wiergate. Tumultuous applause greeted it. If the hand indeed speaks for the heart, I vow there was longing in that applause."[118]

In this isolated timber town, the company was very concerned with inter-racial "morale." Wiergate had: "three separate and distinct towns. Here is a situation that requires delicate steering. Caste lines can be drawn in a city with its variety of interests and distractions; but nowhere does caste flourish as in an isolated community where the little things are magnified out of all proportions." "Chief" Myer, mill superintendent, was the key man in all this, "the official daddy of nearly two thousand souls, the buffer and father confessor in one—his responsibility covers the whole range from godfather to chief mourner."[119]

Concerned with "delicate steering" and "morale," company management carefully screened movies beforehand, censoring any depiction of sex, crime, or violence. If censors turned out to have missed something sexy or violent, the projector promptly "broke down." (Wiergate residents recalled that they saw a great deal of Shirley Temple during these years.) Anglos sat below, and blacks and Mexicans sat on opposite sides of the balcony in the Wiergate theater, which management clearly intended to symbolize the expected harmonies of the workplace. At first, minorities had been reluctant to attend the free movies, but: "the company met this situation by delegating Mexican and negro missionaries—trusted men—and some quiet proselytizing was done. They come out now."[120] Company management always attended movies—always—making a formal show of Wiergate social solidarity. Superintendent Myer sat with the Anglos for one of the three weekly movies, with the Mexicans for the next, and with the blacks—though a little bit apart—for the third.

Interior of the Wiergate movie theater. The company showed several movies a week to a multiracial audience. Blacks and Mexicans sat on opposite sides of the balcony, Anglo-Americans took seats on the main floor. *Courtesy of the Newton History Center, Newton, Texas.*

Bentley concluded: "Not too near, not too far; it required a lot of finesse; [Myer] is the only man in the organization who can thus trifle with the racial status, and he has a motive. Everything is done with an eye to morale. The foundation stone of a remote settlement like Wiergate of necessity is morale. The familiar notices posted through the woods to 'put out that fire!' might apply equally well in a lumber community. One tiny match might start a serious conflagration. It has worked out so well at Wiergate that labor troubles are unknown."[121]

Chapter Three

FEUDAL TOWNS

B ECAUSE of the effectiveness of the lumber companies' control of their towns, few serious racial incidents marred the sixty-year history of Texas boom-era lumbering, and no mob of outraged workers ever looted and burned a company's office or commissary store. In truth, visitors often remarked upon the degree of companies' social and economic control over their mill towns. In 1915, liberal journalist George Creel penned an exposé entitled "The Feudal Towns of Texas" for *Harpers Weekly*, viewing that control in a harsh light: "The town of Kirbyville is admirably equipped to serve as an illustration. The motive and controlling power in this community of about two thousand people is the Kirby Lumber Company, and the source of its autocracy is an ingenious institution termed the 'merchandise check.' The system controls not only the men who work for the Kirby Lumber Company, but every person doing business in Kirbyville."[1]

Creel's objectivity is perhaps suspect, but federal investigators for the United States Industrial Commission also visited Texas and Louisiana sawmill towns around 1914 and said equally harsh things about them. Fresh from studies of western mining camps, lumber towns of the Northwest, Appalachian coal-mining communities, and textile villages of the East, investigators considered Southern timber towns by far the worst of the lot and professed shock at the abuses going on within them. The federal agent who visited Kirbyville reported:

The time certificate and the merchandise check, especially the latter, are the most reprehensible thing your investigator has discovered in his work of investigation in this country; the merchandise check controls the town, it compels all the townspeople to buy the necessities of life in the commissary store of the Company at whatever price the Company chooses to make.[2]

Of the towns in general, the same man observed:

We find that many entire communities exist under the arbitrary economic control of corporation officials charged with the management of an industry or group of industries and we find that in such communities political liberty does not exist and its forms are hollow mockery. Free speech, free assembly, and a free press may be denied as they have been denied time and again, and the employer's agent may be placed in public office to do his bidding.[3]

Ultimately, the company's control of its town was "feudal"—territorial—as another Commission investigator emphasized:

Invariably the corporation owns all the land within a radius of a mile or more around the plant, depending on the amount necessary to maintain absolute control of everyone and everything directly or indirectly connected with its operations. As all the inhabitants are economically and territorially dependent upon the corporation, every vital activity in the community can be dominated by it. No individual or institution of any consequence escapes, not even the church. The people have little if any voice in the usual social, religious and public affairs of the community. Any one desiring to exercise the simplest right, which in ordinary peaceful American communities is regarded as natural and unquestioned (such for instance, as the use of public streets) must fight for them in these industrial towns. The form of government prevailing in these communities is avowedly absolutistic. Some of these towns are not even incorporated so that they are the private property of the company. By owning all the ground and buildings the company has undue power over the inhabitants, no matter who they are.[4]

The "inhabitants," many of whom had lived in the company towns for generations, tended to take company control for granted and to view their communities in a much more favorable light, but company records often support the federal investigators. For example, Silsbee, the first of the Kirby towns, incorporated in 1906 in a citizen vote, but Kirby Lumber Company never allowed the Silsbee incorporation to be enforced, "and for 30 years the town operated as if it never had been incorporated."[5] "Employees were almost owned by the company they worked for," sawmill-town resident Guy Croom admitted, and this economic and social control manifested itself in many policies—for example, in Gilmer Lumber Company's practice of docking employees' salaries for debts owed to Houston creditors at a charge to the creditors of three cents on the dollar. Alexander Gilmer's employees approved such arrangements (or were fired) in a form surviving in the company's records: "Mr. A. Gilmer: Please deduct one half of my wages each week until further notice and pay the same to Teague and Rim. Stem Foley (his mark)."[6] Nor was the Gilmer Lumber Company policy all that unusual.[7]

However, as company records and personal accounts also make abundantly clear, despite all the companies' efforts, they often had less than perfect control of the individual workers in their towns. The sawmill work force was unstable, volatile, and peripatetic, inclined on the least whim to walk the main-line tracks to a new job in the next sawmill town. Many lower-level sawmill workers behaved like the fiddle-footed tenant farmers from whose ranks many of them had come, often moving to a new town and a new job every few months. In 1923, for example, over 14 percent of Texas lumber companies' workers left for somewhere else every month.[8] Furthermore, while sawmill people distrusted outsiders and unfamiliar organizations and proved difficult to recruit by the Brotherhood of Timber Workers, they were also individualistic, combative, and decidedly undocile, and they gave the big companies recurrent headaches with "flash strikes," drunkenness on the job, gambling, fistfighting, and the ultimate Southern bad habit of arson.

As mill superintendent W. A. Smith affirmed, labor was often discontented and easily aroused in the mill towns. "With a bunch of men way out in the woods somewhere, they'll run things if you don't, and they want to know what the rules are to be and who's boss. You can't be halfway firm about it!"[9] Smith's town of Deweyville never organized for a union, but for many years Smith found it prudent to carry a gun on the job to aid him in occasional one-on-one confrontations with his employees. Itinerant barber Roscoe Crouch visited various company mill towns and timber camps and found the workers a rough-living, hard-drinking, and somewhat dangerous lot.

> One night I stayed out on Steepbank Creek, the front for Pineland, and they put me in a shed. Must have been twenty-five cots in there, and every one of those men seemed to have an individual jug. I drank a lot of coffee that night and had the big eye, couldn't sleep. Ever little bit somebody'd take a drink from his jug— glunkety, glunk, glunk, just like a bunch of frogs. Temple Lumber Company operated Pineland. Them men didn't have any more sense than an ox, but they was tough. What I mean, them timberjacks could drink all night and work all day, just keep going.[10]

Strong drink often led to fighting, usually conducted in the old Southern tradition of "stomp-and-gouge." Opining that "people fought a lot more then than they do now," a former resident of Waterman in Shelby County recalled one mill-town fight that began with two men and ended with eight. "Harvey and Delton Martin got into a fight in the road between the Waterman post office and the store," George Williams told. "Pretty soon, it turned into a gang fight, and about eight men were involved. It lasted about thirty minutes. One of the men, who wore spurs because he was riding a horse, jumped on top of another and began spurring him in both sides. I guess sawmill people were just rougher than other folks."[11] Another man wrote of the Kirby town of Bessmay, Jasper County:

> Twenty-five years ago [1910], people in Bessmay were much different than they are today. The company manager always carried a gun for protection, while many residents also carried guns, at least secretly. The Sunday pastime for the boys who stayed at the hotel was to station themselves on the second floor porch and shoot at box cars. If a cow or a hog came by, it was just too bad, for the boys were pretty good marksmen.[12]

Certain of the Kirby towns—Call, Bessmay, and one or two others—caused problems for the successions of mill superintendents who tried and failed to control and reform them—"reform" being primarily defined as "increased production." In his letter of resignation in 1913, one defeated mill manager reminded Kirby executive C. P. Myer that Myer had told him when he took the job that neither he "nor the Company ever expected to get a man to operate Bessmay satisfactorily, but that you thought I could do more with it than any one else you had in mind." However, after a hard try at reforming Bessmay, the superintendent had had enough, concluding that "three years and six months of this is enough for an iron man."[13] A decade later, another Kirby mill superintendent attempted to reform troublesome Call, noting that: "It is generally conceded here that a new day is dawning, and as a rule the majority here understand that their remaining here depends on an honest effort. Of course, there are a few disgruntled employees here as will be found at any plant in this country where there is a man in charge who expects results and has backbone enough to see that his policies are carried out."[14] However, a few months later, the stern new superintendent was on his way out. One reason was simple; he had lost a fistfight. After the superintendent got into an argument with a white sawyer on the mill floor, fired him on the spot, and attempted to replace him with a black sawyer, the discharged Anglo "proceeded to give him [the mill superintendent] a good thrashing, not doing him any damage." The white sawyer's crew then refused to work for the new boss, a black man, who fearfully declined his battlefield promotion, and the mill shut down. For Kirby Lumber Company, mill shutdown was an unpardonable sin, and another Call superintendent soon departed.[15]

No individual so affected the general tenor of life in the hierarchical society of the mill town as the person at the top of the pecking order, the resident owner or mill superintendent. Refusing to obey the orders of certain other superintendents would have been unthinkable. Joe Marriot, the hard-driving head of the Kirby town of Bessmay, was described by one of his enemies as a man who "never married, never took a drink, never smoked a cigarette, never had sex, and associated mainly with a pack of dogs that followed him around."[16] Nacogdoches County mill manager W. H. Whited not only enforced strict discipline in the mill but also public morality, insisting "that all of his employees be morally and physically clean." At Whited's town, wives and daughters of questionable virtue might get a man fired and his family evicted.[17] Southern Pine Lumber Company executive E. C. Durham "was a nice fellow. He didn't have much to say to the men that worked on the job unless they got ugly and didn't behave themselves. Then, he would tear them up like a sow's nest."[18] People regarded W. B. Clint, manager of the Walker County Lumber Company sawmill town of Elmina, as the true "hooking bull" of the place. Guy Croom recalled that Clint "was about as stern a man as I ever saw, he walked and looked as if he spit it would burn a hole in the floor." On one memorable occasion Clint returned by train from a trip to Houston to find his woods crew wandering around the commissary due to a "flood in the woods." Clint summoned the timber foreman and told him to get his men back to work, since "It doesn't rain where I sawmill."[19] Diboll superintendent Watson Walker had at least an equal reputation to that of Clint and was held in general awe by mill-town residents. Herbert Weeks explained: "When I was a kid, I thought Mr. Walker and the Devil were one in the same person, partly because he put alligators in the millpond and things like that. But I was afraid of him, everybody seemed to be afraid of him. In the summertime he wore a white linen suit, white gloves, and he walked through every bit of this plant, and when he come out the far end of it, he had not a speck of dirt or dust, anything, on him."[20] Like Watson Walker, superintendent Cecil Smith of Deweyville ruled the sawmill town as well as the sawmill. Lois Roscoe said of Smith: "He managed the town, you might say, and was beloved by every one of its town folks. It was his town. If the school board or anyone else had any trouble, they called Mr. Cecil, and he straightened them out, always with kindness and love for the townspeople. He attended church and was always finely dressed. We used to talk about how he made us think of a governor and Deweyville was his state."[21]

Even the most authoritarian superintendents could have control problems in mill towns whose owners permanently resided somewhere else. Many managers agreed with W. A. Smith, who opined, "Where the men were reasonably satisfied, labor trouble didn't happen. The main trouble was in those mills whose owners were absent and had superintendents looking after the men."[22] John Henry Kirby came close to falling into this category. Kirby resided in Houston (if he was not off on a money-raising trip to the Northeast) and visited his twelve to fourteen mill towns at infrequent intervals. Company hotels maintained special suites for the "Prince of the Pines," and the rare visit of the prince provoked anxiety attacks among local mill management. However, Kirby's usual practice was to remain at the Houston office and to function as tyrant to his produc-

Watson Walker, superintendent of the Diboll sawmill, ruled his mill town with firmness and courtly Southern manners. *Courtesy of the Temple Archives, Diboll, Texas.*

tion chiefs, mill managers, and woods superintendents. Production was everything to Kirby, and he kept constant, relentless pressure on upper management to go faster, produce more, and keep on running, no matter the shape of the machinery. Sometimes he made his executives' salaries contingent on production. A bitter story circulated about John Henry Kirby's ruthless quest for efficiency. Kirby dreamed one night that he had died and gone to hell, where he found two big black men carrying him off. Asked where they were taking him, the men replied that they had orders to throw him in the Lake of Brimstone. Kirby at once commanded: "One of you lay off, and the other get a wheelbarrow. We don't need two men for this little job."[23]

At other towns—Ratcliff, Groveton, and others—the owner showed up even less frequently than John Henry Kirby, and at some the owners never visited. No surviving resident of Ratcliff recalled an inspection by the head of the Central Coal and Coke Company from distant Kansas City, Missouri, and Chicago businessman Stanley Joyce only rarely visited his backwoods town of Groveton. However, when Joyce's party of "elegant young ladies and solid looking men" did arrive on his private train, it created a local sensation. People in the town had looked forward to the visitation for weeks, though some feared for their jobs. The train remained in Groveton for several days, while Joyce and his executives inspected the mill. Fine meals were served in the dining car every evening, and "from time to time choice recipes were passed around Groveton that 'leaked out' of the diner." During the day while the executives worked, as Groveton resident Willie Burch recalled, "the ladies would walk around Main Street, go into stores, look around, purchase merchandise, converse with the natives. It was said that at meal times and at night the ladies would entertain their mates with hilarious tales of how the natives talked, dressed, and looked."[24]

Towns where owners remained continuously in residence developed in distinctive directions according to the idiosyncrasies of the individual owner's personality. Although not all owners could be John Henry Kirby, each operated as feudal "prince" or "princess" of his or her own part of the pines. If Hal Aldridge wished to build a "palatial mansion" to lord it over his town of Aldridge, no one opposed him, and if W. T. Carter of Camden wished to work on greasy mill machinery in his undershirt, or the sporting Rice brothers wished to take the field for local bear hunts, no one objected. At Olive, owner and mill manager J. A. Sternenberg chose to create a little Garden of Eden for himself on the premises. The *Galves-*

John Henry Kirby, known as the "Prince of the Pines,"
created an empire of sawmill towns employing thousands
of southeastern Texans. *Courtesy of the Texas Forestry
Museum, Lufkin, Texas.*

ton Daily News noted: "Mr. Sternenberg spends most of his time in a
house surrounded by trees, flowers, vines, with all the finest varieties of
grapes, and is now planting a fifty-acre vineyard."[25]

Millowner's wife, then millowner, Lillian Knox of the Knox Lumber
Company town of East Mayfield, Sabine County, also specialized in gardens. After husband Hiram Knox died in a curious suicide (somehow
managing to shoot himself directly in the back of the head with a long-
barreled revolver), and after Mrs. Knox had been no-billed by a grand
jury, she assumed full control of East Mayfield. East Mayfield was land-
scaped, and, in a park adjacent to the company offices, Lillian Knox kept
deer, turkeys, ducks, and peacocks. She lived in a fine house known as

"the mansion" filled with costly furniture, tapestries, imported china, and fine wines. Knox closely involved herself with employee problems at East Mayfield and surpassed all other millowners in personal philanthropies. Knox Lumber Company Christmas gifts to employees ran to thousands of dollars. No family went without a turkey for the holiday meal, and every child born in the town received a handsome gift or a bank account. On special occasions, Lillian Knox hired theatrical and musical groups to come to town for free performances and concerts—once, a white band to play for a black Juneteenth dance (something unheard of, which became the talk of East Texas).[26] During the deadly flu epidemic of 1918, Knox tirelessly sat up night after night nursing the sick, earning her the names of "Lady Bountiful" and "Lady Miraculous" among the townsfolk. The *Kansas City Star* reported on January 6, 1923: "Mrs. Knox was the 'fairy godmother'—quite literally—of the entire district. She gave everybody who worked in town a Ford car. She made large donations to the Hemphill churches. She went into the crude homes of the lumber-camp workers and made herself loved by everyone through her constant smiles and the largess she distributed."[27]

John Martin Thompson and T. L. L. Temple also spent much time in their sawmill towns and practiced many philanthropies, although no one ever bestowed upon either of them the title of "Lord Bountiful." Both were highly religious men who built churches for their towns at the same time that they broke ground for their mills. Management at the Thompson-Tucker Lumber company was a family affair, and the Thompson towns of Willard, Trinity, and Greyburg were well maintained from first to last. The Thompsons prided themselves on the loyalty of their employees, white and black, and the *American Lumbermen* special issue of 1908 on "The House of Thompson" featured many employee photographs and biographies. One photo showed four elderly black men in silk top hats personally given to them by J. M. Thompson for long service to the company—men referred to as "the Big Black Four." Thompson's blacks were different, the *American Lumberman* editor avowed; even the patriarch's former slaves had remained in his service after the Civil War. "The negro of the old days, raised right, is useful to the community and not a menace to society," the editor believed. "John Martin Thompson raised his negroes on strict lines of honesty and took as much pains to instill honest motives into their hearts as if they had been white and related to him by blood."[28]

John Martin Thompson's towns had other peculiarities besides the special concerns with employee welfare. The Thompson family dominated management, the mill superintendent also ran woods operations, the company relied on direct sales and had no marketing agents, and no work ever took place on Sundays. Through more than a half century of Texas lumbering, the Thompson's "rules of business" remained the same:

> To do as they would be done by; to work six days each week; to consider the laborer worthy of his hire; that every man who was worth advancing was also worthy of a stock interest in the business; that any man might come into any position, from office boys to general manager, in any of their companies, by circumstance, but that he must hold and fill that position by work guided by ability; that all these principles must be knitted together by universal harmony and loyalty."[29]

Tom Temple, who founded Southern Pine Lumber Company at Diboll in 1894, had his residence in Texarkana, but he often was in his mill town, poking into every nook and cranny of the operation in an endless quest for greater efficiency. Temple came into Diboll by train, and he traveled light; even toothbrush and toothpaste were purchased anew at the commissary drugstore on every visit. A devout Christian Scientist, Tom Temple hated waste of any kind—waste of lumber and waste of the human soul and body by alcohol and nicotine. He even disliked chewing gum. Once, on a visit to the home of his commissary store manager, he observed the manager's young daughter indulging herself, and finally said, "Josephine, if you won't chew gum anymore, I will buy you a bicycle." She agreed to quit, and Temple kept his promise.[30]

Temple practiced many other personal philanthropies, always preferring to remain behind the scenes. Elodie Miles Edwards came to live in Diboll as a young girl in 1912, and her family was very poor. When she graduated from the Diboll school, Temple worked through Mrs. Frank ("Fannie") Farrenton, the commissary manager's wife, to buy Elodie a "Georgette orchid dress and hat, kid gloves, to go to the baccalaureate," and though she "really wanted to see Mr. Temple and hug his neck" for the gift, Temple remained aloof.[31]

Temple refused to buy his office staff an adding machine, believing it would weaken their numerical skills, and he ordered them to use envelopes from incoming mail to save scratch paper.[32] Employees knew Temple had arrived when they saw him at the mill at start-up time. Dred Devereaux recalled: "You'd meet him up in the shop, out always running around mighty early. He was all over the works."[33] E. A. Farley, formerly shipping supervisor at Diboll, remembered that Temple would hunt

Private office of J. Lewis Thompson, Houston, Texas, 1907.
Courtesy of the Texas Forestry Museum, Lufkin, Texas.

around the planer mill to find little pieces of scrap lumber that had been lost, calculate to the cent how much each was worth, write the value on each one, and lay all of them on Farley's desk.[34] Temple's distaste for waste and quest for efficiency went beyond simple frugality, however; Temple evaluated circumstances with a moralist's eye. As Jesse Parker recalled, Tom Temple sometimes went to the woods to check timber-crew operations, and on one occasion he inspected the mule corral and noticed the mule troughs had no feed in them. He told the corral manager: "Will, let's don't let this happen no more. That's all them mules get, is what they eat. We don't know whether they got enough of it till they leave some in the trough. Let's leave some; then we'll know whether they're getting plenty to eat."[35]

   Fannie Farrenton, Temple's private person in charge of Diboll philanthropies and also a devout Christian Scientist, regarded him "as a very spiritual man," a man for whom the spiritual side of existence came first.[36] Temple's grandson, Arthur Temple, Jr., concurred, noting that: "He was very stingy with himself, but very generous with other people. He considered the people of Diboll his people."[37] Like J. M. Thompson, Temple seemed to have a special relationship with his long-term black employees. One man remembered: "When Mr. Tom Temple used to come to the mill, he would always walk around over the entire plant. One thing that he never failed to do, he always shook hands with all the old darkies. They would get off the job when they saw him, they would get out of the trimmer cage and come down and shake hands with Mr. Temple. They looked on him as their god, almost."[38] And as territorial prince of the Southern Pine fiefdom, T. L. L. Temple's racial attitudes made a difference. After Fennie Simmons became the first Diboll black person to own an automobile, some people cautioned him not to drive it around in broad daylight or park it downtown "because the white people were going to tear that car up and beat him up, too, for driving around in a new car." Simmons told them not to worry, saying: "Now, I got this car from Mr. Temple—Mr. Temple bought this car for me and told me to ride around wherever I wanted to in it. There is not anybody going to bother it."[39] Nor did they.

Robert W. Wier, owner of Wier Long Leaf Lumber Company, came to his town from Beaumont less frequently than Temple visited Diboll, but Wier made the most of his visits. Very often, he stayed in the home of mill superintendent Emmett Lee while in Wiergate, but the family saw little of him. Wier visited Wiergate to check on operations and not to socialize, and he preferred to remain unobtrusive. Lee's daughter Grace recalled: "I hardly saw him, he was out with the men at the mill and in the woods. He went all over that plant, every inch of it. He went out in the woods and rode through the woods with the men. He would talk to them and ask them how they were doing, if they needed anything, or had any complaints. He asked specific questions about their jobs. I think he learned a lot about what was going on."[40]

Mainly, however, Wier left Wiergate affairs to the three very different men who supervised company operations between 1918 and 1942. C. P. "Chief" Myer, the first and perhaps most effective, died in a car accident. Grace Lee's father, Emmett Lee, was the last Wiergate superintendent, an amiable, hard-working man whom his daughter recalled: "was eternally at that office—if I wanted to see him I went and got in line with the men. But days would go by that I didn't see him, he left before I got up and come home after I went to bed."[41] Lee had his eccentricities, and after he rose to power, he began to indulge them. Emmett Lee loved holidays and loved the sound of steam whistles and soon combined these passions. While still assistant superintendent, he arranged for steam whistles all over Wiergate to play the wedding march at the nuptials of his boss's daughter. As his widow recalled, Lee took it upon himself to tune all the whistles in the town: "trains and everything else so they would play the wedding march. Everybody was timed, every man had a string to pull, and it was timed so it played the wedding march. Margaret [the bride] didn't like it."[42] Later, after Lee became superintendent, the steam whistle concerts continued on Christmas and New Year's Eve, and Lee sometimes saluted the arrival of the New Year with the detonation of several sticks of dynamite hanging from a tall pole.

Lee also shipped thousands of longleaf Christmas trees to Houston, decorated a huge company tree by himself, and lighted the whole town for the holidays—all harmless hobbies compared to those of his predecessor Superintendent Booth, who—long unbeknownst to the sober R. W. Wier—loved wild parties and strong drink. The Yankee Booth, while an experienced and well-trained mill manager, also was a heavy drinker, though skilled at keeping it hidden. During the Booth era, consuming large quantities of alcohol at Booth's home became a compulsory activity for Wiergate's upper management. Finally, at one drinking party presided over by Booth with the assistance of Wiergate's quarter boss, a man named "Cap" Nolan, a guest got entirely out of hand, and Nolan accidentally killed him in the process of subduing him.[43] Not surprisingly, soon after this tragedy Wier replaced Booth with Emmett Lee as the head of what Grace Lee termed the "ideal sawmill town" of Wiergate.

Cap Nolan, the wielder of the fatal blackjack at Booth's party, seemed a silly little man to the Lee women, as recalled by Martha: "A little bitty man, but he was dressed up in khaki and boot pants. They kind of ballooned out on the side and [he] had skinny, skinny legs and had the boots laced up."[44] People in the Wiergate quarters did not view Nolan in this way, however; they saw him as an intimidating man on horseback with a big hat, a big pistol, and a mysterious "loaded arm" that made him invincible in a fight. As a black man told Calvin Smith, "I remember that man. When he hit you, don't try to stand up, because ain't no way you are going to stand up."[45] Nor did Nolan hesitate to use firearms. Aubrey Cole's father ran a small store on the edge of the Wiergate quarters, and one day Nolan stepped in and casually remarked, "Loan me a shotgun, I got to move a man out of town." Loading Cole's double-barrel, he stepped out on the street, splattered a black man with small-shot from fifty yards

Superintendent E. J. Booth, millowner Robert Wier, and assistant superintendent
Emmett C. Lee, Wiergate, 1937. Lee became superintendent in 1939.
Courtesy of the U.S. Post Office, Wiergate, Texas.

away, then splattered him again when he didn't walk away fast enough.[46]
Presumably, the man then left Wiergate; sawmill law's common response
to serious rebels and troublemakers of any race usually proved swift and
effective: firing from the job, eviction from the company house, and banishment from the town.

Besides the quarter boss, who sometimes held an honorary commission as a Texas Ranger, mill-town law normally consisted of a resident
constable, who served the local justice of the peace, and a resident deputy
sheriff. In times of tension or labor trouble, as industry historians Maxwell and Baker noted, "the ranger was enforced by deputies, who were
especially hated and were described by union organizers as 'a bunch of
big-hatted boobs who would commit murder or anything else at the command of their chief.'"[47]

In truth, all the sawmill-town law enforcement officials normally were
"company men," often holding day jobs in the mill and being paid by the
company. Such was the arrangement at the Peavy Moore Lumber Company town of Deweyville, where the company lawmen "rode herd on the
town under an agreement with the county sheriff."[48] As at big tenant cotton farms along the Brazos and elsewhere, normally the sheriff contacted

company officials for permission before even entering the precincts of their town. Company-appointed lawmen often became seriously involved in their second jobs. In 1912, Kirby Lumber Company officials at Bronson asked mill employee C. H. Smith to serve as deputy sheriff without additional pay, and "In the process of his duties as deputy sheriff, he shot a man late at night who had started a disturbance in the boiler room and refused to be placed under arrest."[49] A year later, the deputy sheriff and yard foreman at Bessmay became so zealous about his law-enforcement duties that he intruded on the affairs of the nearby Kirby town of Evadale, much to the displeasure of the Evadale mill superintendent, who complained to company headquarters in Houston.

> This man came over to Evadale to watch our negroes and prowling around our quarters, and Saturday night he arrested two of our best negroes for gambling, after breaking into a room on them and turning over the lamp and table. This is the second time that he has tried to make a clean up in the

Wiergate quarter boss "Cap" Nolan (in riding pants and boots, extreme left) also served as scoutmaster for the Wiergate troop. *Courtesy of the Newton History Center, Newton, Texas.*

quarters, and I understand the time before he got 15 to 20 men. It is a very expensive thing to bring men here and have some little Jack Leg Deputy running them off.[50]

Deputies' and constables' law-enforcement attitudes and practices needed to be carefully adjusted to the wrong-doer's position in the status system of the mill town; it would not do to treat a drunken office worker and a drunken day-laborer in the same way. When engineer Claude Kennedy ended up in the Trinity County Lumber Company jail after a Christmas drunk, he left town in a huff.[51] Minorities, especially African Americans, often received rough treatment, and few had anything good to say about mill-town lawmen, but "poor whites" often got much the same. Edwin Nelson told: "I remember seeing John Cunningham, the constable for Diboll, go up to Jerden's and rope Joe Bailey and drag him down the dirty dirt road with his car and place him in the hot calaboose and let him stay all day and night, trying to make him do as he wanted him to."[52]

At Diboll, Wiergate, and most other places, the mill-town jail was called the "calaboose" or the "cattle pen," and often consisted of a small room, strongly constructed of two-by-four boards, in which drunks and fistfighters were placed to sober up and cool off. These were interim holding areas, only; lawmen transported serious lawbreakers to courthouse town jails the next day. The town of Waterman began without a calaboose, but after the mass street fight described earlier by George Williams, the company decided to build one. At the Kirby town of Silsbee, lawman William Badders at first brought Saturday night troublemakers back to his rooms in the company hotel and chained them to the ends of his son's beds, but soon the company built a "sub-jail called a calaboose."[53] People broke out of the wooden calabooses with regularity, but one such attempt at Diboll led to tragedy. A black man locked in the quarters calaboose set the place on fire trying to burn himself out, but, as Pate Warner recalled: "He burned himself up in there. You could hear him hollering for a mile or two. Nobody could get him out, the thing was locked with two Yale locks. They tried to chop him out, but they could not get him out. He burned up in there."[54]

Mill-town deputies and constables often were feared and respected, but the quarter boss was "the man." Normally, such persons were full-time law officers, and, as the name suggests, mill-town law enforcement had a minority focus. After interviewing many mill-town executives, historians Maxwell and Baker reported: "White workers at the managerial level regarded the blacks as more inclined to gamble, drink excessively, and brawl than the whites. One company doctor recalled that it was customary on Saturday nights to be called out to treat stab or slash victims from the 'quarter.'"[55] Trying to put the best foot forward for the *American Lumberman*'s patron, the editor of the magazine's public-relations piece on the Kirby Lumber Company in 1902 nonetheless revealed much about the company's attitudes toward the use and control of black labor.

> They are not without flaw as a source of labor, as many have found to their cost, but with proper supervision excellent returns can be had from their exertions, though they must be guided and controlled. The one who does [supervise and control] the colored laborers of the south must be full master of his men in every sense of the word. Brutality will not answer, though in individual cases it has been found a potent inspiration to faithful performance of tasks assigned. On the other hand, leniency and mildness are often mistaken by the recipients for fear or uncertainty, with a result that either a new force of laborers have to be secured. The average "coon" has a bad habit of "laying off" whenever he feels so inclined. One of the foremen of the Kirby Lumber Company summed up the conditions in a few words: "A darkey," he said, "cannot work with four bits in his pocket. As soon as he has that much ahead he must get a day off to spend it."[56]

The better to serve as "master of his men," with Texas Ranger commission in hand, pistol on hip, and the big company behind him, the quarter boss exercised broad powers to do as he saw fit. Often, such men operated like a cross between the rural sheriff and the horse-riding, pistol-packing "overseers" who still held sway on early-twentieth-century Texas cotton plantations, where most of the sharecroppers were black. Quarter bosses commonly tried to overawe potential challengers by dress and demeanor, thus winning by intimidation: horses, big hats, and large revolvers were standard gear. At Diboll, Darrell "Two-Gun" Singleton carried two big Colt .45s and seemed ready to use them, and, at Wiergate, Cap Nolan rode a horse, carried a gun in plain sight, and dressed like a plantation "driver" or "pusher." Quarter bosses could even afford to kill people in line of duty, as Jay Boren did a black man at Diboll, but, like the rural sheriffs, they could not afford to lose face by losing a fight and having this defeat become public knowledge.[57] Joe Malanders's brother once whipped the Wiergate quarter boss, took his pants, and locked him in his own calaboose, but he returned the man's pants and released him at daylight so the man's reputation would not be destroyed. "Don't tell nobody about this," the quarter boss asked Malanders's brother, and he did not, thus earning the lawman's undying gratitude.[58]

Quarter bosses like Cap Nolan often spent much of their time in the black community and cultivated black friends and "snitches" to keep abreast of what was going on there. Earl Hines observed of Nolan: "He was the quarter boss there at Wiergate, and he had some nigger stooges around that would keep him informed about what was going on over in the nigger quarters. Trouble or any troublemakers over there, he always knew about it."[59]

Often, however, there were other "snitches" around besides those of the local quarter boss. Kirby Lumber Company, other companies, and the Southern Pine Operators' Association all had undercover operatives abroad in the sawmill towns for several decades, occasionally spying on each other and operating at cross purposes, and sometimes it was the quarter boss that got "snitched" upon. For example, an unnamed black operative working for Kirby Lumber Company submitted this report about Bessmay on December 7, 1921:

> I find here as well as at Call, Texas, plenty of white lightning whiskey, with no restriction upon sales, in fact at Bessmay it is sold under the quarter Boss' protection. I talked with a negro here by the name of Williams, and he informed me that the quarter Boss (John Richardson) did not allow anyone to sell whiskey but him, (Williams). Gambling is also wide open for negroes under Richardson's protection as quite naturally he gets his share of the spoils. Grafting which consists of Dance Halls, gambling, whiskey selling and prostitutes are detrimental to any lumber plant and should be cut off.[60]

Quarter bosses controlled access to the quarters by other whites, and many probably also regulated the semilegal and illegal activities going on there. Several persons commented that certain moonshiners and bootleggers operated out in the open in their towns, seemingly without fear of the quarter bosses' interference, and otherwise behaved as if they had the official whisky franchise. According to one man, Bill Murray dominated the whisky trade at Wiergate. Murray openly sold moonshine by the keg or the Coke bottle "Joe," and the black bootleggers he used for assistants held him in awe, probably because of the rumor (perhaps self-circulated) that he dissolved double-crossers in vats of lye.[61] Dave Martinez told, "I'm not saying that he had protection, but I sort of believe that he did, because he never got caught. He would drive in his pickup just as wide open as you please and unload a barrel wherever his customer was."[62] Likewise, Diboll residents Amos Harris, DeWitt Wilkerson, and Mrs. Sidney Walters Kindley all testified about the openness of Diboll moonshining in the early days.[63] Some whisky men operated so close to town that "they'd turn on the light so people could know there was whisky there," Kindley noted, adding, "He [the Diboll law] would walk up and down the railroad tracks and then go home, he didn't want to get mixed up in that."[64]

Some mill managements tacitly approved (or at least ignored) certain illegalities and irregularities in their town's quarter, leaving the quarter boss to regulate matters and keep the peace. Quarter bosses could overstep their bounds (for example, by roughing up the wrong person or banishing someone from the town without the mill superintendent's permission), but they operated with wide discretion.[65] Quarter bosses Ike Green and Jay Boren enforced the formal and informal racial rules of Diboll—for example, that no blacks could cross the railroad tracks to the white side of town after dark.[66] Quarter bosses also functioned like truant officers, rousting out tardy workers to their jobs when they tried to "lay out" in the mornings.[67] Sometimes, the quarter boss (or the constable or deputy) evicted laid-off workers from company houses for failure to pay the rents, a matter so common and troublesome for Kirby Lumber Company that Kirby's legal department devised a special form for the purpose.[68]

After studying justice of the peace court records for the Carter Lumber Company town of Camden, historians Maxwell and Baker found that the most frequent charges were assault and battery, fighting, gambling and keeping gambling houses, petty theft, and abuse of the Sabbath. The latter was punished most severely, at least in Camden.[69]

Drinking, fighting, gambling, and adultery had not been learned in the mill town, however; the turn-of-the-century East Texas countryside from which sawmill people came was a rough place. Born at Lime Ridge community, Polk County, five miles north of Corrigan, Icie Waltman recalled several saloons in Corrigan—and a drinking problem among local farmers. "Every little place that had a post office, then, had a saloon," Waltman said. Farmers would go into town to sell "the little dab of milk, butter, or eggs, or whatever," gather at the saloons, drink, stay late, and sometimes get into fistfights and shootings. Waltman's grandfather had two sons living near him, and one of them, William, always went into Corrigan. Every Saturday, "when it began to get dusky-dark, my granddaddy would say, 'Well, I got to go to Corrigan to see about William.'" And after a while he returned with his dead-drunk son riding in front of him on the family's big red horse.[70]

John Henry Kirby grew up at Peach Tree Village in Tyler County, and in reminiscing about early days there he commented on rural proclivities for gambling and fistfighting. Every "trading point" community had at least one race track, where local farmers raced horses and bet on the outcomes. Peach Tree Village had two tracks, described as "straight, parallel, bridal paths on level ground, carefully plowed and rooted, then packed down, sometimes with a heavy maul, but more frequently by leading horses and mules over them and filling in the softer places with sod."[71] "Card playing" was another common gambling diversion, often practiced away from the house and the womenfolks, sometimes "down in a secluded thicket by firelight, rich pine knot constituting the fuel."[72] Shooting matches and fistfights were other competitive male diversions of the countryside, sometimes gambled on and sometimes not. Rural Texans conducted fistfights under the awesome rules of "stomp-and-gouge," which Kirby well described: "A contestant could not use anything but the members of his body. He could kick, gouge, choke, strangle, pull hair, or resort to anything else with his hands, feet, head, legs, arms, or mouth. He could not use a weapon of any kind, nor a stick, nor a stone, pocketknife, piece of metal, brass knucks, or anything other than his bare body."[73]

Apparently, stomp-and-gouge rules still applied at Copeston, on the edge of Diboll, when Clarence Sanders bit off part of Fukes Fairchild's ear in a fight outside the Green Lantern Cafe.[74] Fistfights were common at the wide-open mill town of Groveton, and workers just leaving the mill precincts at quitting time often matched up waiting youths, paid each a nickel, placed bets on the outcome, and launched a fight. Claude Kennedy had long arms and a reputation as a fistfighter, and his rule was "fight fair, but get in the first lick, and make it count." Kennedy's son noted, "The way they done then, if it got around that a feller was good with his fists, why everybody else that could fight good would want to try him. I expect a feller would have to feel like he was pretty good before he'd want to try Papa."[75] The predilection for hand-to-hand combat extended from the bottom to the top of sawmill-town society, since Irish railroad laborers fought trained bears for drinks in Hardin County bars, and Kirby Lumber Company records document fistfights between superintendents and sawyers, commissary store managers and head cashiers, and other "elite" match-ups.

Male passions occasionally escalated fisticuffs to stabbings and shootings. At Manning, a "big, stout, robust-type fellow with red hair, who was not afraid of anything," named Red Waller, got into a fight with a Mexican man named Peño. Waller was a bully of a man, the sort who volunteered to fight the bear when the medicine show came through, but this time he had met his match. After an argument broke out at the end of the silent movie on Saturday night, Peño pulled out a "pig sticker" and stabbed Waller several times in the stomach.[76] Similar episodes were remembered in every mill town, for example the mysterious killing of the black man known as "Pine Knot" at Diboll.[77] Sexual jealousy often triggered these affairs; former residents told researchers that mill hands had worried a lot about the possible sexual escapades of their supposedly sick or injured cohorts, left behind all day in the housing areas. After a man began work in the morning, he could not come home to check on his wife until the noon downtime.[78] Sometimes family feuds plagued the countryside around the mill towns—Trinity and Shelby, among others, had special reputations as bad "feud counties"—and sometimes these traditional interfamily disputes spilled over into the towns. These affairs of family honor sometimes resulted in "killings," deadly conflicts between consenting adults, which were avoided at all costs by persons outside the blood feud and commonly no-billed by county grand juries. An old man from Burke delivered fresh vegetables every morning to Diboll's Star Hotel, run by Sadie Estes Woods's mother. One day, the man left to get some ice at the ice house, and a man shot him dead in the street. Woods recalled: "Mother run to the front door and told us to come in there quick. Told us, 'You didn't see nothin!' She was afraid they would take us to court. And we ran in the house, and we didn't know nothing, but we sure saw the man shoot him. Diboll was pretty bad. It used to get the name, too, of having the prettiest girls in the world and the meanest men."[79] Also applied to many other sawmill towns across the East Texas countryside, the saying doubtless was regarded by both sexes as flattering.

Gambling was another mill-town proclivity—not surprising in a work force already paid in something resembling poker chips. Veteran lumber-company executive Clyde Woodward recalled that crap shooting was the biggest vice among black sawmill hands, but whites shot crap and played poker as well.[80] Tom Temple's teen-aged son, just testing the waters of Southern Pine employment, once was discovered rolling dice with African American co-workers under the mill dollyways.[81] Baseball contests between mill towns so commonly were bet upon (and fought over) that

Tom Temple once banished baseball from Diboll for a generation. Gambling went on every weekend at Kilraven in a vacant house near the mill, watched over by an approving constable.[82] One family moved into such a house in another mill town and soon began to find so much money in the crawl space under cracks in the floor that a major search was launched, ultimately accumulating several day's wages.[83] The loan-shark business peaked during the weekends, as gamblers and drinkers ran out of money. Dave Martinez's brother, a mill-town constable, discovered a profitable sideline loaning money to destitute gamblers to be paid back a dollar a week. Although the constable did not demand his principal, the interest payments went on and on. Martinez said, "sometimes they would pay him back fifty dollars for the twenty dollars."[84] At Diboll, young African American Willie Massey began company employment at the terrible job of shoveling bark from the bottom of the millpond, but soon he began to get ahead at the expense of black practitioners of the sporting life. Massey was paying off a debt to his father, and after room and board cleared only $2.20 a week, but:

> I was very thoughtful and very determined to succeed, so I would take that $2.20 a week and invest it somehow, let somebody use it, and they would pay me back $5 or $6 on the weekends. I continued this until I got to the place where I had several $20 bills in my pockets at all times. Within the community there was a lot of drinking and gambling going on, but I didn't participate in that sort of thing, but I would let these fellows borrow a little money I had. They would pay me back double on the weekend.[85]

Gambling, drinking, and fighting tended to be related phenomena at the mill towns. Legal saloons, some of them operated by the companies, dispensed beer and whisky until the prohibition movement gradually forced them onto private property in the nearby countryside, then into outlaw status. Even Tom Temple's Diboll had harbored two saloons at the turn of the century, much to the Christian Scientist's disapproval. The nearby saloons remained flashpoints for Saturday night trouble, though often outside the jurisdictions of mill-town law. Millowner Joe Rice had the best of both worlds with his saloon; he moved it out of town so employees could sober up with a mile walk before they came home, and it also drew customers from another mill town a mile away in the other direction.[86]

At a few places, saloons and prohibition battles to vanquish them caused major trouble for the companies. In Groveton, Trinity County

Lumber Company had sold off land on one side of the main-line tracks for a public town, which quickly became the county seat. By 1900, the public side of the tracks featured almost as many saloons and gambling establishments as it did other businesses. Trinity County Lumber Company's opinions about this may be inferred, since the company did not pay its workers enough to support both their families and dedicated drinking and gambling lifestyles. Trinity County had been unusually violent during the Civil War and Reconstruction years, and county historian Flora Bowles believed there were many connections between those troubled times and the whisky wars around the turn of the century. She noted in her 1928 study: "From those days [after the Civil War] to the beginning of the mill operations there had remained among the people a sufficient number of former lawless people, together with some who came with the mill activities, to bring or maintain a condition of disorder. With the passing years, conditions grew worse, until at the close of the century, there was a reign of lawlessness that was appalling."[87]

Whisky drinkers and saloon operators in Groveton for long had the upper hand, outnumbering their opponents and electing county officials "with a clear understanding that they should cater to the wishes of the law breakers who were their creators as officers."[88] Mill workers drew their daily wages "only to spend it in the saloon or gambling den," and the families of these underpaid workmen suffered accordingly from poverty and inadequate diet. "Children were half clad and showed the pinch of poverty in their faces." Groveton merchants stocked few toys at Christmas time, since they knew that the hard-drinking mill hands would have little money to spend for them. Fistfights and killings became commonplace events. Drunks rode their horses into places of business to make purchases from the convenience of their saddles or simply on a lark. "It was no uncommon thing on Saturday for a drunken crowd of gangsters to race their horses through the streets shooting into places of business." Soon, women and children stopped frequenting Groveton streets on Saturdays, and merchants began closing their doors at noon, when whisky consumption picked up, "and repaired to their homes and spent the day in seclusion."[89] After a while, things grew so bad that the Texas Rangers came to wicked Groveton to take up semipermanent residence. After prolonged experience of the town, Texas Ranger Captain Bill McDonald, remarked of the place: "If a whole community has no use for law and order, it's not worth while to try to enforce such things. You've got to stand over a place like that with a gun to make it behave, and when you catch a man, no matter what the evidence against him, they'll cut him loose. In Groveton when I was there, they had only two law respecting officers—the district clerk and the county attorney, and the county attorney they killed. Good citizens were so completely in the minority that they were helpless."[90]

Meanwhile, across the railroad tracks, ruled from afar by the worried Joyce family of Chicago, was one of the five largest sawmills in the United States. Beginning in 1900, the company watched anxiously as the whisky war escalated. Finally goaded into action, the law and order faction began to strike back, and its focus was the saloons. In March of 1900, the Groveton school district held an election to determine whether liquor could continue to be sold within the limits of the district, and the "drys" won. Groveton saloonkeepers defied the law for a while, then moved just beyond district lines on the three roads leading into town and founded new settlements called Tight Eye, Battle Axe, and Last Chance. In several ways, this made things worse than before. Lax law enforcement in Groveton now was replaced with no law enforcement, since these places lay beyond Groveton jurisdictions. Mill workers spent more time away from home getting drunk, since they now had to walk two or three miles back and forth to their whisky and gambling establishments. Roads to and from these whisky settlements became dangerous, and law-abiding people feared to pass through the new communities; the more timid felt themselves trapped in Groveton, with only the railroad as a way out.[91]

This went on for two years, then, in 1902, a county-wide election closed all the legal saloons in Trinity County, signaling a general conversion to illegal back-room bars, bootleggers, and moonshiners. In December of 1903, young Methodist minister Jesse Lee arrived in the town and was immediately offended by the gap between official law and private practice. Soon, Lee preached sermons from his pulpit against liquor and lawlessness, calling the names of the Groveton businessmen who sold illegal whisky. On one memorable occasion, Lee's congregation included all county officers, the entire Texas Ranger force assigned to Groveton, and every major whisky man. Lee blistered the latter in his sermon to provoke them to action in front of the Rangers, but they sat tight. Later, however, they or their agents threatened Lee's life, burned the Methodist parsonage, and threw beer bottles at the minister as he walked the streets at night. An undercover man, hired by the drys to collect evidence on illegal liquor sales, turned up dead.[92]

Finally, the frustrated Texas Rangers pulled out of Groveton in disgust, and the drys, led by Lee, swore a blood oath to close the Groveton saloons or die trying. Ten men met secretly one night, and Lee told them: "I will sign an article of agreement to meet here tomorrow morning at eight o'clock and go in a body to these illicit saloons, smash every one, put the proprietors out peaceably if they will go, and if not, kill them on the inside, nail up the doors of these buildings and tell the owners that if they are ever rented for such purposes again we will tear them down."[93] All parties signed the document, but the next morning the county judge suggested that they first send men to every legitimate business in Groveton and to the offices of the Trinity County Lumber Company to invite additional participation. This proved an excellent idea. At mid-morning, bolstered by the new recruits, a vigilante group of over one hundred men marched into every illegal saloon in Groveton, broke every whisky bottle, smashed every whisky barrel, and nailed every door shut. Nobody was killed, since the whisky men got out of the way of the mob (which afterward formalized itself as the "Groveton Law and Order League").[94]

Historian Bowles was careful in what she said about Trinity County Lumber Company involvement in the antiwhisky mob of 1902 (in 1928 the company still operated, and its woods and buildings remained as vulnerable to arson as ever), but the company probably turned out its entire office staff to join the vigilantes. Such episodes probably were rare in the sawmill towns, where the companies normally kept much better control over community life than at Groveton. Matters were not always serene, however: commissary counterfeiters, outlaw land men, would-be arsonists and saboteurs, racist backwoodsmen at the "front," and such varied organizations as the Ku Klux Klan and the Brotherhood of Timber Workers kept company lawmen on the alert.

At one point or another, nearly every company had trouble with counterfeiters, who often found the base-metal tokens easier to duplicate than the cardboard money. Texas Rangers investigated one such instance at Groveton and found perfect plaster-of-paris dies for producing the $1.00 and $.50 company checks. The phony coinage was so good that even experts could barely detect it.[95] Occasionally, counterfeiters operated on the inside; a Kirby Lumber Company meat-market manager, under an assumed name, once ordered a thousand dollars of paper merchandise checks from a printing company in Orange, Texas. The printers sent the company money into Bessmay shadowed by a Kirby operative, but the ambitious meat-market man became alarmed and never picked it up.[96] Gradually, more and more companies began using hand-signed, edge-sewn, cardboard tokens, since these seemed more difficult for counterfeiters to duplicate.[97]

The higher up a company's chain of command outlaws operated, the harder they were to catch. From the turn of the century until the Great Depression, John Henry Kirby hired spies to watch out for union activists, disgruntled employees, and white-collar thieves, and the reports of these operatives fill entire boxes in the company's papers.[98] Tom Temple was not known for his undercover investigators, but he occasionally employed them. At one point, young Diboll office worker Kenneth Nelson found himself designated as Man Friday for a strange auditor, recently sent to Diboll by Temple. Fat, bumbling Jim Lee seemed an eccentric alcoholic—not the sort of man one would expect the teetotal Temple to employ. Nelson quickly found out that his principal duties included driving Lee to Houston every few days to tank up on Michelob Beer and making weekly runs to the taxi stand or drugstores in Lufkin for liquor. On the way back from Houston, always after dark, Lee ordered repeated stops to relieve himself, always telling Nelson, "Young fellow, you might better stop. I'm going to water Mr. Temple's wheels."[99] Lee drank whisky in his room every night, slung ink all over the company wall beside his work station, and told the same jokes over and over again, but in the end he did his job. He had been sent down to Diboll by Temple to run a check on some of the land men, and after a while he caught a man who had been buying land for himself with Southern Pine money. Jim Lee looked like a fat drunk, but he was really a crack company super-operative in disguise.

Disgruntled employees existed before and after the coming of the Brotherhood of Timber Workers, and company executives and lawmen always worried about arson and industrial sabotage. Kirby purchased Keith Lumber Company at Voth in 1922, and despite official announcements that Keith employees would retain their old jobs, after a while this turned out not to be the case. A new Mississippi mill manager was brought in, and he began to replace Texans with Mississippeans. Soon, emery dust and steel shavings ruined the dynamo and other machinery, and a Kirby operative got a man drunk enough to reveal which former Keith employee had done the deed. This man told that he had "heard Hubert say that if he did not hold his job he would make it hard as hell for the next man and all the rest of the Mississippi gang."[100]

Emery dust in the dynamo was a small thing compared to burning down the mill, however. Sawmills and planer mills were incendiary work-places, but rumors of arson followed many mill fires. Sawmill executives were well aware of the old Southern tradition of revenge arson, though such matters seemed almost too awful to talk about in print.[101] Mill exec-utives expected sawmill night watchmen to exercise eternal vigilance, and according to an industry journal there was a long-standing practice at sawmills of offering a reward of $5.00 "to anybody who could steal the lantern of a night watchmen on duty and take it to the office of the fore-man in the morning."[102] This event, of course, swiftly ended that night watchman's career. Kirby Lumber Company executives often sent letters back and forth, analyzing the possible causes of suspicious fires.[103] Fiery disaster— perhaps even the same arsonists—seemed to follow some mill-owners around. Burned out at his first mill, Hal Aldridge built a new mill town in Jasper County, only to be burned out once more under very sus-picious circumstances. Aldridge rebuilt a supposedly fire-proof new mill at the same site, then in 1914 an arsonist attacked again, with a fire started in the yard but soon put out. This time arson seemed certain, since inves-tigators found a half-empty barrel of kerosene near where the fire started. A year later, someone struck again, and Aldridge's concrete mill proved just as vulnerable as his wooden ones; the big concrete building was gutted by fire, and Aldridge sold out.[104] Franklin Weeks reported that the Hoshall sawmill also burned down more than once, and for suspicious reasons: "One man remembers during a lighting and thunder storm see-ing a man running through, opening the door to the kiln, then to the dry shed, pouring gasoline, and setting it afire as he went."[105] The more arbi-trary a company's policies (and the more absentee its ownership), the more suspicious mill fires it seemed to have. By all accounts, the 4-C mill at Ratcliff was especially troubled by these matters—perhaps because of company attitudes demonstrated by the sixteen-foot-high board fence walling off employees from the nearby town.[106]

As Max Bentley observed at Wiergate in 1921, the companies also wor-ried about "serious conflagrations" of a social nature and the "one little spark" that might set them off.[107] Integrated workplaces and segregated multiracial towns presented the potential for trouble, and company super-visors, relentlessly in search of greater production, sometimes dared to fa-vor the minority over the Anglo. Dwayne Overstreet recalled that "My dad once worked for Kirby at $1 a day—worked for Hi Smith—and when Smith found a black man who would work faster and harder, he fired my father."[108] The higher up the pecking order of the mill this sort of thing took place, however, the more often it caused trouble. When the Call mill manager tried to replace a white sawyer with a black sawyer during the day's run, the Anglo whipped the manager in front of all hands and Kirby officials soon forced him to resign. Nor did the black sawyer fare well. Kirby general manager J. W. Link wrote another official soon after the incident: "I don't believe it is good policy to keep an extra negro sawyer. In other words, I doubt whether the white men will ever stand for a negro during the sawing. A negro is all right as long as he is held within certain bounds, but it will not do to let him get to the top job."[109] Four days later the second Kirby official replied: "Wish to advise that I have already instructed that we discontinue using this negro or another one as an entire sawyer or any other job which is termed a white man's job. You are correct in that we should not do anything to cause any kind of feeling between white and colored labor. We have enough trouble without doing something that is liable to bring on more."[110]

No "race riots" were noted in the sawmill towns in company records or personal accounts, but the companies did have occasional troubles with racist local people at their integrated woods camps and a continuing problem with retaining adequate minority labor at their mills. Dissatisfied black workers might not rebel, but they often left for other sawmill towns, went cotton picking, or even departed Texas for the cities of the North. During the early 1920s, incipient Ku Klux Klan organizations in the towns alarmed the companies by their vigilante actions along the delicate boundaries between the races outside the mill, challenging the companies' control and further disturbing black labor.

Concerns with retaining or recruiting adequate minority labor appear everywhere in the voluminous papers of the Kirby Lumber Company, and every fall during good lumber years industry newspapers filled with laments for wayward mill hands turned cotton pickers. On October 1, 1911, the *St. Louis Lumberman* noted: "The crop is being harvested everywhere, now. The demand for hands to pick cotton has worked hardship on the Texas sawmills already. It is reported from Lufkin, Texas, that 400 negroes, most of whom were mill hands, were shipped to the cotton patches out of that town alone."[111] And in August, 1912, *Southwest* lamented: "The colored laborers of the southwest are now on their way to the cotton patch, and the labor shortage is settling down on the mill men. There is no way to keep the negro from going to the cotton patch."[112]

To combat labor problems during the peak lumber years before and during World War I, John Henry Kirby circulated recruiting posters for

blacks throughout the towns of Texas and Louisiana and sent black recruiters to Brazos Valley cotton plantations and the older Southern states.
One black minister reported: "Since I met your mill managers at Silsbee,
I have worked Central Texas and the farmers on the Brazos. I can get you
labor from the old states. I have put your Houston office in correspondence with laborers and farmers in North Carolina, Alabama, Arkansas,
and Georgia, and in correspondence with many colored farmers in Texas.
I have not quit work. I have got the leading preachers in the state of
Georgia advising the colored farmers to come to Texas and seek work in
the mills."[113] During the war, Kirby used a different set of recruiters to
bring large numbers of Mexicans to Texas to fill the lower-level jobs at his
mill towns and woods camps, and he pressured the U.S. Congress to relax
immigration laws to help him deal with his labor shortages.[114]

The new Mexican labor did not go unopposed, however. In March of
1918, newly arrived Mexicans at a Kirby woods camp out of Silsbee were
"getting along nicely" until, as the foreman reported, their: "tent was shot
into last night by unknown parties, and doubt that we will be able to hold
our crew there. We have no idea who is guilty of this disturbance more
than it is no doubt the old feeling through this section against any foreigners locating or working up here."[115]

By 1918, trouble at the woods camps was an old problem for the companies and one of the things that led minority labor to depart for better
work situations. Although the timber crew at the company front might
appear to operate in the primal wilderness, it was always somewhere, in
some dispersed rural "settlement" well recognized by local people, and
some of these places had long-standing whites-only traditions. Company
control was strongest in the towns (though Kirby Lumber Company had
trouble at Bronson, due to traditional antiblack sentiments at that place)
and weakest in the woods camps—remote, migratory, box-car communities a long way from the quarter bosses.[116] White and black families
resided in close contact at the camps, and this might lead to increased cooperation or to trouble, depending on circumstances and the personalities
involved. A black man reported of the Southern Pine camp of Alcedo,
"The houses, they was in a circle, in other words, the whites and the coloreds mostly stayed right together there at Alcedo."[117] Nothing unseemly
was reported at Alcedo, but at a camp out from Warren, James Addison
Moye recalled: "They wouldn't let Negroes stay on the Warren tram, that
was one place they couldn't work em, crew run em off, crew tarred and
feathered em."[118]

A mixed-race woods crew, Thompson Lumber Company, 1911. During cotton-
picking season, many black employees temporarily deserted their low-paying
lumber company jobs for more profitable labors outside the mill towns.
*Courtesy of the East Texas Research Center, Stephen F. Austin State
University, Nacogdoches, Texas.*

Most commonly, it was the neighboring farmers and free-range stockmen that caused the trouble. Timber camps had their own schools and
stores so as to remain discreetly isolated from the surrounding natives,
and the companies also tried to improve relations with their neighbors by
offering medical help, store services, and free sharpening of farmers'
plows in the camp blacksmith shops.[119] Sometimes, however, isolation
and friendly gestures failed to overcome local people's distaste for strange
blacks and Mexicans in their midst. Kirby camps out from Bronson were
troubled by "pea patch farmers," one of whom placed a careful shot
through the hat crown of the Kirby woods foreman.[120] Slocum, near the
Southern Pine camp of Fastrill, remained a no-go area for African Americans until a passing tornado reformed the place. A black man told: "You

couldn't even stop there and get gas—Uh uh!—until that storm come through there and like to have wiped Slocum away—a twister—you could buy gas then."[121] At Groveton's woods camps, as historian Flora Bowles described: "Sometimes the residents would object to the foreigner or the strange negro coming among them. The Mexican was especially obnoxious, and came in for persecution in one way or another designed to drive him from his work. Many times there might appear upon the trees a poster saying, 'Nigger, don't let the sun rise on you here tomorrow morning.'"[122] In October of 1908, the *Southern Industrial and Lumber Review* indignantly complained:

> Cases of trouble between the sawmill companies and the farmers owning land close to the mills have been the cause of a great deal of trouble during the past year. In most cases the trouble seems to be purely malicious on the part of the farmers. They sell the timber on their lands to the sawmill companies, and when these concerns send their crews to cut the timber, the farmers refused to allow the Negro workers of the company to venture on their land to cut the

A team of black tree fellers at work in the woods. *Courtesy of the East Texas Research Center, Stephen F. Austin State University, Nacogdoches, Texas.*

timber. During the past month, there have been reports of trouble of this nature from the mill of the Carter-Kelly company at Manning. It was found
necessary to get officers to protect the colored laborers while they were doing
their work.[123]

During the early 1920s, the national spread of the "Invisible Empire"
of the Ku Klux Klan brought the KKK into the company towns, where
the Klan seems to have focused its attentions on social irregularities associated with the quarters—domino halls, "barrel houses," illegal alcohol,
gambling houses, prostitutes, and Anglo-American seekers after these diversions. Companies were wary of the Klan, especially at first, but they re-
sisted any organization that sought to compromise their social control of
their towns, and they feared the KKK's impact on black labor.

Former Diboll resident Josephine Rutland Frederick, daughter of the
commissary store manager, recalled that the Klan arrived at Diboll with
an emphasis on "right living, black or white." On the march down the
tracks from nearby Lufkin, they tarred and feathered a man in Emporia
for "trifling on his wife," then: "Just about dark, I was coming across that
little bridge, and I looked up and saw that flaming cross coming down
this track—scared me to death and I ran home. It was horrifying. I saw all
these men in white sheets in a long line coming down the train tracks.
Their policy was at every other house, they would leave a cross."[124] Mrs.
Sidney Walters Kindley affirmed the Klan's focus at Diboll on "intruders
and people that were not acceptable," and recalled that: "one night, when
we were having a church meeting, they marched under the arbor and
asked if they could have charge of the services. They conducted a very
good evening's program, and then they marched out."[125] Black resident of
Diboll Carey Smith remembered a ruder visit of the Klan to the quarter
and its church, focused on white line-crossers and their black associates:
"Old man Burris, he was the law. He would get in there and dance with
those niggers in that [barrel] house all night, dead drunk. Those white
men were coming over here and laying around with the Negro women—
men with white wives over there. They came over to the church house
one night. You remember Buleah? They were coming looking for her to
kill her, white men come in the church. That ain't getting on record, is it?
I don't think I should of said that."[126]

As at other company towns, the Klan in Diboll usurped the company's
power of banishment by ordering certain people out of town. One night,
a man came over from Groveton after being banished by the Klan from

that place and waited to catch the next train out of the county at the Diboll hotel. He was so afraid he would miss his twelve midnight transportation that he "borrowed not one but two alarm clocks and set those alarm clocks so he could catch his train." On another occasion, a lady who was "not acceptable" visited Diboll, and the house where she was staying soon received a note that she must get out of town by midnight. The lady caught her twelve o'clock train, as commanded by the KKK, but she remained defiant, since "when the train started off, she came out on the little back porch and fired a pistol."[127] Probably the unacceptable pistol-packer was a traveling prostitute or "railroad lady," a class of professional that often visited the sawmill towns.

No document records the responses of Tom Temple and the Southern Pine Lumber Company to KKK incursions in its town, but the evolution of Kirby Lumber Company's attitudes to the Klan may be traced in the company correspondence. The Klan first surfaced at Village Mills in 1921, when several company foremen received warning notes to get out of town.[128] Management tended to dismiss this as the work of "idle boys" or even blacks with typewriters; anyone, after all, could send a malicious note and sign it "KKK," but things soon became more alarming. The Klan established a chapter in Kirbyville in 1922, and in July of that year, Rev. Walter E. Rogers, a Beaumont Baptist preacher and front man for the KKK, held a two-day revival at the Kirby town of Call. After the second night's revival, Rogers gave a talk in support of the Klan to an audience of white men and a handful of blacks, condemning moonshine, gambling, and dancing, and warning blacks to "clean up" the vice in their quarter. He also commanded whites living in sin to get married and the white men to keep away from the black women. Black men attempting to seduce white women should be lynched, Reverend Rogers thought, but in return black men should have the right to kill white men trying to seduce their wives.[129]

Reverend Rogers's postsermon lecture threw Call's black community into consternation, as did KKK-signed notices posted in the quarter advising certain persons to get out of town. KKK letters were sent to Elmore Jenkins, the black owner of a barbershop and restaurant, who was accused of allowing domino and piano playing during Sunday services. Another black man operating a dance hall also was ordered out of town.[130]

As Kirby management debated what to do, nervous black families began to leave Call in search of safer employment. A company operative reported that several men had departed, that others were planning to leave after the next payday, and that a black-labor recruiter for Louisiana sawmills had come to Call to fish in the troubled waters.[131]

N. P. Barton, mill superintendent at Call, informed Kirby headquarters that the Klan had some ten members among the mill staff, including such elite employees as the company doctor, the commissary manager, and the saw filer, but he favored eliminating them root and branch, noting: "The Ku Klux Klan are in indirect ways trying to scare some of our negro employees out of town, so far I have kept them pacified. I have no place here for disloyalty and it is my intention to gently fire all men involved directly under my supervision."[132]

Company executives at first reacted with caution. They ordered Barton to hold off on his firings, sent in operatives to investigate the situation in Call, and even asked the Houston Klan to look into the matter. After a while, the company authorized the firing of the Call doctor on other grounds than his KKK membership, and Barton forced the commissary manager and saw filer to leave the Klan, on pain of dismissal. Meanwhile, Barton tried to clean up or gloss over some of the traditional irregularities in the black quarter that the Klan had complained about, for one thing asking Elmore Jenkins to move his barbershop and restaurant off the main road where it would attract less attention. However, when the incensed Jenkins threatened to leave town, Barton talked him out of it and sent company carpenters in to spruce up his premises.[133]

By 1924, Klan activity had subsided in John Henry Kirby's timber towns, and the company's position had hardened. After some initial caution, the company demonstrated its usual distaste for anything or anybody challenging its authority, and KKK organizers found Kirby's towns—with their controlled work force, company lawmen, resident snitches, and visiting spies—very uncongenial places in which to operate. In 1924, vicepresident and general manager J. W. Link summarized Kirby Lumber Company's official position on the Klan in uncompromising terms to Dr. Wier, the head of the company's medical services. "If the Ku Klux Klan has ever served any good purpose, I have failed to find it," Link wrote. "These organizations have engendered hatred between neighbors and friends; they have endeavored to control every political election from Constable to President, they are striving to control the schools. The Klan is undoubtedly based upon religious prejudice and is contrary to the principles of our Government, and I want to see it wiped out."[134] However, moral statements aside, the worst sin of the Ku Klux Klan had been to challenge company authority in its own towns. As the Brotherhood of Timber Workers had discovered ten years before, the only "Invisible Empire" allowed in the sawmill communities was the company's.

John Henry Kirby may have disliked the Klan, but his feelings about the Brotherhood of Timber Workers were nothing short of vitriolic; he once referred to a Brotherhood organizer as "this wolf." In a letter to a friend in Woodville on July 16, 1912, Kirby detailed steps taken by authorities "and a committee of working men" to prevent the organizer from addressing crowds in Houston and Lake Charles, Louisiana, then urged "you and your law abiding citizens, who believe in the church, the maintenance of a family relation, the preservation of property, and the stability of American institutions, to see to it that this wolf is not permitted the use of the people's courthouse in a Christian law-abiding community [Woodville] for the purpose of preaching the doctrines, which he will expound."[135]

For a variety of reasons (among them, the missing of paydays), labor troubles had dogged the Kirby Lumber Company from the beginning, although until around 1911 the Kirby work force remained unorganized, and strikes and walkouts were spontaneous and short-lived. The company, however, vehemently opposed all demands of labor. Kirby official B. F. Bonner wrote John Henry Kirby on October 8, 1903: "The labor agitators are now upon us. They have organized the Trinity County Lumber Co. at Groveton. I will put Nuening actively at work on the plans outlined to you some time ago, and we think we will have a meeting soon from all the large lumbermen."[136] Five days later Bonner further informed Kirby:

> We have had a walk out in planer B today because of passing a payday. Sixty-five men quit and are trying to get others to quit. Perhaps we can corral enough negroes to operate? We took a pretty stiff position, merely stating that we were not the first people to pass a payday. I think passing this payday has been a blessing in disguise. It has demonstrated that not only is there plenty of labor, but that it is a tolerable easy matter to retain it. When you return and finances will permit a full regular payday in all of the mills, I am fully confident it will be an easy matter not only to reduce the wages we are paying, but to put them back down on the 11-hour basis. We would not have a shutdown then over two or three mills, if any.[137]

Bonner's intransigent attitudes toward labor were in no way unusual among the principal mill men and derived from two decades of worker-management conflict. As economist Ruth Allen observed, "Industrial relations in the lumber industry of Texas have never been marked by peace.

The workers in the pineries of the Sabine area have made sporadic but continuous attempts, both organized and unorganized, to protest."[138] Reverberations of the big national railroad and coal-mine strikes of 1877 had been felt in Texas, where in August the *Galveston Daily News* reported that 250 black mill workers at Harrisburg had armed themselves and were threatening to burn the town.[139] In May of 1886, the entire work force of the Eylan sawmill struck, demanding a reduction in weekly work hours from sixty-six to sixty and no change in the base wage of $1.71 a day. After a week, they won out. In 1890, sawmill men in all of the Orange mills walked out in a spontaneous strike, also demanding a reduction in weekly work hours, but they failed to get their demands. Three years later all the Orange mills shut down again, and millowner Alexander Gilmer reported "anarchy prevailing in town."[140]

Between 1900 and 1910, the U.S. Bureau of Labor Statistics noted various informal strikes and shutdowns, some of them involving hundreds of millhands. Sometimes, strikes protested conditions at the timber camps; in 1901, woods-camp men struck Trinity County Lumber Company at Groveton, protesting low wages of $.80 a day and "virtual chattel slavery conditions." Sometimes they protested missed paydays, as at the Kirby mills in 1903. Union men toured the Texas and Louisiana pine towns, circulating disquieting flyers like that of John W. Davis in 1904, which told sawmill workers: "You have created the great wealth that is now enjoyed by the millionaire millowners, who seldom even see their property to say nothing of doing any useful work connected with it. And yet you are the poorest paid lumbermen in America. You work more hours each day for less wages than any other lumbermen in the country."[141] Davis's jibes stung the companies, since many Texas mills were indeed absentee owned and Texas wages ranged well below those of the Northwest Coast. In 1907, economic conditions worsened, many East Texas and Louisiana mills went on reduced running times and wages, and many workers on both sides of the Sabine walked out in a spontaneous general strike, which proved short and unsuccessful. Other flash strikes continued, usually over the issues of daily wages and workday length. During 1908, for example, workers struck the Lufkin Land and Lumber Company at Lufkin, the Southern Pine Lumber Company at Diboll, the 4-C mill at Ratcliff, and the Orange Sawmill Company at Orange.[142]

At all these places, workers achieved little; companies rarely gave in to any of their informal strike demands. Instead, they beat the strikers to the punch with lockouts, refused all their requests, threatened to hire new

workers, and sometimes did hire new workers. Companies also took maximum advantage of their control of the sawmill towns to swiftly fire and
banish troublemakers—tactics that soon would be used against the labor
organizers of the Brotherhood of Timber Workers.[143]

In 1910, disaffected East Texas sawmill hands founded the Brotherhood independent of any other labor group and began a drive to organize Southern pineries, precipitating a three-year struggle that fully revealed the companies' power over their timber towns. A moderate union
by the standards of the time, the Brotherhood explicitly recognized the
rights of employers and discouraged violence. The preamble to the union's constitution stated: "While demanding our rights, we, at the same
time, concede that the employer is entitled to, and we promise him, an
absolute square deal in every sense that this implies. We ask for nothing
which we are not willing to grant. To secure justice we must do justice.
Violence, in all its forms, shall be discouraged. Property rights should be
respected."[144] The Brotherhood was concerned with the "long and trying
hours of labor" and proclaimed its intention to "use every legitimate effort to remove and correct such obvious and patent abuses as compulsory
doctor's fees, hospital dues, the unfair insurance system so universally
practiced, the inordinately high commissary prices, the high rents
charged for the rental of homes, and any and all other unfair and unjust
impositions now fastened upon us by employers. . . . We demand recognition, equal rights, a living wage, a just consideration of abuses, exact and
equal justice."[145] The demands of the Brotherhood for a minimum wage
of $2.00 a day, a ten-hour, six-day work week, pay every two weeks in
U.S. currency, the right to trade outside the commissary, and the right to
choose their own doctors remained unchanged throughout the union's
three-year battle with the companies.

Despite the relatively moderate nature of the demands, industry reac-
tion to them was that of adamant opposition. The *St. Louis Lumberman*
considered the demands such that "no yellow pine manufacturer could do
business under them," and rather than submit "wholesale shutdowns of
plants will be ordered."[146] John Henry Kirby condemned the new union
as "a socialist organization composed largely of foreign-born citizens
which would plunge all the states into anarchy and bring disorder and the
rule of brute force into every community in America."[147] Kirby swiftly
moved to take the lead in the Southern Lumber Operator's Association,
which met in New Orleans in 1910, vowing to "stomp out the Brotherhood." Not only did Kirby mastermind the association's countermeas-

ures against the union, he effectively propagandized for the company position in the media. Presenting himself as a long-term friend of the
worker, he threatened eloquently in the August 1911 *Southwest* magazine:

> I am talking for the man who has a wife and babies at home, the man who,
> perhaps, has been visited by misfortune, the man who may not be a good
> manager, the man whose meal barrel is not full and who could not stand a
> shutdown. It is in his behalf that I would ask his fellow laborers not to push
> upon him conditions that will destroy him and bring tears to the cheek of his
> good wife, anxiety into both their hearts and distress and hunger to the little
> ones who toddle about their homes."[148]

An editorial in the same edition of *Southwest* scoffed at the possibility
that the Brotherhood could successfully organize both black and white
lumber workers, but the prophesy fell short. The union often tried to recruit men doing a particular job at the workplace, and, since mill work
was integrated, especially at the lower levels of employment, it often organized whites and blacks together. Brotherhood membership was open
to blacks as well as whites, though both had their separate "lodges" and
black lodges were forbidden to retain their initiation fees. The Brotherhood attracted capable leaders, and its appeals proved more galvanizing
to mixed-race audiences than the companies had believed possible. Industry spies attended virtually every public meeting of the union, often
recording the speeches word for word. General superintendent W. C.
Keith of the Keith Lumber Company at Voth wrote a Kirby executive
that he had attended a Sunday meeting that Brotherhood president A. L.
Emerson had held in the town: "After his speech he asked for all who desired to be 'saved' to come forward, and the whole blooming crowd followed the bell-wether. We immediately closed down the camp tight, ordered everybody out, and we are sitting idly by, doing all we can to make
the best of a decidedly bad situation."[149] Of black membership in the union, Emerson stated in a Kirbyville speech of January 16, 1912: "The negro
is here and is here to stay and we can't get rid of him. He must live and to
live he must work, beg, or steal. We are all here and we must live and to
live we must work. Now, gentlemen, you need not preach equality to me
about the negro. Who put the negro in the sawmill? You are working side
by side with the negro in the sawmill and you can't get around that. Let
social affairs take care of themselves. Give the negro his lodge room but
let him be under the management of the white man."[150] The companies
used the inclusion of African Americans against the union, but some un-

ion speakers went farther than Emerson in their rebuttals of this charge. Organizer Ed Lehman told one heckler, who had challenged him about "Issiac Gaines and other niggers in the BTW": "Gaines isn't a nigger, he is a man—a union man, and he has proven it by his actions, and that is more than you have ever done in all your boss-sucking life. There are white men, Negro men, and Mexican men in this union, but no niggers, greasers, or white trash! All are men on the side of the union, and all the greasers, niggers, and white trash are on the side of the lumber trust. And you are one of the white trash, now, get out!"[151]

Dutifully recorded by Kirby operatives in the crowds and stored in the Kirby Lumber Company's papers, some of A. L. Emerson's speeches reveal how tellingly he appealed to workers' grievances. Of Kirby's medical programs, Emerson asked a Kirbyville crowd on January 16, 1912: "How many of you men have taken up a collection to send your brothers, fathers, and friends to the hospital? What are you paying a hospital fee for? I believe in a hospital, and when I pay for a hospital, I want a hospital. And not make me pay for something I don't get. Tell me where the hospitals are that the lumber kings are collecting fees to support? And I have seen company doctors of such character that I'd rather see a dog come into my home than them." Then Emerson focused upon a central issue for the union, the low salaries paid by Kirby and other companies.

> Haven't I put my name to many papers and petitions to help bury a man working under this rotten system all his life, and his friends have had to bury him? It exists today, and this system goes on. Nothing makes me madder than to have these fellows say, "Oh, he ought to have saved his money." Why didn't they give them the money to save? You poor fellows who are working for one-fifty a day and have five or six in your family, how do you live? You don't live, you just exist. You tell me men can raise a family on $1.25 a day? No! When I saw the poverty in your homes, when I saw that certain look in your faces, when I thought of the injury that was being practiced upon these sawmill men, I thought of you. There is more to live for than cash and gold, and I tell you, the time will come, and the time has come, when the welfare of the home will be looked upon with greater value than gold and silver.

Finally, addressing the Kirby spies in the crowd, Emerson taunted: "Now, if you fellows want to arrest me, just do it, and put me in jail. If you arrest me without a cause, then we will see about it. I am not going to take any foolishness at all. I am going into these places, and if you want to arrest me, pop your whip! You can kill me, but you can't scare me. Now, if you fellows want Mr. Kirby to know this, write. I want him to see it."[152]

Probably Kirby did see it. Long before Emerson's 1912 speech at Kirby's namesake town, the companies regarded the Brotherhood of Timber Workers as a formidable adversary. Emerson was indefatigable in his organizational duties. He informed the 1912 convention of the Brotherhood that in the past year he had traveled over 11,000 miles, made 257 public speeches and 85 talks "in halls and in the woods to small crowds of union men," and had 37 of his speeches "broken up by the companies and their pimps."[153]

Union tactics evolved over time. At first, undercover organizers traveled from town to town, often taking a few days employment in woods and mill, talking to workers about the union, then moving on. Emerson did this himself in the early days. By 1911, one lumberman calculated that the Brotherhood had a network of five hundred organizers in the Texas and Louisiana region, and worried company executives variously estimated the union's total membership at from 18,000 to 35,000.[154] Soon, the union launched an additional tactic to recruit new members, organizing picnics and barbecues out in the countryside close to company towns, such as the one where Emerson and Covington Hall spoke in 1912. Sometimes, such affairs ended with a group going over to confront scabs at a nearby mill.[155] The problem with the mass affairs was that they drew union sympathizers out in the open so the company operatives could identify and even photograph them; so, toward the end of the conflict, union organizers again went underground. Union men often canvassed the territory around a mill town for people with special grievances against the companies and recruited them as local organizers. C. P. Myer wrote Kirby, "They appreciate the fact that when they secure that class of people that they have a permanent worker in our midst and one that has a personal spite against the company and will strive always to create discord among our mills."[156]

The tactics of the Brotherhood also became more extreme as time went on and the influence of the International Workers of the World (IWW) on the homegrown union increased. On August 8, 1912, the *New Orleans Times-Democrat* published an IWW leaflet that served as a primer for various forms of "direct action," the euphemism for industrial sabotage, and the Brotherhood's own newsletter, *The Lumberjack*, soon began suggesting these options. On July 10, 1913, "The Wooden Shoe Kid" wrote in *The Lumberjack*:

> What's the trouble with that saw, the carriage is out of line
> Don't it beat you, man, how the hands kill time.

The engine is running hot, that part needs packing again
I heard the boss say, "I've got a hell of a bunch of men."
The fireman can't keep steam, the carriage has jumped the track
I wonder, what does it mean, machinery acting like that?
Lordy, hain't this awful bad, that shipping clerk is a sight
He sent the timber to Bagdide which should have gone to Cadite!

None of this amused the lumbermen. C. P. Myer and Kirby exchanged letters in 1912 discussing how best to warn their mill managers and camp superintendents about the direct action being advocated. Kirby wrote Myer on May 24, 1912, about the dangers of Brotherhood men "driving spikes into the trees standing in the forest and nails into planer stock, and expensive and delicate machinery might be destroyed, and that emery dust might be mixed with lubricating oil, that property destruction might be brought to millowners and operation otherwise rendered so expensive and destructive that they would eventually yield to the domination of Heywood and his band of reckless anarchists."[157]

Meanwhile, Brotherhood and IWW literature endlessly picked away at the lumbermen, first and foremost John Henry Kirby. Kirby was termed "Con J. Kirby," "St. John Kirby," "Director of the Gun Toters," "Sultan of East Texas," "the Peon's Pal," and "the Texas Jackass." Emerson said that Kirby "is so crooked he can't lay straight in bed at night."[158] The poets assaulted Kirby, as well. Before moving on to verses aimed at other lumbermen, a union poet warned:

We are coming, brother Kirby, we are coming in our might
Hear the thunder of our legions now emerging from the night.
We are coming brother Kirby, we are coming good and strong
And the day isn't distant when you'll sing another song.[159]

Nothing the Brotherhood did frightened the timber men quite so much as its strike at Merryville, Louisiana, in 1912 and 1913. There, the worst happened, and the union successfully organized not only the mill but the mill town as well, taking full advantage of long-standing resentments felt by private businessmen for the overbearing company. Shop window after shop window posted, "We support the Brotherhood of Timber Workers." Some four hundred men and women picketed each incoming train at the Merryville depot, singing union songs, talking to passengers about conditions at the mill, and soliciting donations for the cause. Other union people formed a longer picket line along the railroad tracks, shouting and throwing leaflets through the train windows in an attempt to inform and convert scab workers being brought in. At the mill gates, a line of well-dressed ladies formed the final gauntlet, armed with long hat pins which they attempted to stick in the legs of passing scabs.[160] Merryville was a large mill of the American Lumber Company, and after the company locked workers out and began to bring in scabs, C. P. Myer urgently warned all his mill managers to be on the alert for trouble caused by the fifteen hundred discharged Brotherhood men spreading the contagion of unionism into East Texas.[161]

By early in 1913, however, the power of the Brotherhood of Timber Workers was on the wane, and the union never successfully organized a single Texas mill. At the onset of the union challenge in 1910, companies swiftly closed ranks to oppose it, using the pre-existing Southern Lumber Operator's Association as their fighting arm, and throughout the combat they made full use of their awesome power over the sawmill communities to battle the union on their individual turfs.

Documented by the U.S. Bureau of Corporations in a monumental report of 1914, Southern lumber companies, national lumber companies, and the railroads formed an interlocking network that gave credence to the Brotherhood's claim that they battled not independent lumber companies but a "Southern lumber trust." As labor historian Geoffrey Ferrell accused (and to an impressive degree, substantiated), this linked network of companies was involved in "undermining competition, fixing prices, curtailing production, manipulating the press, influencing legislation, and battling labor organizations."[162] Ferrell, no friend of the big companies, successfully documented the extent to which the lumber companies traded with each other, exchanged personnel, sat on each other's boards of directors, exchanged information, socialized with each other, and arranged for sons and daughters to marry each other. The networking was formal and informal, economic, financial, social, and familial.[163] The informal network of the Southern lumbermen took organizational form in a secret society called the "Concatenated Order of the Hoo-Hoo," to which virtually every major Southern lumberman belonged. The Hoo-Hoos held around ninety "concatenations" a year. A photograph of one such gathering published in the November 1914 issue of *Southwest* showed men dressed in long black robes and pointed hats, with each robe and hat adorned with a picture of a black cat inside a white circle. Officials of the Hoo-Hoos were designated as "Snarks," "Bojums," "Scrivenaters," "Jabberworks," and "High Priests," with John Henry Kirby holding the appropriately elevated title of "Snark of the Universe."[164]

Kirby also led the Southern Lumber Operator's Association, which swiftly evolved a collective strategy for fighting the union. Where union organizers were most active and successful, the companies closed their sawmills in preemptive lock-outs. Then, after a period of weeks or months, they reopened the mills with workers willing to sign nonunion pledges ("yellow-dog contracts"). Those who would not sign the contracts, or who were thought to be union members or sympathizers, were "blacklisted" in the lumber industry. A Southern Lumber Operator's Association "labor clearing house" was set up in Alexandria, Louisiana, and it circulated thousands of names among association members. The blacklist proved very effective. Ima Windom, former Brotherhood member, claimed: "They blackballed every last one of em, they blackballed em all over the United States. Because, this uncle of mine, do you know he never got another job. Every time he'd go for a job somewhere else, it'd come up."[165]

To obtain employment from a company, besides the nonunion contracts, workers were required to sign special Southern Lumber Operator's Association forms requesting information from previous employers. The form authorized the former employer to furnish the job seeker's complete record to his new company, to tell why the employee left and "whether my conduct and services were satisfactory or not" and also to "give any other information, including your opinion, concerning my personal character, conduct and qualifications for the position of . . . . I now represent and declare to . . . . that I am physically and mentally competent to perform all duties connected with the said position, being fully experienced therein and thoroughly familiar with the duties thereof." Before the job seeker's witnessed signature, the form stated "I hereby release . . . . and you from all liability for any injury or damage whatever on account of furnishing the above information requested by me."[166] The document thus served multiple purposes; it asked about union activity at the last job, released the former employee from damages for slander and false information, and, finally, used the section affirming physical competence, mental competence, and job experience to protect the new employer from personal injury lawsuits. As George Creel summed it up, "In order to get employment, a timber worker must sign away his right to organize, his right to sue under the law for defamation of character, and his right to sue under the law for injuries received in the course of his work."[167]

With the association's new fighting documents in hand, Kirby Lumber Company took the lead in the battle with the union on the Texas side of the Sabine. During the late summer of 1911, Kirby closed his mills at Roganville and Bronson "until the infection caused by the so-called Timber Workers Union has been entirely eliminated and until they can be started without union labor."[168] Kirby executive C. P. Myer reported, "We discharged during the month of August about 250 men suspected of being members of the B.T.W. or sympathizers with them."[169] Kirby himself wrote C. B. Sweet that "we have got Emerson on the run, and if we stay put and keep the infected plants inactive, the whole thing will be abandoned in another two months."[170] A month later, the company reopened the mills with imported labor, although this caused trouble in Bronson, where a "whites-only" tradition prevailed. Myer wrote Kirby's legal office on September 6, 1911: "In order to operate the mill we found it necessary to ship in some Mexicans, which aroused the 'sleeping dog' in some of the people in and around Bronson. Some people expressed themselves as being in favor of running the Mexicans out of town and making the people that brought them in there work in the lead."[171]

At each town, and using many different tactics, the company made full use of its power over the community to combat union organizers. The union men did not lack courage or cleverness, and most were former sawmill hands and knew what they were up against, but they proved no match for the companies in their own towns. Both the Southern Lumber Operator's Association and individual lumbermen like John Henry Kirby maintained extensive networks of operatives (individuals derisively termed "spotters," "suckers," or "pimps" by union men), and these drifted around sniffing out insurrection and recording every speech of A. L. Emerson and other union men. The purpose of these "reporters" was harassment as well as information-gathering. Emerson told one crowd on July 4, 1912: "Kirby spends too much money paying men to come to our meetings, he spends to much money hiring spotters. There is a good bunch of them in this crowd right now. He spends too much money in paying sheriffs and deputy sheriffs to protect these spotters."[172]

Kirby Lumber Company records include hundreds of operatives' reports and many exchanges between company officials and operatives. Spies were everywhere in the mill towns from 1910 to 1914. C. P. Myer wrote the Southern Lumber Operator's Association manager in January of 1912 about his concern with secrecy, noting that "I should keep the present man moving from place to place, staying at each place long enough only to obtain information and when he has made the entire rounds for him to be replaced by another man."[173] On a few occasions, association spies got on the trails of Myer's own men, threatening to expose them. Myer complained about such a matter on January 12, 1912: "I was very much disturbed over this, as I cannot afford to have him turned up. When Operatives are withdrawn from service they are but very little better than the organized union labor men—they get the 'sore-head' and give up their 'guts,' telling everything they know and some things they do not know."[174] Sometimes even Kirby mill managers went undercover. The Bessmay mill manager reported to Myer, "When the labor trouble started in Louisiana and East Texas, I went in disguise night after night and kept continually on the watch out, riding all over this community keeping in close touch with every body and every move that was made."[175]

Operatives used various "covers" in their work, the most common that of new worker in the mill. Some feigned union sympathies—for example, by wearing "Don't Scab" buttons—and some had multilayer covers, as did the man posing as a *Texas Farm Journal* reporter posing as a worker. "Reporters" like this man covered every Brotherhood gathering, public speeches, "secret" meetings, and whatever, and often took photographs of the union's public affairs—a circumstance so unnerving that at one meeting the largest part of the crowd stood out of sight in the woods.[176] Myer may have originated the photograph tactic, since he mentioned it in a letter to B. F. Bonner on January 18, 1912, and demonstrated its effectiveness in three photos of a crowd taken a few minutes apart by one of his operatives. By the third photo, the crowd of nervous union sympathizers had grown notably more sparse.[177]

The companies also tried to co-opt rebellious workers they could not otherwise quiet, another aspect of their clandestine activities. Myer wrote Kirby on January 10, 1912, that if two local union leaders could be "bought out cheap, it would be in the best interest of the Tyler County Lumber Company to have them away from that place." Kirby correspondence suggests that some of these co-opted Brotherhood men, or perhaps ones who were secret operatives from the beginning, rose in the union's leadership circles, attended its national conventions, and reported its inner plans.[178]

The companies' power over their towns also was used to deny union men access to workers. Companies often exchanged information about Brotherhood organizers and their travel plans, often giving other companies' towns advance warning about the organizers' arrivals. Such men might be put off the company railroad, told that the company hotel had no room for them, or run out of town by "goon squads." In some Louisiana communities, companies erected stockades topped with barbed wire around the mill and workers' quarters, and elsewhere workers were ordered to remain in their homes during the times of Brotherhood meetings upon pain of dismissal. Outside of some towns, signs like this were posted: "Private property, all unionists, socialists, peddlers and solicitors, keep out; under penalty."[179]

Meetings in progress might be harassed by repeated photographing of the crowds, by sending brass bands to play, or by "tinpanning"—beating tin pans, saw blades and other noisemakers to drown out speakers. At one meeting, company men beat on a large circular saw blade carried on a cart "with clubs carrying a bolt at the end." A union man recalled that they also employed "tin disks, with handles, which they clashed together, cymbal fashion. All these, with smaller saws carried by the men, added to the boom of the big saw, made about as infernal a racket as I ever heard. We could not hear ourselves think, much less talk."[180]

Another company tactic was to organize antiunion clubs among loyal workers in the mill and businessmen in the town—this by way of inoculation to prevent the horrifying worker-businessman solidarity of Merryville from ever repeating itself in Texas. Kirby's manager at Browndel reported a company-sponsored workers' antiunion meeting "attended by practically every employee of the Company at this place—I believe that any organizer of the B.T.W. who comes here will be roughly dealt with."[181] At Kirbyville, businessmen met to draft and publish a petition appealing to workers not to join the Brotherhood, and in the Temple Lumber Company's town of Pineland, sister city to Diboll, an anti-Brotherhood "Committee of Thirteen" was formed—as usual, with company encouragement and support.[182]

Some of the local "workers' committees" were nothing more than company "goon squads," or so the union claimed. Brotherhood men repeatedly accused the companies of strong-arm tactics in their towns, where quarter bosses and deputized workers not only took action to protect company property but to attack and intimidate union organizers, members, and supporters. Union writings complained of beatings, floggings, and "water cures," the pummeling of restrained men with a high-powered jet of water. A. L. Emerson was in fact severely beaten more than once, and Emerson, H. G. Creel, W. A. Fussell, Covington Hall, and other Brotherhood leaders all received repeated death threats. The most violent episode of the conflict occurred at Grabow, Louisiana, on July 7, 1912, when workers attending an Emerson speech and company men in a nearby office building got into a major gun battle, leaving several persons dead. The companies termed this affair a union riot, and the Brotherhood called it an attempted assassination of Emerson, but in the end Louisiana juries failed to convict anybody. According to most accounts, the first person shot had been a man standing just behind Emerson on the speaker's platform.[183]

The Kirby Lumber Company papers contain little clear evidence of company-inspired violence (though that is exactly what one might expect for good legal reasons), but on July 27, 1912, Kirby instructed Myer: "Have Hooker get in touch with the sheriff of Newton County and see that a suitable number of reliable deputies are detailed. It might be well also for Hooker to select a dozen or two of his own men, who are loyal to him and to us and dependable in a crisis, to have charge of things in the event of any effort on the part of the Timber Workers to capture our barbecue and bring on a riot."[184] A few months before, the mill superintendent at Kirbyville had written Myer that certain measures had been taken to discourage a local man sympathetic to the union from discomfiting the company by luring local blacks away to the cotton fields. "Will Christian made a statement yesterday evening that he was going to get my negroes to the cotton fields between then and Tuesday, that the mill had to be shut down and that was the only way it could be done. Some of my boys waited on Christian yesterday evening, and I do not think he will attempt to carry out his threat. I am having the quarters watched, however, both day and night."[185]

The Grabow trials and the Merryville strike exhausted the Brotherhood's shallow bank account, and the companies' overwhelming resources, money, manpower, and social control of their sawmill towns broke the union. By February 1, 1913, the *St. Louis Lumberman* noted: "So pleased have some of the companies been with the situation the past several months that they have voluntarily raised the wages of their employees. The raise has not been very great, but enough to strengthen the ties between the workmen and their employers and to make conditions generally pleasanter."[186] Years later, Brotherhood organizer Covington Hall recalled: "We could not hold the line; the men were getting worn down, and the lumber companies began to make concessions in higher wages, always coupling it with: 'Now, if you continue to stick with that damn Union, we'll close the mills, and this time keep them closed.' This was a bluff, of course, but effective in the conditions we were battling."[187]

After the Brotherhood's defeat without organizing a single Texas mill, the previous pattern of informal strikes resumed, as at the W. R. Pickering Lumber Company town of Haslam on May 21, 1923. Strikers walked off spontaneously, their wage demands were refused, the ringleaders were fired, and steps were taken to trace them to their next "landing place" to make sure nobody rehired them. Kirby Lumber Company stepped in to print a circular giving a description of the Haslam ringleaders, black and white, and send it to all their towns.[188]

Reports circulated that IWW organizers might have been working the Haslam area before the strike, but company undercover men failed to confirm this. John Henry Kirby and the Southern Lumber Operator's Association believed in operatives and continued to use them throughout the 1920s, though they usually found nothing more to report than employees' grousing and complaining. An association report of 1924 summed up intelligence activities at thirty-five company towns to report "no attempts to organize at any point," and Kirby's Operative #15 had nothing more to tell about Voth than that he heard a disgruntled mill carpenter say, "The company store here is robbing the people, as everything here is about 25 percent higher than Beaumont—this company is known as a cheap company everywhere."[189]

The natives of sawmill towns remained restless and often dissatisfied throughout the remainder of the cut-and-get-out era of Texas lumbering, and their wages remained very low—not only as compared to sawmills in other parts of the country but as compared to other industrial occupations in Texas.[190] Clearly, as historian Ruth Allen caustically remarked, the failure of unionization in the sawmill towns was not due to the "happy satisfaction of the workers."[191] The Kirby Lumber Company papers contain various instances of the exchange of wage scales with other companies, presumably so the wages might be standardized and workers might have little reason to try to better themselves elsewhere. Nevertheless, the denizens of the feudal towns of East Texas continued to express their dissatisfaction in the only way they could, by "voting with their feet" for mill towns a few miles farther down the railroad tracks. A Southern Lumber Operator's Association survey of ten Texas mills in 1923 reported astonishing rates of worker mobility—an average *monthly* turnover of 16.8 percent for Anglo-Americans, 13.5 percent for blacks, and 14.1 percent for Mexicans.[192]

Chapter Four

THE CORNBREAD WHISTLE

L ANTERN firmly in hand, Diboll night watchman Jim Richards walked the dimly lit expanses of the Southern Pine sawmill and planer mill in the hours after midnight. The huge mill machinery lay silent; like most mills, Diboll rarely ran at night. Only the big boilers remained alive, their pressure partially up in anticipation of the workday to come.

Sometime around 2:30 A.M., Richards turned aside on his rounds of mill and town to halt before certain houses and sound the first wake-up calls of the coming day. As part of his duties, the night watchman visited the homes of the woods-train crews, the sawmill and planer mill boil-ermen, and other early risers to make sure they had responded to their jangling alarm clocks. Myrtle Rushing's husband worked on the log train, which left very early, and the train's crew had to rise hours before to fire the boiler and get up steam. Rushing recalled that Jim Richard's custom was to call from outside the yard fence: "He'd holler, 'Heh, Jimmy. Come out by me?' He would holler as he passed by, and it would wake us up. He had a voice like a lion. I told him one time, 'Oh, I almost hate your voice.'"[1]

Along the dark streets of a hundred mill towns this night in the summer of 1922, other night watchmen did the same. At Sabine Tram's town of Laurel, commissary manager W. A. Smith rose early to get ready for his timber-crew customers' obligatory purchases of "chew tobacco," snuff, and work gloves before their train departed for the woods.[2] At Di-boll's Star Hotel and the company boardinghouse in Elmina, the cooks rose at 2:30 A.M. to start fires in their wood stoves and begin preparing breakfast and lunch buckets for the woods crews. At the Star, young Mar-jory Pickle Davis rose reluctantly in the summer dark to light her stoves—

fiery tyrants soon to dominate the sweaty workday of the hotel cooks.[3] Others served more powerful fires. At about the same time as Marjory awakened, half-asleep mill boilermen walked dark streets to their duty posts at the great steam engines, soon to rouse into life. At Wiergate, eight big boilers, fueled by sawdust, shavings, and chopped-up wood scrap from the "hogs," powered the 750-horsepower Corliss steam engine that turned the twenty-foot flywheel. At Groveton, Claude Kennedy fueled his hissing boilers, which powered another great Corliss steam engine—"Texine," named for the mill superintendent's daughter. Kennedy wore heavy cotton "long-handle" underwear even in summer, believing (as his son explained) "If he could get them full of sweat in hot weather, he could stand it better around them boilers."[4] Already, at four o'clock in the morning, "Mr. Claude" had begun to sweat. Jim Whiteside's father stoked the mill boilers at the Kirby Lumber Company town of Honey Island, Hardin County. After steam was up, Whiteside monitored his pocket watch until 5 A.M., then took a certain satisfaction in sounding the wake-up whistle for the sleeping woods crew, the first whistle of the mill town's daily round. Close to the source, the thundering steam whistle shook the ground and vibrated the internal organs of listeners. Then, after the huge sound reverberated away to silence across the dark countryside, all the roosters in Honey Island began to crow.[5]

Sometimes, others joined mill whistles and roosters in rousing the town. At the Diboll quarter, musical mill hand Ed Jones, an army bugler during World War I, walked outside his home after the first whistle to play a rousing reveille for his fellow African Americans. At about the same time, Anglo newsboy Edwin Nelson amused himself by throwing *Houston Chronicle*s against the houses of black subscribers in the Diboll quarter with all the strength in a baseball-trained right arm.[6]

For miles in every direction from a hundred mill towns, farmers also rose and went about their business to the reveille of distant steam whistles. At Chester Treadaway's farm at Rock Hill near the Angelina County mill town of Ewing, the Treadaway family tried to be in the field or on their way by the time Ewing's 5 A.M. wake-up whistle blew.[7] Everyone lived with steam whistles ringing in their ears during the boom-era of East Texas logging—mill whistles, locomotive whistles, even the whistles of steam skidders at "the front." Countrymen often resided where they could hear the daily whistles of several mill towns—whistles easily distinguishable by differences in direction, loudness, pitch, timing, and number

An eighteen-foot flywheel run by the mill's main power plant, a five-hundred horse-power Corliss steam engine, Diboll, 1908. Belts from the main drive shaft behind the flywheel transferred power to the band saws, circular saws, and other mill machinery.
Courtesy of Temple Archives, Diboll, Texas.

of blasts. Company and main-line locomotive engineers had their individual "highball whistles," readily identifiable by most who heard them.[8] At many a dark farm at night, children lay in bed and tried to be the first or last to hear and identify a distant locomotive whistle, passing in or out of hearing in the silence.

Each company's own thundering whistle schedule dominated its town, however. Visitor Hamilton Pratt Easton wrote of Wiergate's:

There is considerable significance to the whistles one hears from the sawmill, planing mill, and woods engine in a sawmill town. At five o'clock in the morning at Wiergate, the sawmill whistle awakened the woods crew with four long blasts. Then at six o'clock it blew again to rouse the mill crew and, if the planing mill were to run that day, its whistle followed that of the sawmill. The two whistles were quite distinct, that of the planing mill being higher in pitch. A third blast, at six o'clock, which chilled the heart of any tardy member of the woods crew, came from the woods engine, which was ready to leave for the logging camp. The sawmill whistle gave two short blasts at 6:45 A.M. to warn the mill men that they had only fifteen minutes more in which to reach their works. Whistles also blew at the beginning and end of the noon hour and at closing time in the evening. The whistle blast to indicate fire was called a "wildcat." It was an ear-piercing, eerie shriek which was terrifying to any hearer.[9]

Also terrifying to mill people were the special "injury whistles" sounded by logging trains rushing injured men in from the woods. At the sound of these special sequences of whistle blasts from trains still a mile or so away, mill-town doctors dropped what they were doing and rushed down to await arrival of the injured. Everyone knew what this whistle meant, and at Fastrill, as Louise Rector remembered, "When that whistle would blow, it used to scare everybody, and we'd all run down there to see who it was, to make sure it wasn't one of ours."[10]

From 5 A.M. on, mill-town men, women, and children arose to their appropriate whistles, wives prepared breakfasts, and the men left for their daily duties at woods and mill. Most families ate breakfast together, but some men had jobs requiring them to rise so early and return so late that their children saw them only on weekends.[11] Guy Croom sometimes rose early enough to eat breakfast with his railroad engineer father, who left the mill town of Hyatt at 6 A.M. six days a week running the woods train and returned at 7 P.M.—if all went well. In the case of derailments and delays, the woods crew did not return until late at night or the next day, sounding a special whistle as the engine approached the town to let their families know they had arrived. After six long workdays, a good part of Croom's Sundays were taken up with unpaid maintenance and repairs for his engine.[12] Other men worked equally long days, however. Troubleshooter millwright crews commonly logged eighty-hour work weeks. In his jobs as commissary manager and mill superintendent at Deweyville, W. A. Smith often worked from 5 A.M. to 10 P.M. and did not see his children for days at a time. Once, when Smith came home earlier than usual in the evening and picked up his youngest child, she did not recognize him and burst into tears.[13]

For many families, biscuits were the daily bread for the morning breakfast. Housewives baked cornbread for the noon meal, after the daily sounding of the "cornbread whistle." Mornings at the Croom household began with the lighting of the family wood stove, the grinding of home-parched coffee beans on the wall grinder for morning coffee, and the making of the daily biscuits. Mrs. Croom's preparation of biscuits had become second nature to her, as her son described.

Making biscuits was something she did every morning as regularly as a goose goes bare-footed. She made biscuit dough in a big wooden bowl, filled with sifted flour except for a place in the middle. First, she grabbed a handfull of lard, poured in milk, then baking powder if she was using sweet milk, or soda with buttermilk, and a little salt. Then she squashed that lard, milk and other ingredients through her fingers till it was well mixed and then began kneading flour into it until it was just right. She did not use a dough board or rolling pin, but rather, she pinched off a hunk of dough just the right size for a biscuit, rolled it into a ball between her palms, then flattened it to the right thickness. She would then give them a little finishing touch with her knuckles after she put them into the baking pan.[14]

At 6:45, the mill whistle thundered "fifteen minutes to start-up," and the workers—stomachs full of biscuits, syrup, coffee, fried eggs, and bacon—moved toward the mill. They walked casually if they had plenty of time, jogged or ran if they were tardy; since the whole operation stepped to a single drummer, it would not do to be late. Then, all hands in position, at precisely 7 A.M. the steam-powered carriage hurled the first log into the screaming band saw, and the long workday began.

Nothing about the mill so awed visitors as the action at the saws. Sawyer's son James Lee recalled:

One time I got to watch Daddy work, and I was very impressed and scared by all the screeching noise and the bedlam which I later learned was really controlled by Daddy. He sized up a huge log as it was being dragged out of the mill pond by a chain apparatus to be placed on an awesome piece of equipment called the carriage, which had a workman riding on it but was controlled by Daddy from his sawyer's station. Daddy had only an instant to calculate the way to saw the log to get the most out of it in relation to the company's pending lumber orders before releasing the carriage at blinding speed right into the whirling, screaming saw. What Daddy did was very important, both from the standpoint of doing the essential work of the sawmill and also having this dangerous machinery and human life depending on his skill and judgment.[15]

Twenty years apart, Hamilton Pratt Easton and Max Bentley also observed the Wiergate band saws, and both gave awestruck accounts of the noise, violence, seeming danger, and awful speed of the great machinery. Easton wrote:

The clank and roar of air and steam machinery, and especially the shrieks of the saws as they hit the logs and cut through them like lightening, made most of the noise in a sawmill. At Wiergate the mill resounded with the roar of machinery, punctuated by the special sounds of log-carriages shooting forward and back and the great saws whirring through the logs. These saws bit through a two- or three-foot log in a matter of seconds, or sliced it lengthwise in much less time than it takes to tell it. They cut with deafening, high-pitched screams, and dazzled one with their swiftness. The machinery was so strong in its attack upon the logs that the whole mill actually shook.[16]

Max Bentley also described action at the great band saws as a scene of terrifying noise, ferocious energy, and controlled violence. He watched a huge tree, "the king log," thirty inches in diameter, approach the saws. "Out of the log pond and up the cable trough it came, surely and steadily under the guillotine," then, suddenly, the cut-off saw came down and one log was three logs rolling onto the log deck.

The waiting sawyer jerked a lever. The first section of the king log was steam-kicked onto the carriage. The "steam nigger" whirled it over and over, placed it in exact position. The block setter spun his dial around in response to some lightning finger-signals from the sawyer. The steam carriage drew swiftly away, suddenly stopped, and then hurled itself against the waiting saw. Then a deafening "ZZZZZZZZT!" and two slabs, exactly of a size, fell into a rolling conveyor and were borne swiftly away. Down the line they went to the trip-man who sent them to the edgerman who sawed them again and sent them to the trip thrower, who divided the merchantable timber from the slab next to the bark and sent the good stick to the trimmer. Above the scene of carnage was the trimmerman, seated in a suspended cage, operating seventeen air-driven saws spaced at two-foot intervals and controlled by wire strands. Like a steam calliope he was, playing up and down the keys, his notes on a black-board before him in cabalistic figures: 2×4, 1×6. His music was harsh, fal-setto—but the air he played was readily distinguishable. It was a savage thing, a dirge for all of its note of triumph. It was the funeral march of the king log.[17]

Behind the noise, violence, and seeming chaos of the mill lay an intricate and massive teamwork of men and machines. An *American Lumberman* editor wrote in 1902:

A plant in full operation is a scene of apparently endless confusion. Men dart here and there; the creak of whirring belts and pulleys is lost in the sharper cry of the cutting machinery; conversation has been reduced to a sign manual. On closer inspection, however, it is found that the seeming confusion is in reality the working out of systematic order. Every man has a certain duty to perform and the work of most of the employees keeps them confined to narrow limits. The work of each man is separate and distinct, and yet the different parts are so closely related and are interdependent to such an extent that it is impossible for one or more to shirk their tasks without interfering with the work of others, and in this way they are closely bound together, one dependent upon the other for the prompt fulfillment of each duty as it comes to hand.[18]

At Wiergate and other mills, processing began when the logging trains dumped two daily trainloads of twenty cars each into the millponds. Logs were sorted and pike-poled into position behind various floating booms by millpond workers, "pond monkeys," who leaped nimbly from log to log in their hobnailed boots. Pond men walked the logs with their pike-poles and pulled chosen ones to the "log-haul chain," an endless chain fitted with hooks and lugs that caught the logs and hauled them into the mill.

At the top of the chain, "scalers" stood at the doorway of the mill and made the initial decisions about the most profitable way to cut the logs. As each log passed through the doorway, the scalers looked closely for natural defects or embedded metal objects that might effect the price of the lumber or damage the expensive saws. Then, as the log moved by them to the "cut-off saw," they indicated to the "cut-off sawyer" where to cut it. The circular cut-off saw dropped down from above, and the log was cut.

After that, the "deckman" took over, operating a steam-powered "kicker" to send the log to one of the three "sides" of the mill, depending on the kind of lumber that would be made from it. At Wiergate, logs of small diameter went to the "Dixie" circular saw, logs up to forty feet in length to the band saw on the "short side" of the mill, and logs of forty to sixty feet to the "long side" band saw.

At this point, a log entered the precinct of one of the three "sawyers," who worked in screened cubbyholes to protect them from flying splinters. The sawyer used a steam kicker to load the log on the "log carriage," then moved it into exact placement with a "steam nigger"—"a powerful steam-driven inverted gothic T-bar that could turn or flip the largest log as easily as a boy could toss a baseball bat."[19] The "block-setter," part of the sawyer's team of workmen, rode the carriage and controlled the viselike clamps, or "air-dogs," that held the log in position on the carriage. The block-setter took directions via hand signals from the sawyer and swiftly adjusted the log to exactly his preferred placement. Then, the sawyer threw his carriage lever, the carriage shot into the "double-cutting" band saw, which "slabbed" the log on two sides, making it a "cant." At that point, the sawyer made another lightning decision. He either slabbed the log on the two other remaining sides to make a rectangular timber, the most profitable use he could make of the log, or he quickly cut it up into planks that moved away from the saw on the powered "live rolls."

Scalers pose at the Wiergate mill doorway as a big log is
about to enter. *Courtesy of the U.S. Post Office, Wiergate, Texas.*

Other highly skilled mill men worked the line of moving wood "behind the saws." Planks from the saws still having edges of bark rolled first
to the "edger man," who removed the bark edges and made the planks
into boards of desired width. Then, they rolled on to the "trimmer-saw
man," who cut the boards to exact length, sometimes cutting out a defect
to make two, shorter boards. The black trimmer-saw man at Wiergate
was one of the highest paid black employees, since this job required skill
and judgment in cutting the boards to avoid lowering the grade of the
lumber.[20]

Then, the boards, slabs, odd lengths, and scrap rolled on to the "automatic sorter," which mechanically separated them into regular lumber,

laths, and trash that went to the "fuel hog" to be chopped up into fuel. In earlier times this sorting function had been performed by a "bear man" in the "bear pit." As industry historians Maxwell and Baker described, "there he stood, waste deep in the pit, with the lumber from the edger coming at him in torrents—he must either clear it or be covered up."[21]

From the automatic sorter on, the men who worked the "green" lumber on its way to the dry kilns were known as "rosinbellies" and were part of the "green lumber chain." Waste slabs from all three saws went to "slasher-saws" that cut them into four-foot lengths to make laths. Finished boards after leaving the trimmer dropped onto another conveyor chain to be graded by a "grader," who marked a grade on each board. Low grades of lumber destined to be stacked for "air drying" continued on live rolls to the "yard." Some customers preferred this cheaper, air-dried lum-

Log carriage and high-speed band saw in the Bessmay mill. *Courtesy of the East Texas Research Center, Stephen F. Austin State University, Nacogdoches, Texas.*

Large timbers produced by the Wiergate sawmill. The company sold many such
timbers to railroads and oil companies for use in construction.
Courtesy of the Newton History Center, Newton, Texas.

ber. Higher grades of lumber were processed for thickness and width by
the "drop sorter," then went to one of the six "dry kilns" to steam-dry and
season for four to six days, then went to the big planer mill for smoothing
on all four sides, then went to the "dress sheds" to await shipment.

As the *Gulf Coast Lumberman* noted, Wiergate's timbers received special treatment: "As the timbers are cut they go right through the mill on
live rolls and then continue on their way to the timber dock. Long leaf
timbers are of course one of the specialties of the Wiergate plant. They cut
timbers all the way up to 60 feet in length, and of great size when desired.
They are loaded from the timber dock to the cars, and when the timber
business is active, car after car of big timbers leaves the mill every day."[22]

From mill pond to boxcar, sawmill work was hard, dangerous, noisy,
and dirty, but above all it was unrelenting—forcing each worker to go not
at his own best pace but at the hard-driving speed of production. Some
men could tolerate this, and some could not. Jake Cole began mill work
moving lumber from planer mill to storage sheds at age twenty-five, but he
soon received a battlefield promotion into the planer mill as replacement
for a man who could not stand the pressures of his job. Cole explained:

This old Nicholson boy, he was running a resaw at the upper end of the planer shed, and he resawed heavy stuff, and we'd get in a whole batch of them. Well, the old boy tailing that mess over on the other end, loading the buggies, he'd burn [Nicholson] out—that was his delight—just feed that stuff through there so fast it would just burn him out. And Nicholson quit and walked off, went down to the country and got him a job. So, the old planer boss was looking up and down the road for somebody, and he spied me. Well, I went over there and old Dick tried to burn me out, but I was pretty tough; I was raised on a farm, and I could work. I learned how, and after he found out he couldn't burn me out, he was alright.[23]

Since every job went at the speed of the mill, foremen often interrogated new hands about whether they could keep the pace and do the work. When Joe Malanders applied for a grueling job sorting lumber on the green chain at Wiergate, foreman Kate asked Malanders's brother "Fat Boy" if his younger sibling could do the work. "Fat Boy, can that little man hold your job?" Kate asked. The brother replied: "If anybody can do it, he can. He is tough, he is used to hard work. I'll help him if he gets tired, but I don't think he'll need help." Gritting his teeth, Malanders did the job, noting: "At times there would be nothing but two by twelves and two by sixteens, all heart lumber, and you talk about somebody having a time pulling lumber! But I never had to call on my brother to help me, I stayed there seven years and eight months on that one job until the mill closed down."[24]

Company foremen like Kate often came under great pressure to push harder and get more done, thus raising job stress for the workers under them. A Kirby Lumber Company management conference of August 25, 1919, detailed the performances of various mill and woods foremen and their relative effectiveness in getting work out of their men. Some people were judged as not having what it took and were on their way out, others had done well but had "worked themselves down" on the job and become ill, necessitating replacement. Production—the "bottom line"—was everything, at least at the Kirby mills.[25] Three years later, in 1922, one of the participants in the 1919 conference reported to the main office about a Call foreman described by complaining co-workers as "crabby and rough": "Wish to advise that there is a very good reason for this and that is that he has been romping on all of them trying to get a little more work out of them as well as a little better work, and I am sure there are a good many of them in the mill that don't feel very pleasant towards him; however, I wish to advise that while this man is not exactly what we want in a

Willard planing mill, 1908. The mill's machines dressed and finished the rough lumber coming from the nearby sawmill. *Courtesy of the Texas Forestry Museum, Lufkin, Texas.*

mill foreman, he is the best we have had in the Call mill since I have been with the Kirby Lumber Company. We have not had any others that got the results under the same conditions that this man is getting."[26]

Besides the harsh sound of the foreman's voice, machine noise was another basic reality of sawmill work, although far worse in some jobs than in others. To some degree sawmill people simply got used to the constant din. An *American Lumberman* editor optimistically observed: "People living in mill towns have become so adjusted to the continuous drumming roar of the revolving machinery and the chug, chug of the engine that without it something of life seems wanting. There is a companionship in noise which after once being cultivated can hardly be dispensed with. Those who live within sound of the sea are lonely and ill at ease when beyond reach of the sound of its breakers, and relatively the same is true of the inhabitants of mill towns."27 However, for workers in the loudest parts of the mill becoming "adjusted to the continuous drumming roar" doubtless involved the loss of some portion of their hearing. Around the saws, the "hogs" chopping up scrap wood for fuel, and the planer machines, noise reached ear-splitting levels. In these parts of the mill a crude sign language developed. The sawyer, for example, gave directions to his block setters by finger signals. The planer mill had its own signal system, as did workers in the yards, where the problem was not only mill noise but the long distances separating workmen. Yard and shed workers communicated across hundreds of yards in a signal language of large, sweeping gestures, like Plains Indians.28 Some of the close-range sawmill signals became uniform from mill to mill: a finger touched to the nose meant, "I don't know"; a finger to the ear meant, "I can't hear you"; and a finger thrust emphatically toward the ground conveyed, "Go to hell!"29 Kiln brick salesman Arthur Beale visited many sawmills as part of

Foremen at Kirby Lumber Company's Bessmay mill. *Courtesy of the East Texas Research Center, Stephen F. Austin State University, Nacogdoches, Texas.*

his job and was always going around the mill in search of people he needed to talk to. By necessity, Beale learned many of the sawmill hand signals used to communicate in the ear-drum-shattering din of a plant in full operation. The mill language was extensive and subtle enough that jokes could be told in it. Beale recalled: "It was fascinating to go into those mills and watch the men work, they had a language of their own. There's so much noise, see. You could go right up to some men, and after you watch a while you realize that they're moving their hands ever once in a while. And then someone will start laughing. After a period of two or three years I learned a lot of that language. You could convey anything by signs."[30]

All too often, however, the mill whistle failed to blow in the morning and the sawmill town spent the day in unprofitable silence. Besides being hard, dirty, noisy, and dangerous, sawmill work also was highly irregular and badly paid. Even an elite saw filer making ten dollars a day, six or seven times the pay of a common laborer, got paid only when the mill ran. A Kirby Lumber Company management memo of 1919 detailed the working period from August 1 to August 22 and noted that mills averaged three and one-half days downtime during that time, excluding Sundays. Often, the mill shut down because the supply of logs ran out. The delivery of logs from woods to millpond was a complicated enterprise, profoundly affected by the weather and involving a great deal of machinery. Woods got too wet for crews to cut timber, steam skidders broke down, and logging trains derailed, all lessening the flow of timber to the mill, and with no logs to cut the mill shut down. If the complicated process broke down at any point, the big band saws did not run.[31] No work meant no pay; as C. P. Myer informed John Henry Kirby in January of 1912, due to "weather conditions for the past thirty days and other factors, the men who are employed as laborers at the company's mills and lumber camps have been unable to get in enough time to pay rent and medical and insurance fees, much less to live upon."[32]

In truth, shutdown was as much a part of the experience of sawmill employment as hard, unrelenting work. Evadale mill manager E. T. Hickman informed C. P. Myer in 1913 (echoing many similar letters in the Kirby papers), "Heavy rains past several weeks here has put our woods in such shape that we find ourselves unable to get the logs sufficient to keep the mill going steadily, having lost at mill 2 hours Friday, 8 hours Saturday, and 4 hours Monday, and will probably lose one half of today on account of no logs."[33] During one rainy January, Browndel mill hands logged only an average of 13.37 workdays—typical of all the Kirby mills in that month.[34]

Even when the mill ran, sawmill pay was low, with three-fourths of the work force paid as common laborers at a daily rate under $2 a day—pay that rose little from 1890 to 1930. A few skilled blue-collar employees—sawyers, saw filers, millwrights, engineers, and perhaps a few others—were paid more and received special treatment by the companies, who wished to retain their services. Other skilled mill men were paid at close to the base wage. At Kirby Lumber Company in 1915, saw filers received the awesome wage of $12 a day, sawyers $5, and engineers $3, but then the drop off in wages was sharp; skilled trimmermen, edgermen, and "bear-fighters" all received $1.75—only twenty-five cents more than common laborers in the yards.[35]

At the top of the pecking order of sawmill workmen, an elite few received high pay and special treatment and attained the status of "unfireables." Saw filers, pursuing their esoteric task with a few apprentices, held one such job category, and so did sawyers and a few highly skilled engineers. In a 1916 letter, Angelina County Lumber Company millowner E. L. Kurth personally tried to recruit a sawyer for his Keltys mill, and James Griner's sawyer father often received similar treatment.[36] R. W. Wier lured Griner away from his sawyer's job at the Kirby mill of Browndel, the Browndel mill manager lured him back, then Wier offered Griner even more—an unprecedented wage. His son recalled: "The manager from Wiergate came over and told him if he'd come back he would pay him a dollar an hour. I thought that there was not any more money in the world than ten dollars a day. We moved back to Wiergate and we lived there until they cut out."[37]

Other men received special, hands-off treatment. At Diboll, mill superintendent Henry Temple allowed saw filer Hamp Byerly to leave the plant anytime he wished to go downtown. As one man recalled, the eccentric Byerly: "Would come out on the plant dressed up like he was going someplace. He'd put on his work clothes, and then at noon he'd dress back up in his dress clothes and go up town if he felt like it." Confronted by young supervisor Joe Denmon about his time off the job, Byerly responded: "Joe, I want to tell you something. I've forgot more about saw filing than you'll ever learn." And when Denmon brought this insolence up with Temple, he only drew another rebuff: "Joe, Mr. Byerly is my baby, you just leave him alone."[38]

A few other men, sometimes not especially well-paid ones, had attained the special status of unfireables. When the Kirby mill manager at Bessmay became so aggravated with Joseph Marriot's increasing deafness that he dismissed him on the job, Marriot failed to hear the edict and kept on working. A few days later, time sheets came back from headquarters without Marriot's name on them, Marriot inquired about it, and Kirby management promptly paid him and formally reinstated him on the job. Later, Kirby officials fired the mill superintendent.[39] Sometimes the unfireables were black. Amos Harris entered Southern Pine employment as bark scooper at the millpond, but in time he rose to edgerman and became a valuable jack-of-all-trades in the mill. He explained: "I'd edge, edge lumber, fight the bear, pull trimmers, did everything—millwright sometimes, when the millwright would get sick—had to fix the chain some when it was broke. Back in them days, I done practically anything."[40]

As in the case of Harris, at the sawmill there was no substitute for mechanical skill, and individuals truly gifted in this regard were highly valued by mill management. Engineer Claude Kennedy, despite his customary insolence, hair-trigger temper, and second-grade education, was courted by a succession of mill-town higher ups. On several occasions, the irascible Kennedy worked at the Trinity County Lumber Company mill at Groveton, always leaving after some real or imagined slight. On one occasion Kennedy lost a fistfight, on another he got drunk and was thrown in the calaboose, and on a third his son Fred insulted the mill superintendent. Always, however, Trinity County Lumber Company tried to get Kennedy back. Fred Kennedy recalled an instance that occurred after the family had moved to a Louisiana mill:

> A man came from Groveton in a big spring wagon driving a great big workhorse. I remember he stayed all night with us. He wanted Papa to go back to Groveton and work for the Trinity County Lumber Company again. Said the company would get a house ready for us and send a wagon to move us. I suppose they wanted Papa pretty bad. I've heard men say what a good engineer he was, how he kept the equipment up, and how he could make an engine pull a lot more than the majority of men could. I know he fired the boilers and kept the engines up, both. I think when he wasn't there they maybe had to have two other men doing that.[41]

Claude Kennedy returned to Groveton, but a few months later he and his family were off again. Always, the mechanical Kennedy quickly got another job. While at Groveton, he invented a "gravity oiling system" that allowed him to read the Bible on the job; as chief engineer at the Crosby Hotel in Beaumont, he devised "a mechanical refrigerator that ran on coal oil"; at a mill at Shamrock he rigged a special steam line to heat up saw-dust and enable the mill to burn hardwood scrap; and back at Groveton he solved a complicated instrumentation problem involving electricity and mill machinery that had baffled the college-educated mill engineer.[42] Always, however, the mechanical Kennedy soon moved on to another sawmill town. While chief engineer at the McNary planing mill, Ken-nedy was bending a pipe to make an "elbow" to use in connecting two boilers when a foreman questioned him about it. Flying in a rage: "Papa got a hammer after him and run him off. Then he went ahead and bent the pipe and connected the boilers. Then we left McNary." A little later, Claude Kennedy worked as chief engineer at the Long Pine Lumber Company in Alexandria, Louisiana, and his family lived in a fine, four-bedroom house with three fireplaces, running water inside the house, and electricity. Quickly, however, as so often before, Claude ran afoul of someone at work, and the Kennedy family moved to another mill out in the country and a rundown house with "cracks you could throw a cat through."[43]

Skilled workmen like Claude Kennedy, who were at the top of the blue-collar pecking order, had relative job security, good wages, and the privilege of socializing with foremen and mill superintendents—if they chose to remain at a certain mill. At the bottom level of mill employment, workers had another kind of freedom—a freedom based upon having lit-tle to lose at any given job and mill town. Of 174 men employed at the Thompson-Tucker mill at Willard in 1908, most drew wages as common laborers, including all 40 working in lumber handling in the yard, "yard-ing and shipping."[44] At $1.40 a day, working at a job unlikely to bring ad-vancement in a mill town much like all the rest, "I quit" often proved an easy thing to say. Told by his foreman to help a man repair something at the Carter mill town of Camden, Joe Malanders responded that he was not being paid at the higher wages of a repairman. Asked again to do it, he again refused and was told "You can go on home." Malanders replied:

"Good, I can do that." I walked off the job. He started whistling at me, I didn't even acknowledge him. My wife and mother were sitting in the doors, it was about ten in the morning, and could see me, and my mother said, "I guess Joe has had a fight. Get ready." I told my wife to get the children ready, because we are going to Diboll. I got to Diboll about eleven o'clock. My brother lived there. I went out to get me a job, I wanted work. He said, "How old are you?" I said, "I am twenty-five." He said, "Do you have a family?" I said, "Yes." He said, "Where were you born?" I said, "Listen, do I have to make a confession before I can get a job? Are you going to give me a job, or not?" He said, "Go out there and see the foreman." I went out there and went to work. I didn't stay there long.[45]

As the mill clock at Diboll reached 11:15 on this summer day in 1922, the "cornbread whistle" blew, alerting all the wives of the town to return home to "get the cornbread in the stove" and prepare the noon meal.[46] Many wives did not carry watches, and since mid-morning they had been out and about, visiting with neighbors and shopping in the town, far afield from their bedroom alarm clocks. Wives relied on the whistle to tell them when this time was up. At some point, Tom Temple had brought in efficiency experts to study mill operations, and one of their recommendations had been the elimination of the cornbread whistle, since the experts thought it caused the mill men to slacken their work. Southern Pine tried this, but there "was hell to pay in the town" when noon meals failed to appear on time, and the company reinstated the cornbread whistle.[47]

After breakfast (sometimes the second breakfast, cooked for their children, if the husbands were early risers), sawmill wives set about their daily round of cleaning house, sweeping their bare-dirt yards, washing clothes, tending cows and gardens, and visiting about the town. At the upper levels of mill-town society, women often could afford to hire others to wash and cook for them, leaving them with more time to visit and socialize. After talking to some of these women, Polk County researcher Emma Haynes wrote of the Carlisle Lumber Company town of Onalaska, "The women of this sawmill town, and of most sawmill towns, were fortunate in that they had very little work to do."[48]

However, most mill-town wives did all their own cooking and cleaning, and some did these things and worked on the side. At Diboll, Franklin Taylor's mother made several dozen corn-shucked hot tamales each day for Franklin to distribute after he got home from school. Many times people would not have cash or company checks to pay for these, but most had charge accounts in the commissary, and some trade-off deal would be made—hot tamales for some needed commodity from the store, charged to the purchaser's account.[49] At Ewing, Ben Barlow's grandmother Pearl Braggs was one of those women who cleaned and ironed for the town elite. At age ten and eleven, Ben daily gathered charcoal "clinkers" from the mill's slab pit to burn in his grandmother's "round clay-lined pot with grates on top that she used to heat her irons."[50] Pearl Braggs had special irons for ironing sleeves, collars, and the bodies of dresses, and Ben tended her irons while she worked, keeping them hot, clean, and ready for her to pick up. Pearl's big ironing day was the day after wash day. Pearl washed also, for her family and for others. She used a three-tub method and was highly organized: first, came the wash tub, then the rinse tub, then the bluing tub. She made her own starch by the "Argo method" and "starched the devil" out of everything. At the Braggs's home and elsewhere, Ewing washdays ended in a scene of row after row of very white clothes, stiff as boards, flying on household lines.

By this summer of 1922, only a handful of women labored full- or part-time in the companies' offices or commissary stores as clerks or secretaries. At Diboll, two young office workers had a special job of cutting, edge-sewing, and waxing the company's cardboard "money."[51]

Many mill-town wives had grown up on nearby farms, and those women found their labors lightened in the towns. Although cooking, cleaning, and child care continued, and many still tended small gardens, cows, and a few chickens, heavy field work no longer was required of them; their grueling double-role of housewife and field hand had ended.

One wifely duty had increased in severity, however. Sawmill towns challenged the homemaker with a constant rain of filth from the sky, and homes, clothing, and human bodies all required continual cleaning. Asked if cinders and soot from the mill were a bother, Myrtle Rushing replied: "You better believe it! They were real bad, they would just be so bad sometimes you would just have to wash your clothes over, they would just rain in there—the cinders. We lived right on the street next to the mill, and especially if the wind was blowing in the right direction, it was just too bad. We tried to pick days when it wouldn't be so bad, we had to kind of wait and see which way the wind was blowing."[52] Cinders from the mill also came into Rushing's house through the window screens and rained down from the rafters whenever she slammed her doors. She recalled: "Housekeeping was really hard, you had a day's job every day. It was the same old thing, you really had to work."[53]

Sawmill-town cleaning customs were those of the country farmstead. Wives or children swept bare-dirt yards clean of twigs and leaf debris each day, everybody took a bath on Saturday night, and daily dishwater went right out the window. Guy Croom told: "Mama always threw the dishwater out the kitchen window. You are right, some of it spilled on the windowsill and ran down the outside wall. But why worry about that, everybody else had the same decoration."[54] As in the countryside, children often helped on the weekly, or twice-weekly, washdays. At the town

Women's lives were home-centered in the East Texas sawmill towns. *Courtesy of the East Texas Research Center, Stephen F. Austin State University, Nacogdoches, Texas.*

of Emporia, Naomi Conner's family had limited household water for washing, so her brothers customarily wagoned the heavy wash pot down to the mill pond, filled it up, and got a fire going under it. Then, their sisters took over and did the family's washing.[55] At John Gee's home in Call, water was at the back door, but: "Monday was washday, and I mean all day Monday. The job of rub-boarding the clothes was assigned to the girls. A huge washtub served to boil the wash in. It was my job to keep the pot boiling and take the clothes out with an old broomstick as they were pronounced ready by my mother. My sisters rinsed everything through three waters, but I joined in on the hanging-out process."[56]

Floor cleanings often relied heavily on the mainstay of lye soap. The board kitchen floor in particular took a lot of abuse from stove coals and cooking grease, and Guy Croom's mother always insisted that her children help her give the floor a thorough cleaning every Saturday afternoon, scouring and scrubbing it with strong lye soap.[57]

Human skin got as dirty as clothing and floors in the grimy mill town. Tub baths ordinarily were a weekly affair, though children might be sentenced to "washing up" hands and face at the porch "water shelf" at any time. This shelf, commonly about a foot wide, was supported at one end by a porch post and at the other by a corner of the house, with a support in the center to prevent sagging. A tin pan for washing face and hands, a water bucket with a dipper in it, and a bar of lye soap sat on the water shelf, and a towel—used by all—hung on the nearby wall.[58] Mill-town wives often practiced the old water economies of the countryside, even when they had faucet water at the back porch. As Croom recalled, "Every Monday, Mama rinsed the clothes in bluing water, and if it was summertime she probably decreed that two or three of us would take a bath in that water before she emptied it out."[59]

The houses mill wives lived in also approximated country standards. Homes in the quarters closely resembled the better sharecropper houses on area cotton farms, most mill families lived in homes similar in size and amenities to those of tenant farmers "on thirds and fourths," and the housing of the blue-collar elite approximated the country standards of small landowners, complete with cow barns and chicken houses. Just beginning his sawmill career around 1900, Guy Croom's father had to accept a poor, shabby home for his wife and young family at the mill town of Warren. Guy Croom told: "It was the shabbiest place we ever lived in. The roof leaked and everything around it was in a state of decay. The floor to the outdoor privy was practically flat on the ground, and the door would not close completely." At this home, snakes regularly surprised toilet users and a rotten fence collapsed on Guy's baby brother.[60] However, a few years later at Elmina in Walker County: "We moved into a nice five-room house painted dark yellow, almost brown. This was the first place where we lived that we had electric lights and running water. We had electric lights from 6 A.M. until daylight and from dusk to 10 P.M. The house had no inside plumbing, but water was piped up to the back porch and it was safe, because it was the condensation from the steam-heated dry kiln at the mill. These were luxuries we were unaccustomed to."[61]

Even a medium-quality blue-collar home like this one had simple furnishings: a cook stove in the kitchen and a heating stove in the front of the house; a "wardrobe" for storing clothes (though with a family of seven, most clothing hung on nails around the wall); a "washstand" in the bedroom, "just a flat-top table with a built-in towel rack at the back, drawers on each side, and an enclosure in the middle"; a bowl and pitcher and soap dish on top of the washstand ("the more affluent the household, the bigger the bowl and pitcher set"); a big "quilt box" for storing quilts and other things; a kitchen "eating table" and a few chairs; and a "cuspi-dor" on the floor for the use of snuff dippers and tobacco chewers, "a real trap for little children to trip over and a perfect booby trap for a crawling baby."[62]

Later, Guy Croom's engineer father rose into the mill-town blue-collar elite of sawyers and saw filers, and his home at the Rice Brothers' mill town of Hyatt, Tyler County, around 1910, resembled the nearby res-idences of the mill manager and company doctor. After Mr. Croom de-parted the house at first light, Mrs. Croom not only cleaned the house but managed "a big garden spot, cow pen and chicken yard with barns, chicken house, etc., and raised a big flock of chickens." Two cows were milked every day, and in season Mrs. Croom practiced various food pres-ervations typical of the country farmstead. She salted down cabbage in a wooden barrel; dried, thrashed, and weevil-proofed peas and butterbeans and stored them in bags; dried figs, peaches, pears, and hot peppers in the sunlight; and filled a frame "potato bank" with sweet potatoes.[63] At Wier-gate, James Griner's mother did much the same at the family's elite six-room sawyer's home, with its ice box, kerosene kitchen stove, cow barn, and chicken house. Wier Lumber Company encouraged its employees to have gardens, even providing free seed and the use of a "canning house." Like the Crooms, the Griner family worked a large garden and kept a yard full of chickens. "The company would build you a chicken house if you wanted one," James told, "and they'd build them with a row of nests in them."[64] At Diboll, Tom Temple also encouraged gardens, providing free garden space and a canning house, and he allowed employees to pur-chase milk cows on no-interest credit.

Shotgun houses in the quarters and boxcar houses in the woods camps lacked these subsistence amenities, and housewives there had to make do with primitive circumstances. After Jewel Minton married her teen-aged husband at age fourteen, the young couple took up residence in a boxcar house at the Southern Pine lumber camp of Buggerville. Initial furniture for the Mintons was "a little iron bedstead, a buffet with a mirror in it, an old willow settee, a little chest of drawers, and two homemade cowhide-seated chairs." The chairs only "cost a dollar a piece, but that was a day's work."[65]

Timber camps were remote places close to the logging fronts, where the families of the woods crews lived in reworked boxcars—"house cars," designed to be moved about on the railroad—and even wooden-floored tents.[66] The Trinity County Lumber Company built its camp houses in

Better-quality company houses, Thompson Lumber Company, 1908. *Courtesy of the East Texas Research Center, Stephen F. Austin State University, Nacogdoches, Texas.*

one-room sections, transported them on flatcars, and joined them together to suit the size of the families. A two-section prefabricated commissary, each half the size of a flatcar, was reassembled at each new camp,
as the woods crew followed the ever-moving "front." Trinity County historian Flora Bowles interviewed several camp housewives during the
1920s about their lives in the decades before, and she offered this description of the woman's world.

> The houses of the people were near the railroad track and the commissary,
> usually about fifty feet apart. Within the house there was but little furniture,
> and this was of a cheap sort. There were a few cheap chairs and some shelves
> placed against walls as receptacles of items of clothing and other things. The
> dining and kitchen were one. In this was a wood cook stove and an indifferent
> aggregation of cooking vessels and a pine table such as is used in an ordinary
> kitchen for the convenience of the cook. These, with the plain iron beds, con-
> stituted all the furniture necessary. The women of the woods led a monoto-
> nous life. They arose early in the morning and worked until late at night, be-
> cause the men of their household left home before daylight and returned for
> their suppers after dark. The woman's daily occupation was something like
> this: she prepared breakfast and dinner for the workmen; she cared for several
> children; and she drew and carried water, cut and carried the wood, sewed for

Portable boxcar houses at a logging camp being loaded on a flatcar for railroad transport to a new camp location. *Courtesy of the Temple Archives, Diboll, Texas.*

her family, washed and ironed their clothes and tidied up the house, and prepared the supper. The woman of the woods camp usually wore a long loose dress of coarse gingham which reached to their ankles. The shoes worn by them were heavy and high topped with buttons on them. Their long hair was arranged on the back of their heads in a knot, which was held in place by a tucking comb or wire hairpins. Some of the workmen have followed the occupation all their lives and know no other home than a portable house in the woods. The children seemed to enjoy the wild woods, climbing trees, riding the saplings for horses, listening to the song birds in the day time and watching the squirrels as they scampered from tree to tree, and at the midnight hour, listening to the scream of the panther and the shivering cry of owls.[67]

Like other former woods-camp children, Rivie Vansau of Angelina County had pleasant memories of growing up in several of Southern Pine's timber camps, especially Walkerton. Since they lived immediately beside the tracks, even more than sawmill-town children, woods-camp children paid attention to the passing trains. Vansau recalled: "To us kids, the heroes were the engineers. They blew the whistles on the trains for us, we knew by the whistles which train it was." They even developed their own names for the various engines, calling one "The Old Shay." Situated in the deep woods, often far from roads, everything for the woods camps came in by train, including tank cars of Neches river water, ice, commissary goods, and special orders. The camp commissary stocked mainly staples, such as cornmeal, beans, flour, lard, dried fruits, overalls, and heavy work shoes, but at Christmas it featured toys shipped in from Diboll, and in baseball season it carried baseball equipment. At Walkerton, Vansau attended a one-room school built "across a branch on a hill" a few hundred yards away from the camp. The handmade seats were long benches with a long, wide pine plank that formed the desk for a whole row of children.[68]

Jake Cole and his wife enjoyed living in a boxcar house at a Wiergate timber camp while Jake "fired skidder" in the woods crew. Their home had two bedrooms, a kitchen, a dining area, a wood stove, and a wood heater.[69] Hazel Woods Wilburn grew up in another Newton County lumber camp, living in two boxcars close to her father's work station, the mule corral and ox lot. Trunks provided storage for the Woods family, kerosene lamps provided illumination, and "the company took up two ties from under our kitchen, dug a large hole, lined it with sacks, and brought 100 pounds of ice every day to keep milk and food."[70] Ervelia Jordan lived in Southern Pine's boxcar timber camps for years, and her family's move from camp to camp became a routine. She recalled: "The section crew would come in. I'd put a sheet or a table cloth in the sink, put my dishes in there and wrap them up. I would fasten the cabinet doors so they wouldn't come open. The men would tie the beds down, take the rollers off them, and tie the other furniture down. I would walk out and go spend the day somewhere, maybe shopping. When I got to the new camp, everything would be in its place. I'd walk in the house, and that was the end of it."[71]

Woods-camp families rarely had gardens or livestock, though a few housewives kept chickens that roamed the surrounding woods by day and roosted in trees away from barred owls and gray foxes at night. Woods camps and the poorer sections of the mill towns thus offered a fertile ground for produce peddlers, who came into town to market milk, eggs, and fresh vegetables to the commissaries and door-to-door in the town. People from the Beulah community so commonly peddled these things in Diboll that the wagon track into town became known as the "Buttermilk

Road."[72] Watermelons, syrup, fresh river fish, chickens, chittlins, coon and possum carcasses (the by-products of fur trapping), and hide-bottom chairs also were sold in camps and towns by country people, and, at Southern Pine's remote White City camp, locals openly brought jugs of homemade whisky to sell to company men.[73] At the mill towns, the quarters were the special target of many of the peddlers from the country-side, since black employees rarely had space around their houses for gardens, chickens, and milk cows.

Most companies permitted this informal trade to go on at their towns because commissaries rarely kept such perishable foodstuffs and—since customers normally paid peddlers in company money, redeemable only at the commissaries—the stores got additional business out of it. Only rarely did peddlers arouse companies' suspicions, as in the case of the patent-medicine man rumored to be a Brotherhood of Timber Workers organizer that Kirby lawmen ran out of Call in 1912.[74]

Full-time, professional peddlers also showed up on the homemakers' doorsteps. At White City, a "sewing machine drummer" occasionally

A lumber camp in the woods. Loggers and their families lived in boxcar houses, tents, and other temporary housing. *Courtesy of the Texas Forestry Museum, Lufkin, Texas.*

stepped off the company train to market his unlikely wares in the big woods. Once, this man missed his train back to Diboll and persuaded Vina Well's mother, who ran the boardinghouse, to take one of his machines and pay for it by allowing him free room and board over a certain number of trips.[75] On another occasion, a Jewish peddler with fancy tablecloths, fabrics, and baby clothes drove up in a White Steamer automobile at the Kennedy family's home in Groveton. Learning that Mrs. Kennedy's infant son had been born "already circumcised," the peddler made a great commotion over it and gave her a fine set of baby clothes.[76] Gypsy traders selling willow-limb furniture, fortunes, and dubious horses showed up at Diboll from time to time as they did at other mill towns,[77] and so did the "tin peddlers," "dry-goods peddlers," and "spectacle peddlers," as Guy Croom recalled. Usually arriving by train, such men often went about on foot in the towns, their bodies draped with their wares. The tin peddler "had sort of a harness over his shoulders that had hooks on it. On these hooks, he hung sauce pans, wash pans, dish pans, kitchen spoons, tin dippers, baking pans, pie pans, coffee pots, etc." Likewise, the dry-goods peddler: "carried his wares strapped to a harness that fit over his shoulders. His wares consisted of bolts of cloth, such as calico, bleached domestic, cotton flannel, etc." Often, this man gave a housewife a free piece of cloth to allow him to set up his heavy fabrics in her home for neighbors to examine. As Croom recalled, an eccentric spectacles peddler known as "Scotty" also made the rounds at Village Mills, Warren, Hyatt, and other towns. Scotty sold spectacles from a huge pile, liniments, and a special soap much favored by greasy handed mill men, "Grandpa's Wonder Tar Soap." At the end of the day, machine-shop workers put a bar of this soap in a bucket of water, threw in a red-hot piece of iron, waited a few seconds, then washed up.[78]

Normally, however, housewives did their morning shopping at the commissary or sent their children to do it. Guy Croom recalled being sent on expeditions for bulk soda crackers, flour, green coffee, cornmeal, black pepper, sugar, and navy beans, which, with cornbread, "made up a good part of our diet in the winter."[79] Bacon, hog lard in buckets, and fresh meat sometime were purchased by the Crooms. At Hyatt, with no refrigeration, the company butcher butchered only once a week, bringing the meat into town to sell. Croom recalled: "I can still see him poking along the road to his shop in his wagon, with the meat covered with freshly cut sweet gum boughs. The jolting of the wagon kept the boughs and leaves shaking, which in turn kept the flies away. Then there would be a rush and a line of people at the market door. I would be there with 35 cents, enough to buy two-bits worth of round steak and a ten-cent soup bone."[80] Families had to be careful about their meat purchases, however, especially in Kirby Lumber Company towns. On one occasion, the company butchered "culled" oxen from the Kirbyville woods camp and sold them at Bessmay, where nobody knew where the meat came from.[81]

At high noon at Diboll and a hundred other towns, the mill whistles blew for lunch, and band saws, planing machines, hogs, and all the mechanical juggernauts of the mill slowed and paused. Some men returned home for their meal, while others remained at the plant to eat a syrup-bucket lunch. Claude Kennedy sometimes stayed with his boilers, sometimes came home. One of the Kennedy boy's chores was to carry the lunch bucket "across the dolly run to Papa." This required the wearing of shoes, since the dolly run had a multitude of splinters caused by the work horses' shod feet as they pulled the lumber dollies, and it was covered with tar, which stuck to bare feet and burned like fire. When Claude Kennedy came home to eat at noon or in the evening, food was monotonous, based on his likes and dislikes.[82] As federal studies attested, sawmill families like the Kennedys still ate like the country tenant farmers many of them had once been, a diet running strongly to the "three M's" of meal, meat (fat pork), and molasses.[83] Fred Kennedy recalled: "What we eat, most every day, was dried field peas or dried beans—butterbeans was papa's favorite—bacon or fatback, and cornbread and syrup. Sometimes she'd fry steak, roll it in flour and fry it, and sometimes we had fried chicken."[84]

As the lunch hour moved on toward the back-to-work whistle at one o'clock this day in 1922, workers began to walk slowly back to the mill from their homes or to polish off the last items in their lunch buckets. On an occasion some years before, a Diboll sawyer named Fogg had finished his lunch near his work station at the band saws, then decided to investigate an unusual sound his trained ear had detected in the operation of the carriage at the end of the morning run. As the carriage and saws powered up for the 1 P.M. start-up, Fogg "got in to see what was the matter, and the carriage got loose, the lockbar turned and run him right into the saw and cut him all to pieces." According to Diboll tradition, workers rushed the remains of sawyer Fogg in a no. 3 washtub to the mill doctor, who said, "Why bring that to me?" In any case, as Clyde Thompson told, "Fogg wasn't shown at the funeral."[85]

Mill hands had many stories of Fogg and others like him on their minds as they moved back into position for their jobs among the danger-

Dry-goods department of the company store at Willard. *Courtesy of the East Texas Research Center, Stephen F. Austin State University, Nacogdoches, Texas.*

ous sawmill and planer-mill machinery. Should they grow too comfortable and complacent among the whirring blades and whizzing belts of their familiar work stations, they stood a good chance of losing limb or life. Of a person who took chances in the mill, workers might ominously remark, "He's got more guts than you can hang on a fence," and after a time they might report of such a man, "He was put to bed with a pick and shovel."[86]

Most mill-town residents had their lives touched by industrial accidents. Claude Thompson's wife Ossie recalled: "My uncle lost an arm over there at 19 years old. He was oiling a machine and his sleeve got caught and just carried his arm. If he hadn't been such a strong man, it would've ground him up to his shoulder. He braced himself and just pulled his arm from under it."[87] Sometimes, oilers lost more than their arms, as James Ellis told: "I seen another man, he was an oiler at a sawmill, he greased them pulleys. All that stuff under the mill, there, he'd keep it oiled up and running. We called him 'Rubberbelly.' And he was down there—couldn't do nothing much else—oiling them cars, and he got tangled up in that belt, in them pulleys, and it whupped him to death there. And he was going down the elevator chains, going out to the flour pit, and the sawyer saw him and blowed the whistle and stopped."[88]

Sawmills and lumbering operations were awesomely dangerous workplaces throughout the early twentieth century. In 1913, the chairman of the American Red Cross estimated that every year in the nation's lumber camps alone 1,920 workers were killed, 8,256 permanently disabled, and 70,272 temporarily disabled.[89] East Texas lumber operations certainly were among the most dangerous. Even after excluding those injuries caused by "unavoidable catastrophic accidents" (whatever was meant by that), the Kirby Lumber Company reported 2,574 sawmill and lumber-camp injuries requiring hospitalization among its approximately 4,700 employees from September 1, 1912, to September 1, 1914, an annual accident rate exceeding 25 percent.[90]

As lumber-industry historian W. T. Block observed, "the concept of occupational safety was unheard of in the early sawmills of East Texas." If you were injured or killed by one of the built-in hazards of the trade, it was your tough luck or your fault. "One might say, if one wishes to avoid an industrial accident, one studied for the ministry. Write-ups about accidents and mill deaths were so commonplace in the newspapers that the reader's eye scarcely blinked."[91]

Nonetheless, the newspaper and trade journal accounts of sawmill accidents truly chill the blood. On March 5, 1905, the *Beaumont Journal* noted a rash of accidents at the E. B. Hayward sawmill near Nacogdoches, after only four months of operation. "Tom Weeks, while feeding a planer at the Hayward mill Saturday accidentally had his hand cut completely off. This makes the twelfth man hurt by accident at the mill, including one that fell from a scaffold and was killed outright." Two weeks later the paper added: "For one cause or another, the band saw of the big Hayward mill was demolished last Thursday, and the edger ('bull edger' or 'gang saw') also was put out of commission for several days. When a big gang saw breaks, it is a dangerous customer and generally succeeds in cutting half a dozen men in two before it is stopped."[92]

When a thirty-foot band saw running at high speed slipped off its "dogs," as at the Hayward mill, a terrible scene ensued at the saw carriage. According to Arthur Beale, the conventional wisdom about this situation advised workers around the saw to freeze in place. "Sit perfectly still. If you run, it will hit you, it whips like a snake. Some of those saws are 30-foot in circumference, or more, it's gonna go somewhere. And you take a big piece of metal with teeth on it whipping around that way, it will cut you to pieces if it hits you."[93] At Call in 1919, perhaps the block setter forgot to freeze. *Southwest* reported: "John Williams, block setter on the carriage at Call, Texas, for the Kirby Lumber Company, lost one of his arms while engaged at his regular work on the carriage on September 7th. The band saw was in motion when it suddenly slipped from its position on the mill and fell on the carriage. It was revolving rapidly when it fell, and it struck the arm of Williams, completely severing it from his body."[94] When band saws or circular saws struck nails or railroad spikes deeply embedded in logs, equally drastic things might happen. Saw blades sometimes shattered into deadly shrapnel, maiming or eviscerating nearby workers.[95]

Southwest and the *St. Louis Lumberman* had many gory accidents to report. In September of 1912, *Southwest* told that a worker at Jones mill had died "when he struck a circular saw, the top of his head being cut off." Debris thrown from the saws also could be deadly, and the *Lumberman* noted on March 15, 1913, that a Texas man had been badly injured "when a splinter fully as large as a man's thumb entered the man's eye and travelled upwards for three or four inches." Other journal accounts detail fingers amputated due to "old and defective revolving knives," fractured skulls and crushed hips due to flying debris, an arm broken by entanglement with the saw, and a man who fell against the saw and suffered his "heart cut in two."[96]

Boiler explosions were another kind of ultimate sawmill accident. In one incident, the engineer "had a roaring fire of boards under the boiler when he saw that the water was very low in the gauge. He opened the injector and within a few seconds a terrific explosion occurred. A portion of the plate from the boiler carried half of his head away, killing him instantly."[97] Lumber industry journals regularly reported bodies and body parts hurled many feet; "workmen about the yards, blown from the stacks where they were piling timber, with wreckage scattered up to half a mile away"; houses in the town damaged by flying debris; a mill smokestack found half a mile from the boiler explosion; and other epic consequences. Of one Texas mill in 1909, *Southwest* reported that: "One of the boilers was blown across the Trinity River and landed 1,800 feet on the further side of the river and over 2,000 feet from the place of explosion. It was buried deep in the side of a hill when found."[98]

Mills and company railroads operated very close to employees' homes, so when a boiler exploded or a train derailed this could have drastic consequences for workers' families outside the mill. Ervelia Jordan of Diboll dreamed of a train derailment, then the next day her nightmare came true.

> I dreamed things lots of times, and it happens. I dreamed that they let flatcars get away and runned into our house. It was about ten o'clock, and I had put the baby to bed. I called Pat [her daughter], and I looked and saw her coming toward the house. I heard this rumbling noise, and it hit—I screamed, I hung on to a screen door, and the porch went just straight up and down, stood on end, and all I had to hang on was my left hand. I was hanging there, and when I looked out there was fire—these light wires was broke, just kept jumping. I ran back to get the baby, and she was alright, but I heard Pat saying: "Mama! Mama! The train's cut my arm off!"[99]

East Texas sawmills and timbering operations were so dangerous, and safety precautions so commonly ignored by the companies, that accidents waiting to happen may be readily seen in photographs taken for the *American Lumberman* public-relations articles done for Texas companies. For example, in the journal's special edition of 1902 about the Kirby Lumber Company appear photographs of a man releasing logs from the inside of a tilted flatcar at the "rollover" (blurring slightly in the photograph, as he moves to jump over the "skidder logs" to safety), black laborers in the yard working among dangerously tilted lumber stacks (falling lumber killed and injured many workers), a heavily loaded logging train tilting badly on the usual unbedded tramway roadbed, and other examples.[100]

Kirby officials probably saw and approved every photo appearing in the *American Lumberman*. Lumber-industry management long regarded the dangers of the job as unavoidable and believed that most accidents occurred because of worker carelessness, not because of unsafe procedures and dangerous machinery, and that stringent safety requirements would put their companies out of business. In 1914, Kirby vice president C. P. Myer wrote with distaste of the new workman's compensation law forced on the company by the State of Texas and expressed the widely held opinion that professional safety inspectors required by the law tended to make "recommendations that will either increase operating expenses or reduce the efficiency of the plant."[101] Companies' "safety first" campaigns did not appear, even in a halting way, until the 1920s. Asked about safety, fifty-year Southern Pine employee Jesse Parker laughed and said, "In that day and time, nobody thought anything about safety first. We didn't know what it was." Then, by way of example, he told how the Temple woods crew got to the front from the timber camp every morning. "Our conveyance then, we were riding what they called 'skeleton cars.' It was just a car that was a frame with no floorboard on it. We got on that, and the engineer pushed it ahead of the engine. It was dark, and we didn't know what we was going into, we didn't see the trees or houses or anything else. That is the way we went in and that is the way we came out."[102]

Despite fire hazards and badly maintained physical plants, John Henry Kirby's mills in particular followed a policy of "damn the machinery and keep on running." Disgruntled mill manager J. H. McDonald wrote this revealing account of the situation he had inherited at the Kirby town of Bessmay, around 1910.

> I found the boilers in the worst condition I ever saw boilers that were being operated, found scales in them caked together so hard that they had to be broke up with bars and picks before they could be passed out through the manhole. The engines were in bad shape. Both bandsaws were jumping so bad the sawyers could hardly stand by them and saw, foundation under band, niggers, and trip were so rotten they were working around through and through; other parts of the mill were just as bad. The Sawyer drops and kiln platform were so rotten they were dangerous to walk over when running. The planing machines were in bad condition. There had been holes cut through the floor of the planing mill and shavings shoveled through them until the shavings were piled from the ground to the floor, which is about 6 feet, making the worst fire trap I ever saw.[103]

Such conditions took their toll on Bessmay's workers, especially new men just arrived at the dangerous, bewildering sawmill. In 1918, young African American Vastine Polk abandoned his mother's twenty-seven-acre cotton farm for life as a mill hand at Bessmay. After lying about his age, the fourteen-year-old boy began work on the sawmill crew, but during only his fifth day on the job Polk's raincoat became caught in the unshielded machinery. A protruding shaft whirled him around and around until he struck his head on a chain carrier that "tore him up very badly." Vastine Polk died a few minutes later.[104]

Over time, Kirby accident statistics improved somewhat from the 25 percent annual casualty rate of 1914 (equal to that of some combat infantry companies). During the first three months of 1923, however, 118 Kirby Lumber Company employees suffered disabling injuries and 5 were killed.[105] And during 1925, 582 (12.2 percent) of the Kirby work force of 4,767 sustained injuries, 7 workers died, and mill hands at Voth suffered a casualty rate of 26.3 percent.[106]

The state did not intrude on companies' medical claims policies until the first workmen's compensation law of 1913, and companies' legal staffs spent much time settling injury claims. Kirby employees were required to pay $1 to $1.50 a month for the mill-town doctor's services and $.50 to $1 for accident insurance. Injury claims were negotiated soon after the injury—too soon, many accused; sometimes the injured worker still lay wracked with pain in the doctor's office, waiting for his train to the hospital, when the company lawyer approached him with a deal. How much a person got for a given injury partly depended on the severity of the injury, partly on the injured man's job status and how well he negotiated his case. A mashed finger might be worth $15 at Call and only $4.35 at Silsbee.[107] A black laborer with both feet crushed by the wheels of a train received only $250 at Village Mills, despite his permanent disability.[108] A Browndel man with a lacerated left testicle asked the company for $1,000 compensation, but finally settled for $20.[109] Perhaps more shrewd, J. W. Lawrence obtained a personal lawyer and had better luck in receiving Kirby payment for an injury sustained jumping from a train—$1,700 and free use of a company house.[110] Typical of many accident settlements noted in the Kirby papers was that of black planer-mill employee Bob Smith, who lost three fingers of his left hand: "by carelessness allowing them to catch in the Feed Gear of one of our Planing machines at Planer 'H' Beaumont, Texas. I don't anticipate any trouble from the case, but I believe it would be policy to let his wages continue until such time we are able to get him back in service, and request a release from liability."[111]

However, the higher the status of the injured worker, the more likely he was to get a lawyer, ask for a high compensation, and give the company trouble. Failing to settle with Kirby over a leg severed on the job, millwright L. K. Barber embarrassed the company by asking the ladies of the United Charities to solicit donations around the mill town to buy him an artificial limb. Spurred into action by this prospect, Kirby executive B. F. Bonner wrote:

> It appears to me that it would be a great injury to the Company on this and other cases to have these women chasing around town raising money, dollar at a place, to buy this poor unfortunate fellow a leg, as they will no doubt express the matter. Our Doctor Wier has a cast of this man's leg already for getting the

artificial limb and he says that the man will get around in good shape on the artificial leg, and he believes that it would be the best kind of investment to put the $110 into the limb. Even though the man sues us, he says he would present a good appearance and would not appear to be injured in any great extent.

The doctor's judgment perhaps proved correct, since the man received only $500 for his lost leg after his day in court.[112]

Even some black mill men dared to oppose the company. George Nolal, who had received "two holes knocked in his head" while blocksetting on the log carriage, soon became dissatisfied with the slow handling of his injury claim and told an acquaintance that they "were fooling with the wrong Negro." Illiterate himself, Nolal said he planned to get somebody to write a letter for him and "if they did not pay up he was going to get a lawyer on a fifty-fifty basis and give them Hell." Unfortunately, the man's friend was a Kirby operative and so declined repeated requests from Nolal to write the letter for him.[113]

With the Texas workman's compensation law of 1913, which set up the Industrial Accident Board, and the strengthening amendments to the law in 1917, 1923, and 1927, companies' attitudes toward safety issues began to change. At first, employers could "subscribe" to the program, or not; if they did, workers could not file for damages for injuries on the job, but neither could the companies use their three traditional common-law defenses against injury suits—"negligence of a fellow-worker," "contributory negligence," and "assumption of risk." As time went on, the increasingly rigorous state laws and the insurance companies began bringing greater pressure on insured companies to install safety devices.[114]

Companies had always practiced "safety first" with regard to mill-fire dangers, however—though how much good this did them is not certain. The *American Lumberman* editor and photographer visited Thompson-Tucker Lumber Company during 1908 in preparation for the journal's glowing piece "The House of Thompson," and the editor noted the company's many provisions for fire safety at its towns of Willard, Greyburg, Doucette, and Trinity. Deep lakes fed water to elevated tanks, which fed the big Gardner duplex fire pumps, which serviced thousands of feet of six-inch and four-inch pipe. The company employed four men as night watchmen at each mill, and "arranged at proper intervals about the plant and lumber storage places" were "128 water barrels and 120 fire buckets for quick emergency service."[115] The praise soon rang hollow, however: not long after the *American Lumberman* team came through (but too late for a correction in the article), Thompson-Tucker's Doucette mill burned to the ground.

Despite all the companies' efforts to deal with this particular "industrial accident" problem, fires plagued bonanza sawmill towns from first to last. Between 1902 and 1906, for example, the *American Lumberman* reported twenty-eight major mill fires in Texas sawmills, and in one week alone during 1916, the *Gulf Coast Lumberman* reported seven lumber mill and yard fires in East Texas.[116] Quite often, state-of-the-art fire-fighting equipment seemed to make little difference. At the Keith Lumber Company mill at Voth in 1916, a sawyer discovered a "hot box," a smoking bearing near where he was working, but the discovery was too late to prevent a small explosion, and in a few minutes fire engulfed the sawmill. Only the planer mill was saved by men playing a constant stream of water on the connecting dollyway from the mill.[117] Something very much like this had happened at Browndel a few years earlier, where the fire-suppression system also had worked perfectly—the night watchman discovered the fire just after it started, men quickly rushed to the spot with hoses, the pumps worked correctly, but the mill burned to the ground anyway.[118] "A sawmill burned down quicker than any other kind of factory," Deweyville mill superintendent W. A. Smith explained, and the fine, dry sawdust from the planing mill, lying about on mill timbers, "is about as good kindling as can be found."[119] Brick salesman Arthur Beale happened to be in a planer mill near Marshall when a fire started on a hot windy day, and he reported that nobody gave a thought to water hoses or fire buckets; they ran for their lives. Beale said, "The planer mill caught fire on the southeast end, and practically before we would get out the north end, the whole thing burned down."[120]

Over the years, Diboll had its share of mill fires and injuries. Between 1912 and 1914, for example, on-the-job injuries totaled "606 non-fatal and 2 fatal,"[121] perhaps including the unfortunate sawyer Fogg, but on this hot summer day in 1922 nothing special had occurred—only the usual small personal tragedies of mashed fingers, splinters in hands, and foreign objects in eyes had occupied the Southern Pine medical staff. The clinic nurse had received a start, however: while removing an object from a man's eye, she noticed something strange about his other one, examined it over his objections, then screamed loudly when the man's glass eye popped out and rolled across the floor.[122] As in the case of cotton ginners, over the course of long careers around the machinery, sawmill men like this one tended to lose body parts. Disabling injuries peaked in the Texas sawmilling counties, some of which nearly doubled the state's average of 6.3 percent permanent disablement among adult males.[123]

Finally, at Diboll and a hundred other towns, the six o'clock whistle blew "quitting time," and the great engines of the mill began to shut off for the day, the boilers powering down to the minimal steam pressures they would keep throughout the night. Improvident workers, the "old boys that lived right up against their pay," rushed to draw company money for a day's work at the company pay windows.[124] Some Kirby employees also had drawn a half-day's pay at the noon lunch break, and the company reluctantly allowed this practice.[125] At the Rice Brothers mill town of Hyatt, mothers called their children in from the street at the sound of the last whistle, since they knew the dollyway mules soon would be released to stampede home to corn and water at their mule corral. As Guy Croom recalled: "At quitting time, 6 P.M., all they had to do was turn those mules loose and they went galloping down the road back to the corral and feed trough. Those mules seemed hellbent on running over anything that barred them from it." Croom remembered mothers closer to the mill crying out the warning to mothers farther down the road, "Here come the mules!"[126]

Then there was supper, and not so long after that, sleep. Men were dead tired after a hard, hot day in the mill, and few found the energy to read or socialize for very long. Sitting for a while on the front porch of their mill houses seemed recreation enough for most of them. As they sat there in the gathering dusk of this summer evening, the ringing in their ears from the eleven-hour day among the great machines gradually lessened, their hearing slowly returned, and their wives' and children's voices began to make sense.[127] On many evenings at this time, Guy Croom's mother and father sang a few old hymns on their porch before going to bed, and they later learned that neighbors sometimes had slipped up, unobserved, to listen to them. For most people, weekday amusements were few in the sawmill town.[128] Then it became "good dark" and most people turned in. Houses were close together, and people heard their neighbors going to bed, heard their bedsprings creaking, heard them snoring and talking in their sleep. Often left alone while her land-man husband roamed East Texas on company business, Mrs. Sidney Walters Kindley took comfort in the small sounds she heard from the Weise's on one side of her and Mrs. Farrington on the other, since "they were both good neighbors."[129]

Chapter Five

DANCING ON THE MILLPOND

———

L ONG after Claude Kennedy had turned in for the night, worn down
by another long hot day tending his engines, the Kennedy children
wandered their mill-town neighborhood, playing with the sons and
daughters of neighbors and roaming the dirt streets of Groveton in the
summer dark.[1] Children knew only the mill town, and for them it was
simply home. At Honey Island, Dwayne Overstreet "played in the black
cinders that came out of the smokestack" and found the mill town a familiar, friendly place. Overstreet told: "When I was a kid, I thought
everyone loved me, because there wasn't much malice around. Oh, there
was a fist fight once in awhile, but no real malice. You could ride your bicycle anywhere, around anyone's house or yard, on other people's property. In a sawmill town, you walked everywhere you wanted and on other
people's property. We hunted and fished wherever we wanted. No one
locked doors or locked up anything."[2]

Mill towns normally had been situated at remote locations in stands of
virgin timber, so the countryside remained close by, accessible to all, even
if it was now cutover land. Pate Warner recalled that Diboll boys often
went in swimming at White Oak Creek, near the town. "There were
three or four pretty good holes down there and everybody went down
there. You'd have an old pair of overalls, or something like that. You didn't
have any money to buy a bathing suit."[3] At Wiergate, sawyer's son James
Lee swam in cool Cow Creek pools in the nearby woods, after the company's fine swimming pool grew tepid in the hot summer, and he also
hunted, fished, crawfished, and frog-gigged around the millpond.[4] At the
poorer mill towns, as at Carmona in Trinity County, visited by geogra-

pher William Chambers in 1931, field sports like these sometimes were almost the only recreation available. Chambers wrote: "Recreational life at Carmona is intimately related to the forest environment. The wild game of the area includes deer, squirrels, foxes, wolves, turkeys, quail, and rabbits. Ducks and geese are hunted on the mill ponds during autumn and spring. The supply pond from which boiler water is obtained affords favorable places for swimming. Fish are caught here and in the log pond, and trips are also made to the Trinity and Neches rivers."[5]

At Carmona, Diboll, Wiergate, and a hundred other places, wild lands remained near. On Saturday afternoons in the autumn, Diboll management dismissed the office staff (and themselves) for a squirrel-hunting party and picnic on the "Neches River squirrel grounds" just east of town. And at nearby Emporia, a few miles north of Diboll, fox hunters gathered on the front porch of the commissary at night to loose their dogs into the cutover lands around the mill and listen for the first fox to "jump." When this happened, and the hounds began to "give mouth," they "lit out after the dogs."[6] As in these cases, companies often encouraged field sports as an alternative to other male diversions, and Sabine Tram at Deweyville even went so far as selling guns to boys and men at cost.[7]

Dave Martinez and his brothers at Wiergate did not hunt just for pleasure, but to put "meat on the table." He told, "We hunted what we needed, we would go out there and kill a couple of rabbits and two or three squirrels and come on back home. Hunting was a pleasure, but it also was a necessity."[8] After school in the summers, the Martinez brothers' forest excursions also often had subsistence purposes, since they cut wood for the family wood stove; fished in Cow Creek; and picked blackberries, mayhaws, and persimmons for their mother to make preserves.[9]

Racial and class lines sometimes relaxed on these excursions, and black boys gathered and fished and hunted with white boys, and laborers' sons "fooled around the woods" with the sons of mill management.[10] Kenneth Nelson and his friends often went down to Ryan's Lake, an old oxbow lake just west of the Neches River, to gather mayhaws, fish, hunt, and camp out. The mayhaw bushes grew in the "back part" of Ryan's Lake, and, as Nelson told:

> You'd take the seine and stretch it out across the water where it was running to you. Another would go up and shake the bushes, and the mayhaws would fall out, and the water would carry them down against the seine. You'd go along with a syrup bucket and dip them up and put them in the tub. You'd bring

Two young bathers pose on the diving board at the
Wiergate swimming pool, late 1930s. *Courtesy of
the U.S. Post Office, Wiergate, Texas.*

them back to Diboll and sell them after you got all you wanted for your
mother or grandmother to make jelly. And if you shook a water moccasin out
of the tree, why, he went right on down in the backwater with the berries.[11]

Nelson and his friends also hunted year-round at Ryan's Lake, paying
no attention to the game laws or the difficulties involved in harvesting
white-tailed deer with single-shot .22 rifles. On many a weekend in the
summer, they left after school on Friday to set up a fishing camp at Ryan's
Lake. "We walked and carried our bedrolls and our grease and our frying
pans," he recalled. "We ate what we caught and cooked. Aunt Nettie
Weeks always made us syrup cookies. We would have some biscuits with
some salt pork in it to take with us in case we didn't catch anything. We
always caught fish, though."[12]

As did the Saner-Ragley Lumber Company at Carmona, most companies began cutting immediately outside their towns, then moved ever further afield, building main-line tramway to follow their logging fronts and leaving cut-over wastelands behind. At the "ideal sawmill town" of Wiergate, however, the company did things differently, as mill superintendent's daughter Martha Lee Bowers recalled. Wier Long Leaf Lumber Company cut inward toward its town, leaving the beautiful virgin longleaf groves around Wiergate standing until the very end. As did many other Wiergate children, Bowers remembered long days spent wandering the ancient pine forest.

> We had a lot of freedom—they'd just let us go. We'd always pack lunches. The woods were wonderful, the longleaf pine was slick and clean, and you didn't have a lot of undergrowth. We could walk for miles over every log, every creek. We roamed all over those woods—I don't believe there was a spot we missed—and we always knew at least what direction was home. My friends all had older brothers and there was always gunny-sack swings on long ropes on the side of some hill on a tall tree, and a flying jenny and a trolley—back in the woods they had tied a cable with a pully on it with a tow sack, and we'd ride. They'd put nailed boards on the trees so we could climb up and ride down. We smoked grapevine—I know we smoked all the grapevine in East Texas. We did it in the summertime—that was a ritual just like marbles and barrel hoops and washers—there was a season to every one of them. We built play houses from that pine straw. We piled it up and made rooms, we'd make beds and chairs. The fun was in the building, I don't think we ever played with them much when we got them built.[13]

Many children's pastimes in the mill towns duplicated those of early-twentieth-century rural children everywhere, though other activities took advantage of the special resources of the sawmill town as "playscape." Mill-town children sailed the tin lids of syrup buckets, Frisbee-style, played ring games, and made many of their own toys, including wooden wagons wheeled with tin cans, popguns of hollow elderberry stalks firing chinaberry "bullets," and "rubber-gun" pistols launching rings cut from innertubes.[14] Mill operations produced a huge amount of wood scrap, and children used this raw material to make model railroads running on back-yard tracks, "stick horses," "scooters," "tom walkers," and many other things. At a certain time during the year, a craze for one or another of these things would sweep the town, and everyone rushed to rig one up from scrap wood. One child on tom walkers soon spawned fifty more, running races on the streets or competing to build the tallest possible version.[15] At Diboll, as everywhere else in the age of steam, railroads fascinated children, and depot agent's son L. D. Smith took advantage of an unlimited supply of mill scrap to build an elaborate model railroad running a great distance. Smith remembered, "It ran all the way through our back yard, through Mrs. Steed's back yard, into Raybun Carrol's back yard. I tore the pickets off the fence and would go through the fence."[16]

At night, on Saturday afternoons and Sundays, and anytime adults were not watching, the sawmill itself provided wonderful play opportunities. Children slid down sawdust piles on boards, walked the logs floating in the mill pond, clambered about on the forbidden elevated wood dollyways, and leaped from lumber stack to lumber stack in the yards.[17] The huge draft horses "with feet as large as a small pie pan" some companies used to pull lumber carts on the dollyways especially attracted children. At the horse lot, as Arthur Tuorila recalled, "We'd be up on a board fence, and we'd jump on them and ride around the lot—our legs would almost stick straight out across their wide backs."[18]

Probably no part of the mill's industrial plant interested children so much as its railroads, but here the differences in fathers' job statuses affected childish play. Many children walked the tracks on a lark, perhaps holding a stick with a partner on the other rail and competing with other pairs to see who would be the last to fall off, and many also put crossed nails and pennies on the tracks to be smashed into interesting shapes by passing locomotives. On Sunday afternoons at Diboll, some of the bolder boys and girls even retrieved the "pump car" from the mill shop and pumped it back and forth on the rails.[19] However, rank had its privileges in railroad play, and only young Arthur Temple sometimes got to drive the gasoline track car on Tom Temple's main-line tracks.[20] Likewise, Vivian Warner played about on her engineer father's idle Texas South-Eastern locomotive on Sunday afternoons, and depot agent's son L. D. Smith even got to run the train. On the trip to Lufkin: "Mr. Bob Cook was the engineer, and Junior and I would ride the engine all of the way to Lufkin. One of us would be the engineer going to Lufkin, and one of us would be the engineer coming back. We would even get to blow the whistle and ring the bell."[21]

Smith also became one of the fortunate boys sometimes allowed to roam the mill during operating hours and pull the rope to sound the cornbread whistle. Wiergate commissary-manager's son Calvin Smith received extra ice cream in his sodas from druggist Earl Hines, rode the tailgates (and stole ice) on the big ice wagons delivering block ice from ice

Virgin longleaf-pine forest close to Wiergate. Children from the town often played
in the nearby woods left uncut until the very end. *Courtesy of the
U.S. Post Office, Wiergate, Texas.*

house to home ice boxes, and had other special privileges.[22] However, head-timekeeper's son Edwin Nelson perhaps enjoyed the greatest advantages. No sooner did the noon lunch bell ring at Diboll School than Nelson rushed down to the company offices to volunteer his services. In rapid sequence, he picked up the "time books" from shipping office, planer mill, shed crew, dry-kiln crew, hardwood-mill crew, and regular-mill crew. As he went about, he yelled at various men he knew in the plant. Then, time books delivered to the office, young Nelson hurried to the boiler room to blow the "quarter whistle," leaping high in the air to grab the cable and make the thunderous sound. That accomplished, he rushed to the depot "to catch the T.S.E. switching the planer. I would ride the train down to the store and helped them switch the cars at the planer. I would just make the bell at school before being late."[23]

At some point, usually during the summer vacation, play in and around the father's job station turned into a boy's first mill employment. As his first job, Guy Croom carried water buckets with a special yoke to workmen at the Warren machine shop his father supervised. Guy had often visited the shop, but now he found the buckets heavy, the eleven-hour days long, and the machine-shop men a thirsty lot. However, there were compensations, since young Croom now got to blow the "work whistle and quitting time whistle," and after a while a friendly engineer let him run his big switching engine on the sly.[24] Fred Kennedy's first job of "feeding the hogs" in the mill came after being caught once too often playing hooky from school. At age fourteen, Fred preferred exploring the millpond or anything else to attending Groveton School, and one day the mill foreman spotted Fred riding the company railroad to visit a carnival set up at the logging camp and reported this to Claude Kennedy. Losing patience with his hooky-playing son, Kennedy put Fred to feeding scrap wood to the screaming hogs.[25]

Fourteen-year-old boys sometimes did not make perfect mill hands. Fred Kennedy preferred feeding the hogs to conjugating sentences on the school blackboard, but one day, rushing to the commissary for a candy bar during a brief morning work break, he accidentally knocked a black boy off the porch in front of the mill superintendent and came under direct criticism. Fred explained: "I had learned to cuss pretty good by then, so I gave the man a cussing and called him a nigger lover. He went and told Papa I'd have to leave, he didn't want me around there no more."[26] Banished from Groveton for this unforgivable offense, Fred soon chopped cotton on a relative's farm.

Fred Kennedy had begun mill work at a better-than-average job, since his father (soon also banished from Groveton) had been chief engineer. Males commonly started work as teen-agers on the dollyways, and, as De-Witt Wilkerson told, boys would be boys: "I've been out early on frosty mornings—frost would be all over them dolly runs—and they'd run them little old jitneys, they was Model A Fords is what they were, up there on that slick frost, and get on the brake, and just wheel it around, just spin it."[27] Other willful youths often sported around the company millpond, even while on the job. Dave Martinez remembered young "pond mon-keys" at Wiergate putting on a show for passers-by: "People going along the track would sit there and watch them. They would jump from one log to another, roll this log, and one would go across the pond from one log to another. He would do his little jig out there on the log, jump from one log to another. Sometimes he would run across that pond."[28]

Some companies prided themselves on their towns' recreational facil-ities, which might include community centers, movie theaters, athletic fields, swimming pools, and even lighted dance pavilions. At many other places, however—the shabby average mill towns like Kilraven, Carmona, and Ewing—recreations remained informal and impromptu, centered around the commissaries, boardinghouses, and millponds.

Aside for a few oxbow lakes along the river valleys (and Caddo Lake in far northeast Texas), natural lakes were rare in the pineywoods counties of East Texas, and company millponds attracted much attention. Sawmill people fished, swam, frog-gigged, duck-hunted, picnicked, baptized, and courted in and around their towns' millponds, and they sometimes even danced on them. Trinity County Lumber Company of Groveton built a circular board dance pavilion in the middle of its largest millpond, and people cavorted there to big bands during the Roaring 20s.

Fishing and frog-gigging remained much more common uses of the company millpond than dancing the Charleston. John Gee recalled long nights spent catching the giant bullfrogs that thrived around the marshy edges of Call's millpond, and how, after John Henry Kirby's mills failed during the Great Depression, the tasty frogs were pursued in earnest.[29] Calvin Smith gigged bullfrogs around the Wiergate millpond, sometimes so many that he sold them in town, and James Griner caught frogs by the sackfull migrating from Wiergate millpond to Cow Creek. He explained: "We could catch them migrating from the pond to the creek. They had to go by this slab pit where they burned old ends of lumber and everything. If we could see and we had a net, we'd net them as they were going down-

Although millponds doubled as recreational sites for swimmers, fishermen, picnickers, and courting couples, industrial uses dominated areas nearest to the mill. *Courtesy of the Temple Archives, Diboll, Texas.*

hill. We'd get a towsack full of frogs."[30] Fishing the pond on Sunday afternoons became a common recreation of many sawmill people—men, women, and children. On one occasion, Fred Kennedy and his older brothers discovered that a dam on one of Trinity Lumber Company's ponds had failed, leaving many fish stranded in a shallow central pool. Although the Kennedy boys dutifully left home each morning with school books and lunch buckets, for days they turned aside to join other hooky-players "grappling" by hand for fish in the millpond. To hide their operations, boys from the mill-town side of Groveton sold their catch on the private-sector side of the tracks, and boys from that side sold their catch in the company town. Despite this precaution, after a while Claude Kennedy discovered the truth, "strapped" his fishermen sons, and expelled them to the countryside to hoe cotton.[31]

Companies with double millponds, one to service the sawmill with logs and one to serve as reservoir for the lower pond in dry seasons, provided the best swimming. While the lower pond might be full of floating logs and debris, the upper pond remained pristine and unspoiled. Manning's upper millpond attracted swimmers and fishermen from the town, the surrounding countryside, and even the county seat of Lufkin.[32] Diboll's murky millpond offered dubious swimming (though many swam there anyway), and residents of the town often walked the railroad tracks to swim and picnic at the scenic upper pond of nearby Emporia.[33]

Diboll's millpond offered another problem for swimmers. Perhaps fearing deaths by drowning or outbreaks of typhoid caused by "the lake draining off the Negro quarters,"[34] or perhaps just disliking naked youths in his millpond, mill superintendent Watson Walker took steps to discourage bathing. Pate Warner had found some alligator eggs near Ryan's Lake, hatched them under a "broody hen" (who repented of her broodiness when the first reptile began to "pip out"), and kept them around in a tub to show off. After a while Warner tired of his exotic pets, and Walker asked him, "Pate, what are you going to do about those alligators?" "I don't know, sir," the boy answered, and Walker said, "If you don't mind, put them in the mill pond."[35] Thereafter, the alligators flourished, and only the most intrepid of Diboll's youths went swimming in the company pond. The matter was resented. Herbert Weeks, who admitted that he thought of Walker somewhat as he thought of the devil, once shot one of the reptiles and nailed it head-down to a tree "for Mr. Watson Walker to find," and a "French boy from Louisiana," recently moved to Diboll, taught local boys "to ride the alligators."[36]

Commissaries were another focus point for community recreational life. Although only a few of them served as launching places for packs of foxhounds, as at Emporia, all did double duty as social centers for their communities, and some provided the only recreational gathering point. Manning, a relatively large company town possessing a movie house, nevertheless lacked a true "community hall"; consequently, the Manning commissary served as the center for social activity. At Carmona, Kilraven, and Ewing, the commissary was the only gathering place. Ewing resident Chester Treadaway recalled that women and children met there during the day, and that men packed the place just before work and at the noon hour. As at Ewing, commissaries provided large front porches and numerous benches and chairs, and these attracted many idlers.[37]

Diboll possessed a community center and movie theater, but at night people always "gathered around the store."[38] During the day, the Diboll commissary's drugstore served as a meeting place, as did the drugstore at Groveton. At Wiergate, people frequented the ice house adjacent to the commissary in the hot evenings to buy ice sodas for a nickel, ice-cold watermelons for fifty cents, and ice cream by the quart.[39] At Groveton, young people customarily stopped by the commissary shoe shop on the way home from school, and at that place, as at Wiergate and everywhere else, Saturday was the big day.[40] Major entertainments sometimes appeared on the commissary porches on Saturdays, including style shows that were staged by the lady in charge of the women's-wear department and featured not only belles of the town modeling "hats, dresses, and other accessories" but also the ever-popular Buster Brown and his wonder dog, Tige.[41] As Pate Warner recalled, this representative of the Brown Shoe Company of St. Louis, which made only children's shoes, "Was a little midget feller. He wore a little cap, and he had a little bulldog named Tige. He would come to Diboll every six months or so, and all the kids would gather around."[42] Buster Brown also came to the Groveton commissary, and Willie Burch remembered how he amazed the crowd by his tiny stature and sailor-suit dress—but Tige normally stole the show. Wonder-dog Tige walked on his hind legs, smoked cigarettes, found hidden objects, and sat upright in a small chair. After Buster Brown took the Brown Shoe Company act to another mill-town commissary, he invariably left behind mothers buying Buster Brown shoes, puppies named Tige, and the sounds of free Buster Brown whistles heard far and wide.[43]

Commissaries also seem to have been the center of another kind of social action, the classic Southern "hoorah," or joke on the job. No one recalled any tricks played around the saws or in the planer mill, and with good reason, but commissary staff had energy and time for such things, and the noise level at the commissary allowed human conversation. Men were supposed to take jokes played on them, hoorahs, in good grace, especially when the perpetrators were their superiors. Presumably, young cashier Earl Hines joined in the laughter after Wiergate commissary manager E. C. Hopkins sent the dead rat up the wire to him in the cash cylinder.[44]

The Diboll commissary was a hotbed for hoorahs, played both on commissary staff and their customers. Clerks positioned an electric contact on a big wrapping table that people sometimes sat on, and flipped a hidden switch whenever a victim moved to the right spot. Sometimes staff hid in caskets on the second floor, then spoke to passers-by in ghostly voices.

Grocery section of the Willard commissary, 1908. Especially in the smaller mill towns, commissary stores also served as informal centers of community social life. *Courtesy of the East Texas Research Center, Stephen F. Austin State University, Nacogdoches, Texas.*

They also used a phony snake to frighten customers, though on one occasion this almost backfired on clerk Jim Fuller. Held in the hand, the snake appeared to be moving: "and there was a lady across the counter from me, and she just put her head on the counter and said, 'Oh, my God!' And she didn't say anything, she just stood there a few minutes. And her boy was standing by her, and I said, 'What is the matter with your mother?' And he said, 'Well, sir, she has trouble with her heart.'"[45] Unchastened, the Diboll commissary staff continued their hoorahs, and one favorite trick was to start a rumor that a circus train was coming through Diboll at four o'clock. A crowd always gathered at the depot, but "it never came, you know, and some people really got mad about it."[46]

On one occasion at Groveton, mill-town people tricked the commissary, though this was less of a joke and more of a serious enterprise. Claude Kennedy's boys and other children of the town discovered an old wrecked skidder boiler in the brush near town where the company burned its worn-out merchandise checks. Much company money lay around on the ground, and the boys used it to purchase their hearts' desires at the commissary, soon setting up a wonderful camp in the woods, complete with dishes, cooking utensils, and all the food they could eat. As Fred Kennedy told: "We even bought a cast-iron cook stove. One of the big boys bought it, and was paying for it by the week to keep them from getting suspicious. He acted like it was for his mother."[47] The campers needed recreational equipment to accompany their cook stove, beds, and mattresses, so they purchased a baseball bat, ball, and gloves, and bought an augur and an ax to rig up a "flying jenny" on an old stump. "We'd go out there and spend the day playing and eating," Fred recalled. "Just boys, wasn't no girls there. I guess this went on for maybe a month before the company found out about it."[48]

Although commissaries, millponds, and boardinghouses remained informal focal points for sawmill towns' social activities, by 1910 most larger communities possessed a hall or community center—typically, a two-story frame structure that served as school by day, union church on Sunday, and recreational center and meeting hall by night. Normally, companies built these for their townsfolk, and it was a poor mill town where people had to cobble together a "hall" on their own.[49] Village Mills, Diboll, Deweyville, and many other places began with these two-story, multipurpose halls, but in time the schools and churches departed to their own buildings and the community halls grew ever more grand.[50]

By the early 1920s, community halls in the Kirby towns featured "dom-

ino parties," "ice cream socials," and even radios. At Christmas in 1922, the
company installed large radios, complete with batteries and headphones,
at Call and all other Kirby towns, and many people came around late at
night to experience these modern wonders. Now, for the first time, World
Series results could be learned on the day the games were played. Unfortunately for hard-laboring mill men, static plagued Call's radio until after
11 P.M., so interested persons had to hang around until nearly midnight.[51]

With the surrounding Kirby towns as his measure, R. W. Wier built a
fine community hall adjoining the movie house at Wiergate. "The life
center of the town," the hall had domino tables, checker tables, card tables, "a big fire and a man to keep it up," a children's room with child-
sized furniture, a ladies' room "furnished appropriately," and a lodge hall,
a large banquet hall, and a well-furnished kitchen upstairs, complete with
silverware embossed with "Wier 3L Company." As James Griner told,
"We'd have our school banquets there, they'd have something almost
every month."[52] In the lodge rooms upstairs, the Eastern Star, Odd Fellows, Masons, Woodmen of the World, Knights of Pythias, and various
ladies' clubs met regularly.[53]

Nearby, in "Africa," the Wiergate quarter, R. W. Wier's African American employees had their own community hall. Companies sometimes
provided blacks with formal social centers in the larger mill towns, but in
many cases the community centers grew up informally in association with
the black sub-commissaries, boardinghouses, or dance halls, often called
"barrel houses." At the big Southern Pine woods camp of Fastrill, black
social life centered around the boardinghouse, which had dance-hall
facilities (or at least a piano) on the premises. As Horace Warren remembered, this area was in use "all time, day and night." He recalled: "They
had to go there and tell the man to quit getting up and playing that piano
before daylight, before the folks would go to work. He would get everybody up, nearly. That place would be full of folks before daylight."[54]

In Diboll and many other places, private enterprise filled the enter-
tainment gap at the quarters. The Diboll quarters had "domino parlors"
and various "outdoor stands," which peaked in numbers during the
warmer seasons.[55] The "Foggy Bottom Cafe" served as a focus for social
life, and Mr. Lignon, the owner, often arranged for special events, such as
prize fights and visiting bands. Diboll had its own black band, led by
trumpet player "Professor" Jackson, which sometimes played at dances
and marched in the streets. A conductor on Southern Pine's Texas South-
Eastern Railroad, Jackson had spent his early life touring with a well-

known band of black boy musicians on the carnival and medicine-show circuit. Later, he played with the W. C. Handy Band and gave early trumpet lessons to Harry James. On one occasion, Jackson repeated that claim to Jake Durham and Durham called his bluff, telling him to wait right there, he was going to get Harry James on the telephone. James, however, confirmed his old mentor.[56]

Movie theaters—"picture shows"—had become common at major mill towns by 1920. Earlier, private tent shows had come through from time to time and shown movies, as at shabby Ewing, which remained without a proper theater until the end.[57] For Diboll and Wiergate, the company theater had been preceded by a primitive, open-air operation, which at Diboll people jokingly referred to as the "Air Dome."[58] A man named Chaney operated this open-air theater at Copestown on the outskirts of Diboll, and since the movie had only one projector the show was interrupted at the end of each reel. While Chaney changed the reel, a boy peddled parched peanuts and a brownish taffy candy called "Johnny Crook" to the crowd. Mr. Chaney was entirely toothless, and some boys would usually provide him with his favorite Thompson grapes just to watch him eat them. With fascinating proficiency, Chaney spat seeds out of one side of his mouth at the time that he inserted grapes in the other.[59]

Permanent theaters had replaced the open-air operations by the early 1920s—sometimes separate theaters for Anglos and blacks, but more often (because of the cost) segregated facilities in the same building.[60] Some people liked to go to "country dances" and "yank a plank off the wall," but Saturday nights were movie nights to most mill-town residents. For Manning males, the Saturday night movie ritual began with a trip to the barber shop before the movie for a shave, haircut, and shoe shine. Robert Poland explained: "Nearly everyone wanted a shampoo to get the sawdust out of his hair. You could even get a bath if you could afford it. Benches and chairs lined the wall inside, and spittoons were available for the snuff dippers and tobacco chewers."[61] After that, cleaned up and having had their first shave since last Saturday, the men filed into Manning's New Lyric Theater, named after the Lyric Theater in distant New York City. Poland concluded: "The silent movies were the thing, with Charlie Chaplin or Fred Thompson. Everyone would come early, before the show started, to hear Jimmie Gibbs play the piano. I will never forget how good she could make that piano sound."[62]

The first generation of sawmill-town moviegoers sometimes grew unruly from overexcitement, as in the case of the eccentric Dred Devereaux at Diboll. Devereaux, who often sat outside the commissary reading his newspaper upside down, as a challenge, also occasionally disrupted the Diboll picture show. Kenneth Nelson explained: "I've been to the picture show where he would be in there, and maybe a Tarzan picture would be on, and old Tarzan would get in a tight, and it would look like he would get hurt, and [Devereaux] would yell out, 'Watch out, Tarzan! Look out, they gonna get you!' He would disturb the whole picture show. He was one of those kind, he thought he was the only one in there."[63]

Courting youths in the mill towns often did some of the same things that they had done in childhood years to amuse themselves, and still mostly on foot: they walked to the train station to see who got off the train, walked the tracks to the next mill town or the river bridge, and even walked around the stacks of the lumber yard in the moonlight.[64] Young Wiergate teacher Grace Lee Amiott once stayed out unsuitably late with her husband-to-be, engineer Emmett Lee, while he showed off by walking logs on the millpond.[65] On a typical night out at Wiergate, Dave Martinez walked his date to the picture show, walked her a quarter of a mile to the ice house afterward for soda water or ice cream, then "you walk on home, that was a big night."[66] Even the rare Wiergate boys with access to automobiles had few places to drive them, since nearby Burkeville and Newton closed down as early as Wiergate on Saturday nights. Nor did they have much money for gas: by special agreement with the man at the company gas station, when young Wiergate males drove up with their date and said, "Fill her up," the pump man watched for finger signals given outside the car doors for the real orders, usually one or two gallons.[67]

Boys and girls had the same difficulties beginning courtship in sawmill communities as in other small towns, where everybody knew everybody else, and one's behavior remained always under scrutiny. After Grace Lee Amiott stayed out with earlier boyfriend Earnest White beyond Wiergate's ten o'clock lights-out, the boy's mother told everybody in town, and the teen-aged teacher nearly lost her job.[68] At the sawmill towns where Guy Croom grew up, socializing between the sexes began during early teen-age years, with "socials," "hayrides," "country parties," and nocturnal visits in season to nearby cane mills and watermelon patches.[69] Perhaps the earliest courting experience was the chaperoned walk home after church, the mother following behind the young couple with her lantern. One Diboll woman followed so closely that, it was claimed, "you could always tell the boys that had been out with her girls, because the seat of their pants was scorched."[70] Boys sometimes also asked and received permission to escort girls home after "socials"—party-game affairs at private homes, where boys and girls played "Ring Around the Rosey," "Drop the Handkerchief," "Go Forth and Meet Your Lover," "Post Office," "I Kneel Because I Love You," and other games.[71] A little later, youths participated in hay rides and organized trips to cane mills and watermelon patches. The countryside remained very close to the sawmill towns, and Willie Burch recalled that at Groveton young people often went out for "cane juice drinking parties." Mixed groups walked or rode to a nearby cane and syrup mill at night, after it had shut down for the day. Some pushed the pole around the juicing mill, while others fed stalks of cane into the mill and others caught it in a bucket. Burch explained, "They caught the juice in a syrup bucket, then they lined up and passed the bucket down the line, each one drinking as it came to him."[72]

At some point in the progression of their courting lives, mill-town youths began to attend real dances. Sometimes these were private affairs in homes cleared of furniture, with traditional Southern "fiddle music" dominating all.[73] Families constantly moved out of mill towns, so one or more company houses usually were empty and available for dance parties. Houses under construction, with only their floors in place, provided even better dancing facilities.[74] Sadie Estes Woods attended her first dance at a crude, open-air dance platform some boys had built a few miles out from Diboll at Ryan's Lake. Woods's attendance at these affairs ended soon after her mother learned that party-goers had both danced and swam, and some had danced in their swim suits.[75] Guy Croom took part in private "balls," where courting pairs and young married couples combined resources to rent country schools and hire outside bands. Such affairs often began at 9 P.M. on Saturday nights, since sawmill men often worked until 6 P.M., and "the problem of getting rid of the sweat from the day's work was not easy without a bathtub, and shaving a week's growth of beard in cold water was no simple matter, but necessary to put up the best front possible."[76] Croom recalled that the uneasy alliance between courting pairs and married couples often broke down during the ball, after the married people grew dissatisfied with the other group's immature behavior.

To varying degrees, companies facilitated their employees' desires to dance. At one extreme, Fastrill blacks in their boardinghouse had little more than a piano and a broomstick, but they made the most of them. Horace Warren remembered: "We didn't know nothing about no bands, then. Only band we knew anything about, a feller take a broom handle, rub it on the floor, sound like a beat. But they would jump for it, the cat's whiskers! Oh, they danced! And I thought I was a blues singer, I'd get up and try to sing."[77]

Southern Pine sometimes went much farther than this, however. The company occasionally held "Diboll dances" at some place in the countryside along the tracks of the Texas South-Eastern, and these affairs attracted people from both Diboll and Fastrill, as well as other woods camps. Workers swiftly erected a dance pavilion and band platform, and on the appointed Saturday flatcars loaded with people and beer rolled in and young Oscar Allen and the Allen family band played far into the night for the Southern Pine employees.[78]

However, nothing Southern Pine did along the T.S.E. tracks came close to matching the elaborate, permanent dance pavilion of the Trinity Lumber County at nearby Groveton. There, as Willie Burch recalled, a six-foot-wide pier reached to the center of the millpond: "joining a huge open dance pavilion. The structure was round, with built-in seats inside the perimeter. Steps led to the water on three sides. Boat clubs had anchored their row boats around the building and others were fastened to the pier."[79] Dances were held on the pavilion during the summers of 1925 and 1926, with big-city bands from Houston and Beaumont often coming up to play for them. Burch recalled that the structure had other recreational uses, as well.

> Practically each Sunday afternoon, a group of young people went kodaking and landed at the lake. The pavilion was opened at all times, so this was a fun place. Some of the boats were accessible, so the group would row the boats out into the lake, get them as close together as possible, let down the anchors, and sing for an hour or more. We sang old songs: "Sweet Adeline," "When You and I Were Young, Maggie," "Down By the Old Mill Stream," "Carry Me Back to Old Virginia," and many more.[80]

Sometimes other people arrived to dance for the amusement of the mill-town residents. "Traveling shows" and "tent shows" of every conceivable sort rolled into town on wagons or railroad cars, and one man recalled a group of "gander dancers," who performed a dancing act while balancing on each end of a board centered on a sawhorse.[81] Circuses, carnivals, patent-medicine shows, stage shows, magic acts, dog acts, musical groups, strong-man performances, revivalists, dancing (and fighting) bear acts, tent-show movie theaters, and variety acts of every description all came to the sawmill towns, and some even called on the remote timber camps. Edwin Nelson remembered that Doug Morgan's Tent Show sometimes came to Diboll to put on variety entertainments for two or three nights, and that Molly Bailey's Tent Show, which also played Diboll, was more specialized—a dog act featuring only white spitzes.[82] Dave Martinez recalled a lively medicine show that visited Wiergate with a man selling an all-purpose, pain-killing liquid medication. The master-of-ceremonies poured some of this on a piece of leather shaped like a shoe sole, harangued the crowd for a time, then showed them how it had penetrated the leather, noting triumphantly that, "If it will go through this pure leather, you know it will go through your skin!" After that, a helper worked the crowd, peddling bottles of the penetrating pain reliever.[83]

Among the traveling shows, the Chautauquas were in a class by themselves. Local persons and the companies partially sponsored these week-long tent shows, which featured a mixture of educational lectures and stage entertainments. At Diboll, teachers marched school children in to take their seats in a big tent. Lectures on health, history, and other subjects alternated with entertainments. Flava Vaughn told: "I remember one Chautauqua a woman would do the buck-and-wing and then would play the violin and the guitar, then we would have the lecture at the end. Then we would all stand up, file out, and march back to school."[84]

Mill-town people knew when the passenger trains arrived each day and often went down to see who got off, and with good reason. In truth, during this railroad era anyone or anything might show up at the depot, a fact which made people vulnerable to malicious rumors about circus trains. At the Badders Hotel in the Kirby town of Silsbee, May Badders Overland grew up helping her mother run the company hotel, and she became acquainted with a wide range of circus performers and other railroad-riding professionals. Circus people were amusing but untrustworthy, often departing with bills unpaid. Overland told: "Nine times out of ten, when they got ready to leave, they didn't have the money, so Mama would either hold their clothes or a diamond ring or whatever she could get." In this manner the Badders family acquired over time a monkey named Pete, a trick pony, and a parrot called Polly, but only the parrot lasted very long.[85]

Besides the circus people, traveling whores—"railroad ladies"—commonly got off the train and set up shop in the company hotel, but not if Mrs. Badders spotted them first. Actually, Mrs. Badders did not have to spot them, since: "Every time there was a crooked woman in the hotel, it was guaranteed that Mr. _____ and Mr. _____ would show up. When they did, Mother would say, 'Well, I got a whore in the house tonight. I'll have to check that out.' One evening one of the men showed up with a white starched linen suit on, and mother started chasing after him and ran him through the kitchen. He dove off out into the mud hole in the back where she threw the dishwater and where the pigs were."[86]

Whoremongering, gambling, drinking and other off-color male recreations peaked on Saturday nights, but, as superintendent W. A. Smith recalled, when a mill was running at greatest capacity, with eleven-hour day following eleven-hour day, sawmill adherents of the sporting life had limited energy for such things. Conversely, rainy days and off days were potential trouble times, from management's point of view. At Deweyville, Smith often tried to keep a personal eye on things, especially in the boardinghouses of the single men. Sometimes, they would stay up playing poker from Saturday morning until ten o'clock Sunday night, when the lights went out for the next working day. And when rain closed the woods and shut down the mill, sometimes the men just kept on gambling and drinking. Sabine Tram did not allow alcohol in its Deweyville boardinghouses, but, as Smith said, "You couldn't expect to keep a bunch of men up in their bunkhouses from drinking."[87] Another trouble time for the companies came at their rare cash paydays, since railroad-riding professionals preferred to deal in U.S. currency and detected an approaching payday even faster than the men. For this reason, a Call mill manager wrote Kirby Lumber Company's Houston office in 1903 to suggest a more secretive delivery of payroll money to avoid a rush on the office and so "we would not be infested with a lot of gamblers and prostitutes, as we are every pay-day when pay-master arrives."[88]

Whores and professional gamblers might have been an annoyance, but the recreational beverage alcohol caused companies the largest off-duty problem with their male work force. Historian Geoffrey Ferrell noted, "That timber and lumber workers drank great amounts of 'squirrel cider'—homemade whisky—was evidenced in the fact that both the lumber owners and the Brotherhood of Timber Workers developed programs to encourage and maintain sobriety. Lumbermen and YMCA representatives regularly condemned workers' 'drunken debauches.'"[89] Drunks and lumber work did not mix, but drunks on the job continued to trouble the companies—some of which contributed to their own problems by operating "company saloons" and giving bonus gifts of strong drink, at least in the early days.[90] The papers of the Gilmer Lumber Company contain various examples of the latter—bills sent from liquor dealers to Alexander Gilmer for "whisky for section hands," "drinks for switchmen," and "drinks, etc., for train crew."[91] The Southern Pine switchman who crashed the runaway flatcar through Ervelia Jordan's Diboll home and severed her daughter's arm had been drinking heavily all weekend, people said.[92] James Ellis, another switchman at another timber town, admitted that he often drank on the job, and that on one occasion, because of a terrible hangover, he had lost a finger while trying to couple two cars. Of drinking on the job, Ellis told: "Plenty of us did it. That's the way I learned it, from them old timers older than me. We'd have a time. Now, me and John Dunham, a fellow I used to hook [logs] with in the woods, we carried a pint with us to drink. If I didn't have it, he had it."[93] Federal investigations of 1914 and 1915 support Ellis's assertions, since researchers found repeated evidence of high whisky consumption in the sawmill towns.[94]

On several occasions during the year—Christmas, Juneteenth, the Fourth of July, and perhaps one or two other times, lumber companies gave their employees official holidays, with paid time off, picnics, gifts, dances, barbecues, bonuses, and baseball games. Local events were intended to keep sawmill people at home and in their towns, and to discourage wild drinking excursions on the railroads, a practice commonly termed "spreeing" by mill management—at least when African Americans did it.[95]

Every Texas sawmill town celebrated Christmas and Juneteenth, though only not all of them recognized the "Yankee holiday" of July Fourth. At Christmas, companies gave gifts and bonuses. Wiergate families received Christmas turkeys, free groceries, and packages of candy, fruits, and nuts that they picked up at the commissary. Jake Cole recalled: "That old man [R. W. Wier] would come around the sawmill and the planer mill about twice a year, and he'd shake hands with every hand that was working. Christmas time, he'd give you a turkey or $7 worth of groceries. I took groceries one year because I already had a turkey. I had to make two trips from the house down there to the commissary to carry that $7 of groceries to the house, that's how cheap everything was. Course, we were working cheap."[96] Every Wiergate child also got a sack of fruit, nuts, and candies, as James Lee remembered, "not to mention the turkey that every family got, including picking it out of the pen with a long wire hook."[97] A Houston newspaper observed of the tri-ethnic Wiergate Christmas: "In 'Dark Town' were heard the singing of the negro spirituals, in 'Mexico' the playing of the guitar and the familiar music of 'La Paloma' and 'La Golondrina,' and in 'White Town' was the familiar old Southern way of celebrating Christmas around a large decorated tree in the community hall."[98]

Company largesse at Christmas had become a competitive tradition, and although Southern Pine delivered gifts door-to-door in a freight wagon and Peavy Moore paid employees bonuses of $5 and $10 in gold coins, for once Kirby Lumber Company set the standard for generosity.[99] John Henry Kirby loved Christmas and celebrated it extravagantly. At Christmas of 1917, Kirby's bonuses and gifts totaled $12,000 for his Houston office and $31,000 for his timber towns.[100] In 1922, Kirby Lumber Company's costs for Christmas cards and free turkeys—2,600 of them, one for every family—totaled $25,000, a figure not including the costs of bonuses, fruit and nut packages, children's gifts, and the seventeen new $100 radios delivered to sawmill towns and timber camps. At every town and camp on this memorable Christmas morning of 1922, Kirby's estimated 10,000 town residents assembled around the company Christmas trees to receive gifts and hear an eleven o'clock address by John Henry Kirby himself over their communities' wonderful new radios.[101]

Juneteenth and July Fourth were summer affairs, celebrated in much the same way at every town, with picnics, dances, barbecues, and baseball games. While most companies recognized the Fourth, Peavy Moore Lumber Company at Deweyville did not. As a former resident told: "June 19th, or Juneteenth, was the greatest event of the year, with the mill shut down and barbecue made for all. In contrast, the mill operated full blast on July 4th."[102]

Both summer celebrations were recognized at Wiergate. Preparations began three days ahead of time with the excavation of barbecue pits, with Mr. Dudley, the "carpenter foreman," in charge. Pits were dug and hardwood burned down to coals over several hours, then men placed wire across the pits and slow barbecuing began. At the Wiergate hotel and all over town food preparation went on to supply the several picnics of this three-day, paid holiday. As James Griner recalled, "The company would buy bread and furnish the ice water; there were barrels all over there with big chunks of ice in them." Dances were held at night, picnics by day, and a big baseball game was played on the afternoon of the Fourth.[103]

Sometimes a company's Fourth of July celebration was intended only for its employees, sometimes the whole surrounding countryside was welcome. Carter Hart recalled that the sporting Rice brothers, owners of the Rice Brothers Lumber Company town of Hyatt, liked all-inclusive affairs, and that other millowners in the vicinity rose to their challenge with

Black employees preparing the barbecue for the Thompson Lumber
Company's Fourth of July celebration, 1908. *Courtesy of the
Texas Forestry Museum, Lufkin, Texas.*

grand, regional Fourth of July celebrations. Hart explained that, on one
July Fourth, Village Mills outdid the Rices by ditching and draining its
millpond for a great fish feast.

Village Mills was in the center of six or eight mills. There was a little rivalry
between every mill, friendly of course. Each of them tried to have some
amusement, what the country afforded. One year, Village Mills had a pond
out there, had lots of fish in it. They drained that pond and scooped up the
fish, killed them right then and cooked them. They ran the train out there to

this pond, it was on the tram logging road, and carried people out there. Of course women folks had bread and cakes and pies and things like that but the main thing was the fish.[104]

Blacks often participated in the Fourth of July events, and whites—to some extent, at least—took part in the similar celebrations of Juneteenth. Like the Fourth of July celebration, Diboll's Juneteenth went on for three days, with a barbecue, dance, and baseball game, and the commissary manager's daughter, Josephine Rutland, attended them all. "You could smell the barbecue all across the countryside for a day before it was ready," she recalled. There would always be a little fighting in and around the big baseball game, but nothing excessive. One evening, choirs would sing, and on another a dance was held, and "I would get Chester [Willis] and Josie to take me to the dance. Course, I was just little, but I would sit on the side and watch them."[105]

On both June 19 and July 4, festivities usually culminated in a big base-ball game with a traditional rival, in Diboll's case the nearby courthouse town of Lufkin. Baseball was serious business at the sawmill towns, and for these games companies pulled out all the stops. Tom Temple's son and namesake, T. L. L. Temple, Jr., was assistant manager at Diboll for a time after World War I, and, being an ardent sportsman and gambler, played on the company team. One year, as the big Fourth of July game with Lufkin approached, he took money from the company till, hired some semi-pro "ringers" at Houston to play for Diboll, bet on the game, and replaced the company money after Diboll won.[106]

Peavy Moore Lumber Company at Deweyville provided softball, tennis, and croquet courts adjacent to the Anglo company hotel, and black teacher Artie Brailsford introduced basketball to Wiergate and won the girl's basketball national championship in a tournament at Tuskegee, Alabama. However, despite the competition from other games, baseball remained the king of sports in the sawmill towns.[107]

Sawmill baseball began informally during the 1890s, with homemade bats and balls, no gloves, and pick-me-up teams, but it quickly turned serious. Sawmill-town teams soon played "for blood," with fights between rival fans a common sideline.[108] Although companies sometimes disapproved of the rowdiness and drinking that went on at baseball games (and Tom Temple closed down Diboll baseball for a generation because of it), most found that the national sport helped their employees to blow off steam, helped to forge increased work-force solidarity and morale, and

T. L. L. Temple, Jr., millowner's son, and Temple Weber in Southern Pine Lumber Company baseball uniforms, Diboll. Company
management and the community at large usually took great pride
in the local baseball squad, which often competed with teams
from other mill towns. *Courtesy of the Temple
Archives, Diboll, Texas.*

gave zealous owners a chance to play. After all, these were their teams.
For example, Jonas and William Rice of Rice Brothers Lumber Company
at Hyatt played regularly on the company team, and so did some of
the Thompson family on Thompson-Tucker's famous New Willard
"Trimmers." Most companies sponsored and outfitted black teams as well
as white, and black and white playing fields became standard in the mill
towns.[109] Wiergate for a while had three different teams, leagues, and

baseball fields for Anglos, blacks, and Mexicans, but Mexican players later joined the "whites" to bolster the performance of Wiergate's "All Stars." Like the Trimmers, the All Stars soon became good enough to play semi-pro teams outside the sawmill leagues.[110] Childhood baseball games sometimes were integrated, the black team of a mill town occasionally practiced against its white team, and individual black stars sometimes practiced with the whites, but no sawmill town ever integrated its official black and white baseball squads—however tempting it might have been to do so. Black teams sometimes included super-stars like Fred Nelson, who carried Diboll's baseballers to a national tournament at Wichita, Kansas.[111] Even crack teams like Diboll's sometimes met their match, however. On one occasion the touring Kansas City Monarchs, including Satchel Page, played Diboll. After Page walked the first two batters one inning, he contemptuously called in both infield and outfield, faced the next three Diboll players with nobody behind him, and struck them all out.[112]

Sawmill-town boys (and some girls) began developing their bat-and-ball skills very early in games of "One-Eyed Cat." In this game, the pitcher threw, the batter hit, the pitcher retrieved, and the batter tried to run to the pitcher's box and back to the plate before the pitcher threw the ball to the catcher.[113] As Franklin Taylor explained, an absence of store-bought bats and balls was no obstacle, since "we would save all the string we could get out of the store" and from every store package carried home wrapped with string. "We would take the string off and save it. We would take a sweetgum ball for the center and wrap the string around it. We made our bats. We would go out in the woods and get us a good piece of hickory about the size of a baseball bat, and we would peel the bark off it, and that is what we used for a bat."[114] Later, boys like young Joe Malanders played real baseball and improved their skills. Using a glove made by his mother from an old cotton sack, Malanders fielded and batted for hours every day in the summer at White City near San Augustine, playing with Anglos, blacks, and Mexicans. "I would be out there with them all day," he said. "Sometimes they would have to come out there and get me, we would build a fire around each base and play night baseball."[115]

Serious players like Malanders developed reputations that soon reached beyond their home mill towns, and, as Lamar Tinsley reported of Ewing, "a good player could get a job most any time."[116] Guy Croom played for one company team and knew how the baseball squad of the Cowdan Lumber Company at Pollock got its hard-hitting catcher,

Morris Moses. Pollock "needed a catcher so the team got Morris Moses to move from Keltys and work in the commissary and do catching for them on Sundays."[117] Nobody knew young Joe Malanders at Wiergate when he showed up looking for work, and the foreman at first told Joe he had nothing available, but then the conversation took a familiar turn. Having second thoughts, the man asked: "Tell me something, do you play ball?" "Yes." "Can you pitch?" "Yes." "Are you left-handed?" "Yes." "I tell you what you do, you go over and see Mr. Talbot, he will put you on." As Joe soon found out, baseball men at the sawmill sometimes did not have to work as hard as less-talented company employees, especially on the day before a big game, since they needed to be "rested up."[118]

Only at the very end of the cut-and-get-out era of Texas lumbering did other team sports begin to challenge the mill-town passion for baseball. Diboll added a six-man football team in 1938, and, led by coach "Door Knob" Allen, they played similar squads at Pineland, Hemphill, Shelbyville, and Indian Village.[119]

Football had first appeared at the sawmill towns some thirty years before, when a Village Mills school teacher got his hands on a strangely-shaped pigskin ball and encouraged his students to throw it around at recess. This soon caught the attention of woods superintendent R. G. Woods and mill superintendent F. F. Welker, and these natural rivals proposed a football game between Village Mill's woods crew and mill crew. Uncertain if football would prove a suitable sport for Anglo-Americans, Woods and Welker set up the first game between blacks, to try it out. Teams from the mill and lumber camps were selected and began to practice, after a fashion, as Carter Hart recalled, "at the slab pit where they burned the slab." Word went out about the trial football game, and on the appointed day "the mills closed down for twenty miles around, and that was just unheard of," and many people from Nona, Kountz, Olive, Trian, Plank, Warren, Village Mills, and other towns showed up.[120] Rules were imperfectly understood and minimally enforced. The sooty slab pit "field" had two goals and a center point, but no yard markers, as Hart described.

> One man run from each side and kicked that ball. It had to be kicked off the ground, and then after it was once kicked, why they did everything they could; take it away from each other, try to take it to each goal just like they do now, but they didn't have no ten-yard lines, nothing like that. They just had two posts down there, and they had to get that ball across that line between those posts. I don't think they had any rules. Woodward had a book of rules, but I don't think they even looked at it.[121]

Wiergate's black basketball team and managers. Only at the very end of bonanza-era lumbering did other team sports begin to compete with baseball. *Courtesy of the U.S. Post Office, Wiergate, Texas.*

Never quite managing to score, the black players wrestled back and forth with the ball in the slab pit for well over an hour, sweating profusely, tearing their shirts off, and covering themselves with dirt and charcoal. Play never stopped, and gradually players were injured or became exhausted and the teams declined to three and four on a side. Finally, a group of judges declared the game in favor of Welker's mill hands. Carter Hart explained, "They claimed the reason Welker's niggers won was they were smaller and more active and could get around them logging niggers. That was the first football game ever played in Hardin County."[122]

Apparently, it was a considerable time until the next one. After observing the battle in the slab pit, most sawmill men, Anglo- and African American alike, had decided that they much preferred the noble sport of baseball.

Chapter Six

CUT AND GET OUT

———

S OMETIME in 1928, geographer William Chambers visited the Saner-Ragley Lumber Company mill community of Carmona in Polk County, Texas, and found a pall of doom hanging over the town. As at many mill towns before Carmona, and despite all efforts to continue operations, "cut-out" loomed on the horizon. Chambers wrote, "When the original [10,000-acre] forest holding was cut over, the purchase of additional stumpage perpetuated the life of the industry. But the timber reserve is again nearing exhaustion, being estimated as sufficient only for eight month's continuous operation."[1]

Carmona presented a shabby prospect in 1928. For years past, Saner-Ragley had refused to spend any more money for maintenance than absolutely necessary to sustain an operation on its way out, and company employees had evidenced similar attitudes. The visiting geographer found the results of these years of neglect to be depressing. Chambers observed:

> Carmona is situated in an expanse of typical southeastern Texas cut-over and fire-swept forest land. The residential area is beside the mill. The rather small, old, unpainted wooden buildings have paper and galvanized iron roofs. They are arranged in rows along sandy streets which divide the land into rectangular blocks, and are overrun with grasses and weeds except where traffic keeps them bare. All buildings except the church and school are owned by the lumber company. None of them are painted, and their weather-beaten aspect is an expression of declining value and increasing neglect as timber reserves approach exhaustion. Employees move so frequently that they have small incentive to improve their rented homes by planting trees, cultivating shrubs, repairing fences, and developing the lawn. Deterioration is the inevitable result of temporary interest in the residences by both their owners and tenants.[2]

Carmona had lasted twenty years at the time of William Chambers's visit just before cut-out, a respectable life span for an average mill town created as a result of "temporary interest" by the company that built it, used it, and soon would disassemble or abandon it. Permanency never had been intended or even believed possible for Carmona and places like it; sawmill towns were temporary communities assembled by companies whose policy was "cut and get out." Lumbering, like coal mining, remained an "extractive industry," and when the local vein became exhausted a company moved somewhere else in Texas or—increasingly, as time went on—to the distant Northwest Coast. By 1910, William Carlisle's mill town of Onalaska in Polk County had cut out, sold out, and relocated, as had his two previous towns. Carlisle liked the name "Onalaska," since he founded successive sawmill towns called that in Wisconsin, Arkansas, Texas, and Washington state.[3]

Most companies saw no alternative to a policy of cut and get out. Since the Southern lumber boom had begun during the 1870s, companies had bought stumpage rights to blocks of timberland along the new railroads, built mills and tramway systems, and cut their virgin pine groves as fast and efficiently as they could. Buying land made no sense to most companies, since regeneration of pines on cut-over land seemed a dubious possibility, and in any case the next crop of marketable saw timber remained at least a third of a century away. And that would be three and a half decades of paying for land, paying taxes on land, paying for more careful logging to protect the seedlings, paying for thinning the hardwoods so the pines would not lose the competition for sunlight—money spent with no return and no assurance that the person setting the policy would ever live to see the trees turned into profit.[4] When the Southern Pine Association cosponsored the first "Cut-Over Conference of the South" in New Orleans in 1917 to discuss the problem of cut-over lands, the possibility of reforestation scarcely was considered, so unattractive and economically infeasible did it seem.[5]

Far better to keep operations clean and simple, most lumbermen believed—to buy stumpage, build temporary towns, cut out, and move on. Besides, the cheap lumber prices of competitors following these policies discouraged other companies' experiments with land ownership, "selective harvesting," and "silviculture," as did Southern traditions of the "open range," which allowed landowners only limited control of their own lands. Northern lumbermen had discovered to their consternation soon after relocating to East Texas that Southern customs gave anyone the

right to trespass, hunt, fish, and run stock on the lands of anyone else—
even when that second "anyone" was "Prince of the Pines" John Henry
Kirby or the huge Kansas City Coal and Coke Company. When pressed,
local courts often supported these informal usufruct rights, and fence-
builders and other violators of custom also suffered retaliatory attacks of
arson, another old Southern tradition.[6]

As a consequence, companies practiced cut-and-get-out lumbering,
but the result of this rational economic policy was an environmental disaster that only worsened as time went on. Writing to the U.S. Bureau of
Forestry in 1900, pioneer Texas forester W. Goodrich Jones complained,
"Like the buffaloes, the timber is going and going fast: what escapes the
big mill, is caught by the little mill, and what the little mill does not get,
the tie cutters and rail splitters soon have chopped down."[7] Furthermore,
Jones thought things were getting worse, and the cut-over lands were being left in worse condition than before the turn of the century. During
the first two decades of Texas lumbering, companies had "high graded"
only the tallest and best trees for cutting, usually those eighteen inches or
more in diameter, felled them, hauled them to the mill or railroad with ox
teams, and left behind many seed trees to produce another forest. By
1900, the time of Jones's essay, tramway logging had increased, the devas-
tating steam skidder had begun to replace oxen, and the whole woods operation had speeded up and become more ruthless and wasteful. Companies still high graded, but under this "new method" of lumbering:

> Everything that has diameter of from 10 to 12 inches above the ground is cut,
> and after the saw comes the tie cutter and railsplitter. Felling the trees had
> bruised and broken most of the smaller trees, and with fires twice a year, eat-
> ing and gnawing into the stumps and littered tops and withered leaves, and
> with the sawyer worm attacking all this sap-soured wealth, alack and alas 'tis a
> sad reckoning and accounting the present will have with the future. Hurri-
> canes could not bring greater destruction.[8]

Furthermore, with speeded-up operations came even greater waste of forest resources.

> The tree is cut from two-and-a-half to three feet above the ground. Above the
> stump, say four logs, each 16 feet long are sawed. From the lowest branches to
> the top, say thirty to forty feet, is rejected and left on the ground to rot and be
> destroyed by fires and worms. When these logs reach the mill another waste
> of from 10 to 15 percent takes place, as the outside bark and sapwood, or
> "scantlings," are burned by the hundreds of cords at each mill. We can safely

say that 40 percent of the tree is wasted—shingle mills could cover every house in Texas with the waste of extra fine wood left in the stump.[9]

As woods operations and sawmills modernized and speeded up, companies' investments in machinery increased, and it became even more imperative for them to cut every marketable pine tree as quickly as possible. The Fletcher steam log skidder, first tested at Village Mills in 1895, played a major role in these changes; it raised companies' investment and operating costs, made money by drastically speeding up operations, and left shattered cutovers behind that Goodrich likened to the "shell-torn areas of France" after the Great War.[10]

Interviewed by lumber-industry researcher Hamilton Pratt Easton during the 1930s, retired mill superintendent W. A. Smith agreed with Jones that operations had become more ruthless over time, and Smith

Cut-over acreage, with fellers still "bucking" logs for hauling to the logging tram with the steam skidder. Only the smallest trees are left, and most of these will not survive the skidding process. *Courtesy of the Texas Forestry Museum, Lufkin, Texas.*

blamed this on an increase in absentee ownership. After 1910 or so, the typical owner believed that what happened to his employees after cut-out was in no way his problem. Planning to cut and get out, companies tore the land up with skidders and paid little attention to reforestation. To escape taxes, they tried to cut the woods as fast as possible, whatever the consequences for employees and environment. Selective logging, abolition of skidders, reforestation, and other reforms held no interest for the new generation of owners, Smith opined. As an example, Smith told Easton that "it was even hard to secure the introduction of spark arresters on wood-burning machinery in the forests, because the cost, though slight, cut current profits slightly, regardless of future savings for the companies and an available timber supply for posterity."[11]

The devastation of modern steam-powered lumbering peaked in the longleaf zone, where the open woods presented a perfect environment for use of the steam skidder. After a timber crew had passed through a longleaf forest, little remained. Every tree above ten inches in diameter had been cut, and most smaller pines not taken for saw timber were either destroyed by logs pulled in by the skidder or scavenged for tramway ties or "corduroy" used in the process of lumbering. Pine knots gathered from the forest floor powered the engines of the forest's destruction.[12] Damage was permanent, since skidder logs gouged great trenches into the earth, loosening the sandy pine-barren soils, which eroded to choke the creeks at the next big rain.[13] In the end, all that was left of the virgin forests were "stump pastures" with a few crooked "mule-tail" pines left to swish in the wind.[14] Thinking primarily about the longleaf lands of the South, historian Thomas Clark joined Smith and Jones in a harsh judgment of the effects of companies' policies on employees and environment. "Sawmilling exerted its particular kind of hardening influence upon the men who labored in woods and mills," Clark wrote. "They came to reflect the harsh ends of an industry that seemed destined for oblivion and left more than 150 million acres of forest lands an economic shambles with a sea of stumps as grim monuments to the demise of a precious natural resource, and their shabby sawmill-camp shanty homes melted into the ground along with the sawdust and slab piles."[15]

To sawmill people (many of whom would have been offended by Clark's words), mill cut-out and the end of a community had become an old story, simply one of the realities of their way of life. Many families moved restlessly from mill town to mill town as a matter of course, so to them the end of one place meant little—only a new start somewhere else.

To others, who had chosen to stay on and put down roots in the "Old Carmonas" of East Texas, cut-out brought a great loss—a painful shattering of family and neighborly ties and the end of community.

By the time William Chambers visited Carmona, whole generations of previous mill towns had come and gone, and the pattern of their demise was long set. As at Carmona, woods crews went out to the front every day, and workers were well aware of the shrinking away of the pine forest before their onslaught; the end of the timber, economic life blood of their town, was there for all to see. As cut-out approached, rumors circulated about possible new timberland acquisitions to prolong the life of the town. The company rarely moved to squelch these (and perhaps even encouraged them) and often proved reluctant to announce a termination date, since it was in its economic best interest to keep workers on the job until the last tree was cut, sawed, and loaded on a boxcar. Hope often persisted until the very end. At Olive, as the timber dwindled away, workers organized a new lodge of the Improved Order of Redmen in 1907, the company chartered a special train and took the entire town to visit Galveston to see a huge beached sperm whale in 1910, and in 1912—three weeks before the secret date of Olive's final mill whistle—mill superintendent Charles A. Sternenberg got married in the union church.[16]

Then, suddenly, at Olive and other places, the company announced the shut down of the mill, and the death date of the town became official. Many people left immediately after the announcement, others stayed to attend the rituals of the end—the last log cut, the last log milled, and the last whistle of the mill. Some towns died from simple cut-out, others died after a major fire, when the company decided that its remaining timber reserves did not justify a rebuilding of the mill and town. One variety of town demise seemed about as common as the other among the inflammable mill towns of East Texas. Remlig, Alexander Gilmer's town in Sabine County, died of cut-out in 1924. At the end of the last day of the mill's operation, workers extinguished fires under the boilers, tied the mill whistle down in wide-open position, and the whistle sounded a "dying workcall" for 45 minutes.[17] Aldridge (1915), Browndell (1925), Manning (1936), and many others all suffered major fires and never reopened.[18]

Especially in the case of absentee-owned mill towns like Ratcliff and Haslam, companies' abandonment of their communities often proceeded at great speed, with houses and machinery swiftly whisked away to somewhere else, or sold to someone for salvaging on the spot. Ratcliff's Italian workers and their families disappeared on boxcars in two days for parts unknown, leaving hundreds of bewildered dogs, cats, and goats wandering the abandoned "Dago quarter." Any local person who wished to own a goat now came over to catch one.[19] The 4-C's huge Corliss steam engine and boilers sold to a sawmill in Slagle, Louisiana, and two 4-C locomotives departed for a new home at the Walker Lumber Company.[20] Although companies sometimes offered to sell their rent houses to the families who lived in them when the mill closed, more often they "scrapped out" their entire towns to the highest bidders.[21] At Ratcliff and a hundred other places, the company that had swept in from nowhere with a new town, sawmill, electricity, and employments now swept away to somewhere else, leaving local people almost as dazed as the Italians' goats. Electric light switches in the homes no longer worked, and people got out their coal oil lamps and lanterns. After a few weeks, or a few months, and the work of the salvage crews, sometimes not much was left to show that a community had been present. At Ewing in Angelina County, as historian Bob Bowman noted, "the town's only remains [were] a few concrete leftovers from the town's sawmill, some forgotten graves hidden in the forests, a few water cisterns that mark Ewing's homesites, and an old wooden residence," and a similar description might have been written for the remnants of hundreds of other East Texas lumber towns.[22]

For forty years, sawmill people always had many other towns to migrate to after their old communities ceased to exist, but by 1920 this was no longer true. Company operations rapidly exhausted East Texas timber reserves, and Wiergate, built in 1917, was the last major timber town established.[23] All across the South, sawmill towns had come and gone since 1880, with new ones starting up as old ones died, but by the 1920s deaths far outnumbered births. Writing in *American Forestry* in 1923, R. D. Forbes eloquently sounded the death knell for this way of life.

No wonder the hotel was empty, the bank closed, the stores out of business: for on the other side of the railroad, down by the wide pond that once held beautiful, fine-grained logs of long leaf pine, the big sawmill that for twenty years had been the pulsing heart of this town, was already sagging on its foundations, its boilers dead, its deck stripped of all removable machinery. A few ragged piles of greying lumber were huddled here and there along the dolly ways in the yards where for years lumber had been stacked by the million feet. The mill had "sawed out"—had cut its last log six months before. Within the town grass was beginning to grow in the middle of every street and broken window lights bespoke deserted houses. In county after county across the

South the pinewoods have passed away. Their villages are Nameless Towns, their monuments huge piles of saw dust, their epitaph: "The mill cut out."[24]

Geographer William Chambers and historian Flora Bowles observed at close hand the social and economic effects of the decline and fall of the lumber industry in Polk and Trinity counties. Thinking of Carmona and the much-larger mill town of Groveton, a few miles away, but speaking in general of conditions across the pineywoods South, Chambers wrote:

> The passing of a large saw mill town is a community and sectional tragedy. The company necessarily absorbs heavy losses of "fixed" capital invested in buildings, machinery, railroad, and other equipment that cannot be diverted to another use. Every family in the community is thrown out of economic adjustment. Wage earners and salaried men seek employment in other sawmills, and failing this they must enter other occupations. Local institutions such as the church and school decline rapidly. Usually the community does not secure another economic base and undergoes complete disintegration. As families move away houses become vacant. They may be purchased for as little as five dollars each by persons who wreck them to secure lumber. Failing this fate these old dwellings are abandoned to burn in some woods fire or to slowly tumble down with decay. Thus communities of five hundred or a thousand inhabitants disappear from the face of the earth—the homes, churches, schools, and stores perish, government is blighted by tremendous decrease in value of taxable property, and farmers in the district see the local market for produce wither away.[25]

University of Texas masters thesis researcher Flora Bowles came to Trinity County during the middle 1920s, as the local lumber industry entered its death throes, and she supported Chambers' analysis. After the big mills had moved in beginning around 1880, post-bellum agricultural recovery had ceased, since "the negroes who labored on the farms congregated at the mill centers and were employed by them." Many farm owners moved away in disgust after this loss of labor, and good farmland again grew up in pines. Thus, "the rural sections were retarded by the saw mill industry."[26] Now, during the late 1920s, the mills were cutting out "and leaving nothing to take their place." Only the fact that the mill closings had been extended over several year's time kept Trinity County from bankruptcy. The Josserand Brothers mill at Josserand closed in 1909, and a town of 900 vanished. In 1911, Thompson and Tucker Lumber Company closed down Willard (population 1,200), and in 1919, Saron (population 1,200) closed. With the closing of the West mill at Westville (population 1,000) in 1921, only the lumber operations of the Trinity County Lumber Company at Groveton and the Rock Creek Lumber Company at Trinity remained.[27]

The railroads had brought the companies into Trinity County, now they followed them away. On the main-line track, "instead of ten or twelve trains per day the number has been reduced to one train per day each way, and the traffic was so poor that even these did not meet the cost of operating."[28] The county had only seventeen miles of road that could be called highway, and this ran through the town of Trinity at the extreme south boundary of the county. The rest were mere trails and at times were impassable due to deep sand in the summer and mud in the winter.

As a result of the closing of the mills and the demise of railroad interests, property values had fallen drastically. In 1924, a Groveton man sold an entire block of land in the downtown area, with a good six-room house, two four-room houses, a fig orchard, and other improvements, for only $1000. Cut-out approached for the Trinity Lumber Company on the other side of the tracks, and all knew it. In Bowles's opinion: "The lumber companies have retarded developments, not through design, but as an ultimate and logical result of conditions. Of the 450,560 acres of land in the county, 376,000 are either owned or held under the lumber deeds of five lumber companies. This acreage had never been offered for sale, and as a result agricultural development has been greatly retarded."[29]

In truth, as at many other places across the pineywoods South where the lumber boom busted, the companies had "retarded developments"; Trinity County in 1928 was left with dead mill towns, dying railroads, undeveloped road systems, a decreasing population, an eroding tax base, and plummeting property values. A short time later, Trinity County Lumber Company folded and the railroad actually pulled up its tracks. The local effects of companies' cut-and-get-out policies could be enormous. Company physician Dr. George F. Middlebrook, who had witnessed the death of three major timber towns, aptly remarked, "There is no sound on earth so sad as a silent mill whistle."[30]

Many more mill whistles fell silent during the 1930s. Lumber prices had remained high and stable in the decade after World War I, and surviving mills prospered—if they had timber to cut—but disaster struck with the Great Depression. Prices for the best-quality pine lumber were $42 per thousand board feet during the late 1920s, while costs of production ranged from $23 to $24 per thousand board feet. In 1930, the sale price dropped to $24, in 1931 to $18, and in 1932 to $14.65, while production costs remained the same. If companies operated from 1931 to 1940, most of them operated at a loss.[31]

Some companies shut down very quickly after the great economic downturn; others, with more timber left to cut or more concern for their employees, reduced schedules to two or three days a week and kept running. At Diboll, Wiergate, Ewing, several of the Kirby towns, and elsewhere, companies reduced wages to a base-pay rock bottom of just over $1.00 a day and tried to give every family man at least a day's work each week. Companies also reduced or abolished rents on workers' houses, maintained medical care, offered commissary credit, and took other steps to try to keep mill families from abandoning their towns. Genuine concern for employees' welfare motivated the companies, but there were practical considerations, as well. As Wesley Ashworth of Diboll noted, Southern Pine planned on resuming operations after the Depression and did not wish to lose its skilled work force. He explained: "It was rough back in those days, it certainly was, but the company was really good to employees. They wanted them to stay, because they knew what sawmill hands were back in those days, and those they had were already trained. They knew what it cost to train a new hand, and the company did all it could to hold their people together."[32]

John Henry Kirby felt the same, but his massive operations and many mill towns were more vulnerable than most, and as usual he had been operating close to the economic edge in 1929. By December of 1930, four of Kirby's twelve mills had been closed and the others operated on greatly reduced schedules, and further cutbacks and shutdowns followed.[33] John Henry Kirby's report to Kirby Lumber Company's board of directors in January 1931 made clear just how desperate everything was: "We operated no mills in January 1931, and our Hardwood mills are down for an indefinite period. We made a reduction in the salaries of all monthly employees, from the president to the shipping clerk, of from five to fifteen percent, and reduced the supervisory forces 33 1/3 percent. Corresponding reductions have been made in all classifications, so that our common labor is paid as low as 17 cents an hour."[34]

By 1932, matters had worsened, and John Henry Kirby told an underling, "Not a man should be engaged until the necessity for his service has become imperative and his remuneration should be fixed at the lowest minimum consistent with his sustenance."[35] Workers rehired or kept on were grateful for whatever they could get. A Kirby official reported, "Our employees at all the points visited seemed to be thoroughly happy even with the low wages we are paying them, and I am sure they are going to do their best to render us efficient service."[36]

Kirby's mill town of Call shut down early and operated only sporadically during the 1930s, and remaining residents became truly desperate. As Mollie Eddlemon recalled, after the mill closed about a third of the population went to live with relatives in the countryside, a third went to larger towns looking for work, and a third stayed in Call, fishing the millponds, gigging frogs, hunting squirrels and rabbits, poaching deer, and scavenging the abandoned gardens of those who had left. "Butterbeans were good until the first killing frost," Eddlemon told, "God's blessings were seen in these good crops."[37] Call residents helped each other in this time of need, since "a spirit of total love pervaded the whole town of Call."[38] A black resident, who was lucky enough to have a job working for a local cattle raiser and butcher, distributed discarded organ meats to Call's black community, and another man who worked for a truck farmer distributed produce. As the *Jasper Newsboy* noted on January 29, 1931, outsiders also helped, since the Raymondville Chamber of Commerce sent "four hundred bushels of turnips" to aid the Red Cross in their relief of the "famine struck families" of Call, and Beaumont bakeries contributed two hundred loaves of bread a day. However, mill doctor Virgil Beavers helped Call's residents the most. Beavers's family owned a rice farm in China, Texas, and "he had some rice delivered to Call for all families, white or black, to share in his bounty." Beavers's son Howard: "wore hip boots when he went frog gigging. He filled his boots with frogs before leaving the pond. This made a good meal for several families."[39] After word of this personal philanthropy reached the pages of the *Beaumont Journal* (Beavers's daughter was night editor), Kirby Lumber Company officials became furious at the bad publicity, and "soon, Dr. Beavers resigned and retired to his rice farm."[40]

As the Depression wore on, Kirby Lumber Company went bankrupt and passed under the control of the Atchison, Topeka and Santa Fe Railway, and at Diboll the desperate Temple family struggled to avoid a similar fate.[41] On the eve of the great stock-market crash, Tom Temple's Southern Pine Lumber Company had taken on a $2 million debt to pay for new land and machinery; now, that debt hung over the company like a fiscal Sword of Damocles. Lumber operations at Southern Pine were in the red by 1931, but, like a few other mills, Diboll reduced schedules, cut salaries, and kept on running, trying to offer its employees enough support to ensure their survival and keep them around.

Finally, the elderly T. L. L. Temple could deal with this no longer and gave over control of the company to his son Arthur Temple, Sr. Tom Temple died in 1935, a few months before Southern Pine desperately sold off around 81,000 acres of its timberland to the U.S. Forest Service at the rock-bottom price of $2.75 an acre. To Temple, who believed in buying land and never selling it, these negotiations with the government must have been too horrible to bear.

"We had a terrible time, and the people that worked for us had a terrible time, during the Depression," Arthur Temple, Jr., recounted. During shared nights on the sleeping porch of the family home at Texarkana, "Dad [Arthur Temple, Sr.] never slept. For two or three years he almost didn't sleep at all because he was worried sick about the debt that had been created in the expansion. Dad's entire role was to pay off that debt."[42] At one point, Southern Pine's bankers held a key meeting to determine if they would seize control of the company for missing payments on the $2 million, and the matter hung on a fine edge until one bank official sarcastically asked the others, "Do any of you know how to run a sawmill?" Obviously, none of them did, and by that narrow margin Southern Pine survived the Depression.[43]

As at Wiergate, Keltys, and a few other towns, Southern Pine at Diboll and Pineland stopped collecting rents, extended credit in the commissaries, and tried to give as many people as possible a little work. Diboll people fell back on their gardens and livestock to survive. Beatrice Burkhalter recalled: "Everybody had a garden and a cow, and we had community gardens. The ones who didn't have a [private] place, they had a community garden. That was the way they made a living, and they'd swap out different vegetables. I had a cow, chickens, and a big garden."[44] Nevertheless, E. C. Durham, manager of the company railroad, wrote from Diboll on October 31, 1931: "How some of these men can pay rent, hospital, etc., feed and clothe their families on what they earn is a mystery difficult for me to solve. The fact is, in many cases they are not doing it. The number of under-nourished children to be seen at the schools is almost unbelievable, and the teachers report that some of their lunches are so meager as to make one doubt they are living in a land of plenty."[45]

For every person still semi-employed by Southern Pine, the commissary joined the community garden as a lifeline of survival. The store gave credit, though its own creditors threatened; Arthur Temple, Jr., later found begging letters from his father to Bewley's Flour Mills, asking for one more carload of flour to feed the people after that company had cut off Southern Pine's credit.[46] Determined to keep employees' commissary purchases to essential items, the company developed a system in which customers wrote down what they needed on white slips of paper and these circulated to the timekeeper for approval before orders were filled. Unfortunately for the many snuff dippers and tobacco chewers in Southern Pine's ranks, these items were scratched off the "white horses."[47] Money paid to employees moved in a swift circuit from their pockets to the commissary and back to company pay offices. Commissary clerk Lefty Vaughn recalled: "Everybody made a living and that's about it. If it hadn't been for the store, though, the company would have had a hard time paying off. The people would come and buy from us, and then that money went right back into the office, see, and that kept the mill running."[48]

Not all former Southern Pine employees could be given work, and many of these hung on to their gardens and rent-free houses and tried to find other ways to make a little money. The backwoods along Highway 1818 and the Neches bottoms soon filled with apprentice moonshiners. Rox P. Mann picked cotton at 35 cents a hundredweight and swiftly learned from his father-in-law how to make chairs, hoe handles, and ax handles.[49] Frankie Glass and her husband raised skimpy cotton on bad land and did "custom canning" for their neighbors, sometimes taking their pay in canned produce or flour sacks.[50] Young Claude Welch, born in 1913 and an orphan, joined other desperate youths in a hunting-and-gathering life along the Neches River. He explained: "We built us a little old house on the river at a place called the McCarty campground. We stayed in and out of that house for about three years and fished. We killed hogs regardless of whose they were, because we were going to eat. And we come out at Burke. Burke was a pretty nice little place, there were two or three stores where we'd swap them fish for meal or syrup—anything to get something to eat, because it was rough."[51]

Employees—and certainly the company—fared better at Wiergate, where Wier Lumber Company marketed a product that bridge contractors, builders of oil field rigs, and foreign construction companies still wanted, even in the depths of the Great Depression—structural timbers of longleaf pine. Wier still cut virgin longleaf in the remnants of the 86,000-acre tract acquired from Lutcher-Moore Lumber Company in 1917, and by the 1930s that timber had become a rare commodity. Consequently, although the company cut back operations drastically during the 1930s and profits shrank, it continued to make money for its stockholders.[52] Nor were R. W. Wier's employees entirely unaware of this. Jake Cole told, "That old man never did lose a dollar, he made money even though he didn't run but three days a week."[53]

During most of the Depression, Wiergate operated three days a week, and the company tried to give every man at least one day of work. Harry Eaves told: "They had a man who saw who had the most children, and that man got the most money. They just tried to keep the people alive."[54] James Griner added: "They tried to give everybody one work day a week work so they'd have a little money. People raised most of what they ate. They had ragged and patched clothes, but everybody else did too; so, it didn't make any different. I remember the old saying during the Depression. Bob Wier was one of the owners of the mill then, and there was the old saying, 'In God we trust and Bob we must.' Bob and Tom took care of everybody."[55]

Gradually, economic conditions improved, and Wiergate, Diboll, Keltys, Ewing, and a few other surviving Texas timber towns moved out of the killing ground of the Great Depression. Wier Lumber Company resumed full operations, but every day its remaining timberlands diminished, and cut-out moved ever closer. The great Southern longleaf forest, once covering 230,000 square miles, had declined to a few tens of thousands of acres, and those were disappearing fast. State Senator W. Goodrich Jones, president emeritus of the Texas Forestry Association, had led a campaign back in 1931 to establish a state park in the virgin longleaf. Jones told a *Jasper Newsboy* reporter on January 29, 1931, "What acreage there is left in Texas of the virgin longleaf pine is located in Jasper and Newton counties and is owned by a few individuals and companies." These "individuals and companies," principally R. W. Wier and John Henry Kirby, turned a deaf ear to the conservationist's pleas. Struggling for survival during the Great Depression, the companies valued their remaining acres of longleaf beyond all others.[56]

During 1940, University of Texas doctoral student Hamilton Pratt Easton visited Wiergate to study the operations of the state's last bonanza-era company, still doing things the old way in the virgin longleaf. With full company cooperation, Easton hung around mill and woods operations for several weeks, observing, asking questions, and interviewing mill foremen and officials. Easton found Wiergate a pleasant town, though a little rustic. He wrote:

In 1940, the houses in Wiergate have telephones, pianos, electric lights, drapes and curtains, and radios. The homes are now equipped with running water. Because there is no gas heat, some have large central wood stoves. Around the houses are grass-covered yards, gardens, trees, and shrubs. Pigs, cattle, dogs, cats, and chickens roam the streets at will. Wiergate streets are unpaved except for the county road. Possibly fifty percent of the townspeople own cows. The night milking is usually done by the wives because the husbands are too tired after a day's work.[57]

For several days, Easton rode the logging train out to the front to observe steam-skidder logging operations identical to those seen twenty years before by journalist Max Bentley. Like Bentley, Easton was awed by the power and the violence of the machinery, and the great logs crashing and gouging their way through the forest at the end of the skidder cables. By 1940, nobody Easton talked to was happy about the company's use of the destructive steam skidders, and they filled the young researcher's field notes with seditious comments—the sort of things mill men were willing to say just before cut-out.

Dr. F. E. McAlister, Wiergate company doctor, stated emphatically that in his opinion companies "should not have put a skidder in the woods but should have used teams entirely. If the company hadn't used skidders, the job would have lasted twice as long, because jerking trees with drums, when they are logs five to six feet in diameter and forty feet long, knocks out the small trees. Loaders are all right, but skidders jerk the small standing trees all to pieces!"[58] Skidder foreman J. J. Griffin told Easton that he hated to use the device, but if he did not use it "someone else would." Griffin thought that every time the skidder brought a log in, two or three young trees were ruined, and the skidder operation left a tangled mess behind to become a serious fire hazard. "Skidder operations here will kill more young trees than the government can grow in that length of time," the skidder foreman believed. Nor was that all he had to say about the steam skidder, which to Griffin and Dr. McAlister exemplified the cut-and-get-out company's exploitive attitudes toward land and employees. Easton summed up: "In the opinion of Mr. Griffin and many others, only a few men really profited from the lumber resources of East Texas. Labor in general received small wages, while the people of the state let their patrimony in timber resources fall into the hands of the large companies to be exploited without regard for the future welfare of the state. This disproportionate distribution of wealth was accentuated by the use of the steam skidder."[59]

Professional foresters had condemned the use of steam skidders for a third of a century, but here, at the Wiergate front, Easton saw the last longleaf still being logged in the same old way. Other companies had taken a conservationist stance and abolished their skidders, but they no longer had any longleaf to use them on! Easton observed: "It would appear that the main reason for the disappearance of skidders in Texas logging is depletion of large timber stands, in which skidders could formerly be used to advantage. As the forests have been thinned out or removed, or selective logging has replaced wholesale destruction of a timber stand, it has become economically unexpedient to operate skidders, as well as tramways and logging camps."[60]

By 1940, Easton, Griffin, and McAlister all knew that forests did not have to be logged by steam skidders and that mill towns did not have to die. Selective cutting and careful regeneration of pine trees in cut-over land allowed not only "perpetual forests," as Southern Pine asserted, but permanent towns. Wiergate, and many of the other "nameless towns" before it, might have persisted as living communities. Seventy miles west of Wiergate in 1940 was the Carter Lumber Company town of Camden, where the company used a "perpetual system" to cut timber in a circuit around the mill to "keep timber growing and cut lumber indefinitely."[61] A hundred miles to the northwest lay Diboll, where the farsighted Tom Temple had placed a company credo in *American Lumberman* in 1908 that was fully a third of a century before its time: "This operation asserts that all yellow pine lands are susceptible of a second cutting, with high-class commercial results a possibility, after a lapse of 12 to 15 years after the first cutting." Fifteen years after cutting, "any acre of land cut by this concern will produce 3,000 to 5,000 feet of merchantable pine timber. Unripened yet marketable trees" were to be left for a third cutting.[62]

In 1940, Southern Pine Lumber Company owned many thousands of acres of pine timberland in various stages of regrowth, but Wier Lumber Company, which had purchased stumpage rights in the old bonanza way (agreeing to cut every tree of ten-inch diameter or larger), owned only the 640 acres immediately around its mill.[63] By 1941, the Wier front had moved inward toward the town until only those woods were left, and now—rapidly—they also began to fall. Sounds of the crashing trees could be faintly heard in Wiergate when the wind direction was right, like the noises of a battle front moving ever closer.

These were the woods in which Martha Lee and other Wiergate children had wandered and played for a quarter of a century, but one day mill

Wiergate's two-line, self-propelling steam skidder at work in the longleaf.
Courtesy of Doyle Smith.

superintendent Emmett Lee finally told his daughter the bad news she had been expecting. "I was in the eighth grade. Daddy told us that they announced that they were going to cease operation on a certain day, that's when I started counting down. I don't believe if he had stabbed me with a knife it would have hurt any worse. I counted down, I cried, it didn't do a bit of good. But, oh, I didn't want it to leave, because I knew it was the end of a way of life."[64]

On November 19, 1942, the *Newton Herald* sounded Wiergate's official death knell. Company officials held a brief ceremony at the cutting of the last longleaf pine, a tall tree that superintendent Emmett Lee had kept standing just behind the commissary. A team of African American flatheads selected from the woods crew whipped a big Simon saw through the thick trunk in three minutes, and the last tree fell. This ended employment for woods crew, bridge crew, skidder men, and loaders, though the planing mill and sawmill operated for a short time until all remaining logs were milled. Gloomily, the *Herald*'s editor observed: "The once busy

Tramway spur laid into the last stand of virgin longleaf pine at Wiergate.
Courtesy of Doyle Smith.

Area view after cutting of the last stand of virgin longleaf pine at Wiergate, 1942.
Courtesy of Doyle Smith.

town, which with hundreds of men, making a good living and support for their families, has been slowing down for some time. Now it is very slow, only a few men go to work, and soon a pall will settle over the town as the 'Wiergate Mill' will be no more." Nor was this just a tragedy for the people of Wiergate, as the editor well knew. "Newton County will miss the Wiergate Mill. The residents were a help to the County in every way; their payroll forming the larger part of the county's money in active circulation. The taxes paid on the Mill, and the personal property as well as the many acres of timber lands reduced in value, will be keenly felt by the County."

Quietly, one by one, the families of Wiergate began to depart the dying town for new jobs on the Gulf Coast. A lucky mill town, residents thought, Wiergate had escaped killer fires for a quarter of a century and had supported its people through the Great Depression while citizens of nearby Kirby towns scavenged for butterbeans and bullfrogs. Even in death Wiergate proved lucky; by late 1942, war-industry plants on the

Press-shop manager and his family, Wiergate.
Courtesy of the U.S. Post Office, Wiergate, Texas.

Last tree cut at Wiergate, November 1942. Mill superintendent
Emmett Lee saved one big pine near the edge of town for
cutting in the "last tree" ceremony when the mill ceased
operations. *Courtesy of the U.S. Post Office, Wiergate, Texas.*

coast hired workers by the tens of thousands at better wages than the
Wier brothers ever paid. Consequently, a lot of former Wiergate employees and machinery rolled south: a new rubber plant at Port Neches hired
ten thousand defense workers at ten dollars a day, base wage; Wiergate's
mill whistle soon sounded at the Neches Butane Products Company in
Port Neches; and a Wiergate locomotive engineer, who had hauled the
last load of logs from woods to millpond, followed his old engine to the
Lummus Company, the prime contractor for the new rubber complex,
where he resumed the engine's operation.[65]

Martha and Emmett Lee pose for the camera next to Wiergate's last fallen pine,
November 1942. *Courtesy of the U.S. Post Office, Wiergate, Texas.*

Despite the new jobs, many grieved the loss of community, as had generations of sawmill people before them at the death of so many other
towns. Present at the end, Jake Cole remembered:

> Old man Emmett Lee was superintendent, and there was one big tree close to
> town. When they cut the timber, they cut it back toward town. He saved that
> one tree so it would be the last tree they cut. Those old colored boys, the flat-
> heads, with a cross-cut saw, cut that tree down, the last tree that was cut. People
> went out there to have a gathering out there to see it cut. You know, when
> Wiergate cut out, there were a lot of people that wept, a lot of women just
> cried. They knew that was all of it. They had to go to other places to find jobs.
> Of course, as luck would have it, that was right during the war and everyone
> went down to the coast and got jobs, better jobs. But it wasn't like Wiergate.[66]

From the beginning to the end, druggist Earl Hines had observed the
life of Wiergate from the town epicenter, the commissary, and forty years
after Wiergate died Hines recorded his memories on tape in a self-interview for a Newton County history project. "In the drugstore I could look
out the window and see the workmen going and coming to work, the
woods crew and so on, the mill crew," Hines remembered, and at this point

his voice strangely changed, and he began to call the names for the tape recorder—names of sawyers, saw filers, commissary store clerks, mill managers, log scalers, doctors, depot men, supply-house men, teachers, mill foremen, millwrights, timber men, blacksmiths, logging superintendents, roller men, skidder men, corral men, store managers, postmasters, planer men, butchers, dry-goods clerks, grocery men, bookkeepers, secretaries, cashiers, train engineers, and on and on—a Wiergate citizenry of the dead Hines since has joined.[67]

Wiergate closed officially on December 31, 1942, and on that day Hines stood his last duty at the commissary. He recalled: "On that night I could not force myself to hurry out as usual. With my wife waiting for me in the car outside to drive me home, I kept walking up and down the aisle between the counters—back and forth—for twenty-five years of routine is not easily changed, and I knew I would not be coming back. My familiar daily path had vanished. Most of my fellow workers had already gone."[68] While his wife waited, Earl Hines paced the aisle for a time longer in the silence of the Wiergate commissary, then he turned out the light, locked the door, and drove away.

Notes

Chapter One. Introduction

1. Odom, *Over On Cochino*, 13.
2. Gerland, "The Largest Sawmill in the World," n.p.
3. Bowman, *The 35 Best Ghost Towns in East Texas*, 121.
4. H. S. Filson letter, Gilmer Papers, File 2n14.
5. Roach, *The Hills of Cherokee*, 131.
6. Maxwell and Baker, *Sawdust Empire*, 160.
7. Quoted in Allen, *East Texas Lumber Workers*, 26.
8. Maxwell and Baker, *Sawdust Empire*, 116.
9. Vivian Warner interview, April 25, 1985.
10. Maxwell and Baker, *Sawdust Empire*, 71.
11. Ibid., 124.
12. Kirby Papers, Houston Municipal Research Center, RG D-34, Box 48, File L.
13. Loughmiller and Loughmiller, *Big Thicket Legacy*, 25.
14. Maxwell and Baker, *Sawdust Empire*, 3–5; Clark, *The Greening of the South*, 3.
15. Walter Cole interview, July 9, 1992.
16. Truett and Lay, *Land of Bears and Honey*, 11.
17. Jordan, *The American Backwoods Frontier*; Sitton, *Backwoodsmen.*
18. Owens, "*Big Thicket Balladry*," 203.
19. Block, *East Texas Mill Towns and Ghost Towns*, 2: 16.
20. Jordan, *Trails to Texas*, 1–58, 103–124.
21. Sitton, *Backwoodsmen*, 194–203.

22. Wright, *My Rambles,* 10.

23. Hahn, "Hunting, Fishing, and Foraging," 37–64; Sitton, *Backwoodsmen,* 233–273.

24. Clark, *The Greening of the South,* 11–12.

25. Sitton, *Backwoodsmen,* 66–68.

26. J. Louis Bingham interview, May 28, 1992.

27. Easton, "The History of the Texas Lumber Industry," 47.

28. Zuber, *My Eighty Years in Texas,* 26.

29. Schaadt, *Hardin County History.* 56.

30. Block, *East Texas Mill Towns and Ghost Towns,* 2: 12–13.

31. Maxwell and Baker, *Sawdust Empire,* 17–33.

32. Clark, *The Greening of the South,* 15.

33. Williams, *Americans and Their Forests,* 241–243.

34. Maxwell and Baker, *Sawdust Empire,* 34–50.

35. Block, *East Texas Mill Towns and Ghost Towns,* 2: 17.

36. Maxwell and Baker, *Sawdust Empire,* 39.

37. Bentley, "The Dirge of the Lonesome Pine," n.p.

38. Maxwell, *Whistle in the Piney Woods.*

39. Poland, "Manning in General," 22.

40. Poland, "The People of Manning," 27.

41. Croom, *When the Pines Stood Tall,* 79.

42. Riggs, *Crosscut* (First Quarter, 1995): n.p.

43. Charlie Havard interview, April 12, 1986.

44. Sitton, *Backwoodsmen* 116; Walker, *The Southern Forest,* 105.

45. Charlie Havard interview, April 12, 1986.

46. Flournoy, "History of Manning," 3–4.

47. Allen, *The East Texas Timber Worker,* 91–96.

48. Bowles, "The History of Trinity County," 72.

49. Croom, *When the Pines Stood Tall,* 16.

50. Fred Kennedy, quoted in Holland, *Mr. Claude,* 49.

51. Eddlemon, "The Depression at Call, Texas," 224.

52. Roach, *The Hills of Cherokee,* 131.

53. Flournoy, "History of Manning," 6.

54. Oscar Allen interview, March 15, 1986.

55. Maxwell and Baker, *Sawdust Empire,* 166.

56. *American Lumberman, "The House of Thompson."*

57. Maxwell, "The Pines of Texas," 79.

58. Buber, *Pullman,* 37.

59. Foley, "The New South in the Southwest," 244.

60. Biesele, *The Cornbread Whistle,* 59.

61. Frank Ashby interview, March 19, 1992.

62. Cravens, "Kilraven," 162–166.

63. Ibid.

64. Block, *East Texas Mill Towns and Ghost Towns,* 1: 215–218.

65. Montgomery, "Before and After the Birth of Wiergate, Texas," 331.

66. Earl Hines self-interview, 1982.

67. Quoted in Bowman, *The 35 Best Ghost Towns of East Texas,* 43.

68. Ibid.

69. Jake Cole interview, July 9, 1992.

70. Bentley, "The Dirge of the Lonesome Pine," n.p.

71. Jake Cole interview, July 9, 1992.

72. Bentley, "The Dirge of the Lonesome Pine," n.p.; similar accounts are found in Charlie Havard interview, March 14, 1986; R. J. Rawls interview, April 27, 1986; Boon, "The History of Angelina County, Texas," 120.

73. Charlie Havard interview, March 14, 1986.

74. Bentley, "The Dirge of the Lonesome Pine," n.p.

75. Ibid.

76. Ibid.

77. Ibid.

78. Ibid.

79. Horace Warren interview, January 3, 1986.

80. Quoted in Williams, *Americans and Their Forests,* 252.

81. Roy Smith interview, January 18, 1986.

82. Walter Cole interview, July 9, 1992.

Chapter Two. Panoramas

1. Croom, *When the Pines Stood Tall,* 27; Bowles, "The History of Trinity County, Texas," 107.

2. Bowman, *The 35 Best Ghost Towns in East Texas,* 29–30.

3. Bentley, "The Dirge of the Lonesome Pine," n.p.

4. Quoted in Block, *East Texas Mill Towns and Ghost Towns,* 2: 74.

5. Poland, "Points of Interest in Manning," 29.

6. Hines, "Those Were the Days," 232.

7. Quoted in Inez Thompson Asher interview, July 1984.

8. Icie Waltman interview, March 25, 1986.

9. Pearl Havard interview, August 8, 1985.

10. Croom, *When the Pines Stood Tall*, 11.

11. Rhoda Faye Chandler interview, September 7, 1982.

12. Wayne Overstreet in Block, *East Texas Mill Towns and Ghost Towns*, 2: 75.

13. Wanda Gipson DuBose interview, July 30, 1994.

14. Holland, *Mr. Claude*, 32.

15. Mrs. Sidney Walters Kindley interview, 1984.

16. Boon, "The History of Angelina County, Texas," 103.

17. Holland, *Mr. Claude*, 65.

18. Raimer, "Smallpox, Typhoid Took Early Toll in Silsbee," *Silsbee Bee*, October 9, 1969.

19. Bowman, *The 35 Best Ghost Towns in East Texas*, 24.

20. C. P. Myer to B. F. Bonner, October 23, 1915, Kirby Papers, Nacogdoches, Box 243.

21. Croom, "Reminiscences," *Lufkin Roundup*, April 1973, 18.

22. Ibid.

23. Bowles, "A History of Trinity County, Texas," 103.

24. Haynes, *The History of Polk County*, 147.

25. Frank Ashby interview, March 16, 1992.

26. Myrtle Rushing interview, March 15, 1986; see also Johnson, "Electrification of East Texas Sawmill Towns before World War I."

27. Haynes, *The History of Polk County*, 147.

28. Edwin Nelson manuscript, n.p.; Harold Turner interview, September 9, 1992.

29. Bowman, *Land of the Little Angel*, 156.

30. Ibid.

31. Boon, "A History of Angelina County, Texas," 116.

32. Chambers, "Life in a Southern Sawmill Community," 182.

33. Bowman, *Land of the Little Angel*, 163.

34. Anon., "Deweyville," 360.

35. Kilgore, "The Business District," 11–12.

36. Edwin Nelson manuscript, n.p.

37. Bowman, *Land of the Little Angel*; Pride, "The Origin of Manning," 4.

38. Tinsley, "The Boardinghouse," 22.

39. Kirby Papers, Nacogdoches, Box 273.

40. Ervelia Jordan interview, December 10, 1985.

41. Horace Warren interview, January 3, 1986.

42. Holland, *Mr. Claude*, 88.

43. Cravens, "Kilraven," 164.

44. Maxwell and Baker, *Sawdust Empire*, 139.

45. Quoted in Bowman, *Land of the Little Angel*, 159.

46. B. F. Bonner to J. F. Votaw, July 8, 1903, Kirby Papers, Nacogdoches, Box 23.

47. B. F. Bonner to W. W. Wilson, July 29, 1903, Kirby Papers, Nacogdoches, Box 23.

48. Smith in Easton, "The History of the Texas Lumbering Industry," 178.

49. *American Lumberman*, "The House of Thompson," 38.

50. Easton, "The History of the Texas Lumbering Industry," 177.

51. Ibid., 178.

52. Maxwell and Baker, *Sawdust Empire*, 140.

53. Elveston, "The Manning Church," 18.

54. Grace Lee Amiott interview, January 29, 1993; Elveston," The Manning Church," 18.

55. Curry, "The School of Manning," 19.

56. Poland, "Points of Interest in Manning," 28.

57. Maxwell and Baker, *Sawdust Empire*, 141. For a comprehensive social history of the Texas rural schools, see Sitton and Rowold, *Ringing the Children In*.

58. Poland, "Manning in General," 22.

59. Texas State Board of Education, *A Report On the Adequacy of Texas Schools*, 144.

60. Willie Massey interview, April 22, 1986.

61. Block, *East Texas Mill Towns and Ghost Towns*, 2: 166.

62. James Griner interview, May 19, 1993.

63. Burch, "The Groveton Sawmill," 26.

64. Quoted in Bowman, *The 35 Best Ghost Towns in East Texas*, 24.

65. James Griner interview, May 19, 1993.

66. Releford in Bowman, *The 35 Best Ghost Towns in East Texas*, 23.

67. Aden F. Vaughn interview, June 19, 1985.

68. Hines, "Prime Time," 128.

69. Calvin Smith interview, January 18, 1993.

70. Earl Hines self-interview, June 1982.

71. Ibid.

72. Hines, "Prime Time," 127.

73. Earl Hines self-interview, June 1982.

74. Baird, "Excerpts From the Early Years of a Small Town Doctor," 34.

75. Ibid.

76. Poland, "The People of Manning," 25; Vivian Warner interview, April 24, 1985.

77. Maxwell and Baker, *Sawdust Empire*, 151.

78. Ibid.

79. Bowman, *Land of the Little Angel*, 179; Easton, "The History of the East Texas Lumbering Industry," 83.

80. Weaver, "Labor Practices in the East Texas Lumber Industry," 43.

81. Cravens, "Kilraven," 165.

82. Maxwell and Baker, *Sawdust Empire*, 152.

83. *American Lumberman*, "Timber Resources of East Texas," 64.

84. Maxwell and Baker, *Sawdust Empire*, 151; Kirby Papers, Houston, R6 D-34, Box 58, File 3.

85. General Purchasing Agent to B. F. Bonner, November 9, 1916, Kirby Papers, Nacogdoches, Box 286.

86. Kirby Papers, Houston, R6 D-34, Box 58, File 1.

87. Kirby Papers, Houston, R6 D-34, Box 58, File 3.

88. Croom, *When the Pines Stood Tall*, 68.

89. B. F. Bonner to W. D. Deax, November 26, 1919; G. H. Garrett to E. C. Downman, August 25, 1919; B. F. Bonner to W. D. Deax, November 26, 1919 (all in Kirby Papers, Nacogdoches, Box 273).

90. Metcalf to C. E. Davidson, April 22, 1919, Kirby Papers, Nacogdoches, Box 206.

91. Houston Operative Report No. 274, Houston Investigator Reports, May 29, 1919, Kirby Papers, Nacogdoches, Box 273.

92. F. Mantooth to J. M. Seale, March 20, 1925, Kirby Papers, Nacogdoches, Box 273.

93. Frank Ashby interview, March 16, 1992.

94. Jackie Oliver Morehead self-interview, 1985.

95. Ibid.

96. Quoted in Bowman, *The 35 Best Ghost Towns of East Texas*, 45.

97. Martha Bowers interview, January 29, 1993.

98. Tatum, *River Road*, 14.

99. Johnson, "The Road to Possum Walk," n.p.

100. A. L. ("Babe") McGalin interview, May 14, 1992.

101. Johnson, "The Road to Possum Walk," n.p.

102. M. Wade to Kirby Lumber Company, January 30, 1914, Kirby Papers, Nacogdoches, Box 273.

103. Boon, "A History of Angelina County, Texas," 111.

104. Willie Massey interview, April 22, 1986.

105. Wilk Peters self-interview, 1984.

106. Willie Massey interview, April 22, 1986.

107. Edwin Nelson manuscript, n.p.

108. Horace Warren interview, January 3, 1986.

109. Block, *East Texas Mill Towns and Ghost Towns*, 2: 73.

110. Calvin Smith interview, January 18, 1993.

111. Kitchens, "General Facts About Manning," 9; Johnson, "The Road to Possum Walk," n.p.

112. Gee, "The Call of Texas," 4.

113. James Griner interview, May 19, 1994.

114. Harry Eaves in Bowman, *The 35 Best Ghost Towns of East Texas*, 45.

115. Taylor, "General Description of Manning," 8.

116. In Bowman, *The 35 Best Ghost Towns of East Texas*, 45.

117. Rhinehart, "Persistence Or Change," 1–13. In her careful census study of the demographics of the Kirby town of Village Mills, Hardin County, 1900–1920, Rhinehart concluded that the government census takers had been trying to hit a moving target, noting that, "at any point in time, one third of that working force was moving from one job to another." (p. 11)

118. Bentley, "The Dirge of the Lonesome Pine," n.p.

119. Ibid.

120. Ibid.

121. Ibid.

Chapter Three. Feudal Towns

1. Creel, "The Feudal Towns of Texas," 76.

2. Peter A. Speek quoted in Allen, *East Texas Lumber Workers*, 149.

3. Ibid., 156.

4. Quoted in Ferrell, "The Brotherhood of Timber Workers and the Southern Lumber Trust," 201–202.

5. Houston *Chronicle*, December 7, 1981.

6. Croom, *When the Pines Stood Tall*, 48; Allen, *East Texas Lumber Workers*, 48.

7. See, for example: E. L. Kurth to John Walker, n.d., Angelina County Lumber Company Papers, Nacogdoches, Box 775.

8. Southern Lumber Operators' Association labor report, June 28, 1923, Kirby Papers, Nacogdoches, Box 343.

9. In Easton, "The History of the Texas Lumbering Industry," 267.

10. In Loughmiller and Loughmiller, *Big Thicket Legacy*, 171.

11. In Bowman, *The 35 Best Ghost Towns of East Texas*, 51.

12. Joseph Marriot in Block, *East Texas Mill Towns and Ghost Towns*, 2: 124.

13. J. H. McDonald to C. P. Myer, March 27, 1913, Kirby Papers, Nacogdoches, Box 215.

14. Mr. Barton to J. W. Link, August 31, 1922, Kirby Papers, Nacogdoches, Box 385.

15. Hildreth to J. W. Link, December 7 and December 12, 1923, Kirby Papers, Nacogdoches, Box 385.

16. Ed Reichelt in Landrey, *Boardin' in the Thicket*, 66.

17. Robert Maxwell interview notes, Stephen F. Austin State University Library, n.p.

18. Jim Rushing interview, January 13, 1986.

19. Croom, *When the Pines Stood Tall*, 68.

20. Herbert Weeks interview, September 8, 1984.

21. Roscoe, "I Was a Deweyville-ite in 1938," 103.

22. Easton, "The History of the Texas Lumbering Industry," 267.

23. Maxwell and Baker, *Sawdust Empire*, 105.

24. Burch, "The Groveton Sawmill," 31.

25. Block, *East Texas Mill Towns and Ghost Towns*, 2: 117; *Crosscut*, "The Carter Sawmill Legacy in East Texas," n.p.

26. Frank Laing interview, 1954.

27. In Bowman, *The 35 Best Ghost Towns in East Texas*, 172; see also, Johnson, "Sawmill Women," n.p.

28. *American Lumberman*, "The House of Thompson," 81.

29. Ibid., 86.

30. Joseph Rutland Frederick interview, October 13, 1984.

31. Elodie Miles Edwards interview, June 12, 1990.

32. Edwin Nelson manuscript, n.p.

33. Dred D. Devereaux interview, 1954.

34. E. A. Farley interview, 1954.

35. Jesse Parker interview, 1954.

36. Mrs. Frank "Fannie" Farrington interview, 1953.

37. Arthur Temple, Jr., interview, May 8, 1985.

38. E. A Farley interview, 1954.

39. Willie Massey interview, April 22, 1986.

40. Grace Lee Amiott interview, January 29, 1993.

41. Ibid.

42. Martha Bowers interview, January 29, 1993.

43. Ibid.

44. Ibid.

45. Calvin Smith interview, January 18, 1993.

46. Aubrey Cole interview, August 14, 1995.

47. Maxwell and Baker, *Sawdust Empire*, 144.

48. Anon., "Deweyville," 359.

49. C. H. Smith to John Henry Kirby, March 23, 1912, Kirby Papers, Nacogdoches, Box 206.

50. L. G. Smith to C. P. Myer, October 27, 1913, Kirby Papers, Nacogdoches, Box 219.

51. Holland, *Mr. Claude*, 81.

52. Edwin Nelson manuscript, n.p.

53. Landrey, *Boardin' in the Thicket*, 31.

54. Pate Warner interview, June 7, 1994.

55. Maxwell and Baker, *Sawdust Empire*, 147.

56. *American Lumberman*, "Timber Resources of East Texas," 127.

57. Dewey Ballinger interview, June 20, 1984.

58. Joe Malanders interview, July 8, 1995.

59. Earl Hines self-interview, June 1982.

60. Operative S-17, December 7, 1921, Kirby Papers, Nacogdoches, Box 376.

61. Joe Malanders interview, July 8, 1995.

62. Dave Martinez interview, July 8, 1995.

63. Amos Harris interview, May 22, 1985; DeWitt Wilkerson interview, October 23, 1985; Mrs. Sidney Walters Kindley interview, 1984.

64. Mrs. Sidney Walters Kindley interview, 1984.

65. G-3 Reports, Call, August 11, 1922, Kirby Papers, Nacogdoches, Box 343.

66. Franklin Taylor interview, October 12, 1993.

67. Memorandum, November 23 and 24, 1916, Kirby Papers, Nacogdoches, Box 455.

68. Kirby Papers, Nacogdoches, Box 298.

69. Maxwell and Baker, *Sawdust Empire*, 147.

70. Icie Waltman interview, March 25, 1986.

71. Kirby in Lasswell, *John Henry Kirby*, 26.

72. Ibid.

73. Ibid., 27.

74. Edwin Nelson manuscript, n.p.

75. Fred Kennedy in Holland, *Mr. Claude,* 46.

76. Poland, "Some Events That Happened in Manning," 29.

77. Edwin Nelson manuscript, n.p.

78. Maxwell and Baker, *Sawdust Empire,* 144.

79. Sadie Estes Woods interview, July 18, 1984.

80. Robert Maxwell interview notes, Stephen F. Austin State University library, n.p.

81. Latane Temple interview, July 19, 1985.

82. Cravens, "Kilraven," 116.

83. Franklin Weeks taped address to Diboll Historical Society, n.d.

84. Dave Martinez interview, August 17, 1994.

85. Willie Massey interview, April 22, 1986.

86. Loughmiller and Loughmiller, *Big Thicket Legacy,* 137.

87. Bowles, "The History of Trinity County, Texas," 130.

88. Ibid., 131.

89. Ibid., 132.

90. Quoted in Payne, *Captain Bill McDonald,* 235–236.

91. Bowles, "The History of Trinity County, Texas," 136.

92. Ibid., 152.

93. Ibid., 158.

94. Ibid.

95. Allen, *East Texas Lumber Workers,* 119.

96. George R. Cristie to C. P. Myer, September 1, 1915, Kirby Papers, Nacogdoches, Box 243.

97. Clyde Thompson interview, January 14, 1984.

98. Rhinehart, "Spies in the Piney Woods."

99. Kenneth Nelson interview, August 17, 1985.

100. A. B. Reports, Voth, September 1, 1922, Kirby Papers, Nacogdoches, Box 343.

101. For a discussion of Southern traditions of arson, see Sitton, *Backwoodsmen,* 240–245.

102. Allen, *East Texas Lumber Workers,* 75.

103. For example, C. P. Myer to B. F. Bonner, January 5, 1908, Kirby Papers, Nacogdoches, Box 125.

104. Block, *East Texas Mill Towns and Ghost Towns,* 2: 117.

105. Franklin Weeks taped address to the Diboll Historical Society, n.d.

106. Maxwell and Baker, *Sawdust Empire*, 157.

107. Bentley, "The Dirge of the Lonesome Pine," n.p.

108. Quoted in Block, *East Texas Mill Towns and Ghost Towns*, 2: 75.

109. J. W. Link to H. B. Hildreth, December 8, 1923, Kirby Papers, Nacogdoches, Box 384.

110. H. B. Hildreth to J. W. Link, December 12, 1923, Kirby Papers, Nacogdoches, Box 384.

111. Quoted in Ferrell, "The Brotherhood of Timber Workers and the Southern Lumber Trust," 554.

112. Ibid.

113. J. B. Reynor to John Henry Kirby, March 29, 1913. Quoted in Ferrell, "The Brotherhood of Timber Workers and the Southern Lumber Trust," 555.

114. See President John H. Kirby of the National Lumber Manufacturing Association to the U.S. Congress, July 1918, Kirby Papers, Nacogdoches, Box 354; see also extensive correspondence concerning Mexican labor, Kirby Papers, Nacogdoches, Box 350, Box 354.

115. Westeraby to G. E. Davidson, March 16, 1918, Kirby Papers, Nacogdoches, Box 350.

116. For trouble at Bronson, see L. M. Wade, Southern Lumber Operators' Association inspection report, January 30, 1914, Kirby Papers, Nacogdoches, Box 273.

117. Horace Warren interview, January 3, 1985.

118. Loughmiller and Loughmiller, *Big Thicket Legacy*, 189.

119. Odom, *Over On Cochino*, 15.

120. Operative T-176, Case 455, October 15, 1918, Kirby Papers, Nacogdoches, Box 348.

121. Horace Warren interview, January 3, 1986.

122. Bowles, "The History of Trinity County, Texas," 111.

123. Quoted in Block, *East Texas Mill Towns and Ghost Towns*, 1: 70.

124. Josephine Rutland Frederick interview, October 13, 1983.

125. Mrs. Sidney Walters Kindley interview, 1984.

126. Carey Smith interview, September 28, 1982.

127. Mrs. Sidney Walters Kindley interview, 1984.

128. Conrad, "The Invisible Empire in the Piney Woods," 3.

129. Ibid., 4.

130. Ibid.

131. Ibid., 5.

132. Ibid.

133. Ibid., 8.

134. Ibid., 9.

135. In Ferrell, "The Brotherhood of Timber Workers and the Southern Lumber Trust," 758.

136. Ibid., 508.

137. Ibid.

138. Allen, *East Texas Lumber Workers*, 137.

139. Ibid., 165.

140. Ibid., 166.

141. Ibid., 170.

142. Ibid., 171.

143. Ibid.

144. Ibid., 175.

145. Ferrell, "The Brotherhood of Timber Workers and the Southern Lumber Trust," 144.

146. Allen, *East Texas Lumber Workers*, 180.

147. Ibid., 174.

148. Ibid., 188.

149. W. C. Keith to B. F. Bonner, January 25, 1912, Kirby Papers, Nacogdoches, Box 205.

150. Kirby Papers, Nacogdoches, Box 205.

151. In Ferrell, "The Brotherhood of Timber Workers and the Southern Lumber Trust," 299.

152. Ibid., 155.

153. Ibid., 303.

154. Ibid., 290; Allen, *East Texas Lumber Workers*, 188.

155. Ferrell, "The Brotherhood of Timber Workers and the Southern Lumber Trust," 304.

156. C. P. Myer to John Henry Kirby, September 2, 1911, Kirby Papers, Nacogdoches, Box 205.

157. Quoted in Ferrell, "The Brotherhood of Timber Workers and the Southern Lumber Trust," 329.

158. Ibid., 367.

159. Ibid., 356.

160. Ibid., 342.

161. C. P. Myer to Mill Managers, October 7, 1912, Kirby Papers, Nacogdoches, Box 243.

162. Ferrell, "The Brotherhood of Timber Workers and the Southern Lumber Trust," 660.

163. Ibid., 724.

164. Ibid., 726.

165. Ibid., 768.

166. Creel, "The Feudal Towns of Texas," 77.

167. Ibid., 78.

168. B. F. Bonner to Judge J. W. Terry, September 27, 1911, Kirby Papers, Nacogdoches, Box 205.

169. C. P. Myer to B. F. Bonner, n.d., Kirby Papers, Nacogdoches, Box 205.

170. Quoted in Ferrell, "The Brotherhood of Timber Workers and the Southern Lumber Trust," 759.

171. C. P. Myer to Andrews, Ball, and Streetman, September 6, 1911, Kirby Papers, Nacogdoches, Box 205.

172. Ferrell, "The Brotherhood of Timber Workers and the Southern Lumber Trust," 765.

173. Ibid., 767.

174. C. P. Myer to G. R. Christian, January 18, 1912, Kirby Papers, Nacogdoches, Box 205.

175. J. H. McDonald to C. P. Myer, March 27, 1913, Kirby Papers, Nacogdoches, Box 215.

176. Ferrell, "The Brotherhood of Timber Workers and the Southern Lumber Trust," 768.

177. Kirby Papers, Nacogdoches, Box 205.

178. Ferrell, "The Brotherhood of Timber Workers and the Southern Lumber Trust," 772.

179. Ibid., 770.

180. Ibid., 771.

181. Manager to C. P. Myer, August 14, 1911, Kirby Papers, Nacogdoches, Box 197.

182. Kirby Papers, Nacogdoches, Box 197; Biesele, *The Cornbread Whistle*, 62.

183. Ferrell, "The Brotherhood of Timber Workers and the Southern Lumber Trust," 761.

184. Ibid., 769.

185. J. Herndon to C. P. Myer, September 6, 1911, Kirby Papers, Nacogdoches, Box 197.

186. In Ferrell, "The Brotherhood of Timber Workers and the Southern Lumber Trust," 773.

187. Ibid.

188. W. H. Herndon, May 24, 1923, Kirby Papers, Nacogdoches, Box 343.

189. August 18, 1922, Kirby Papers, Nacogdoches, Box 343.

190. Allen, *East Texas Lumber Workers,* 91.

191. Ibid., 185.

192. Southern Lumber Operators' Association labor report, June 28, 1923, Kirby Papers, Nacogdoches, Box 343.

Chapter Four. The Cornbread Whistle

1. Myrtle Rushing interview, March 15, 1986.

2. Easton, "A History of the Texas Lumbering Industry," 164.

3. Marjory Pickle Davis interview, July 18, 1984.

4. Fred Kennedy in Holland, *Mr. Claude,* 72.

5. Block, *East Texas Mill Towns and Ghost Towns,* 2: 80.

6. Edwin Nelson manuscript, n.p.

7. Treadaway, "The Ewing Commissary," 18.

8. Bowman, *The 35 Best Ghost Towns of East Texas,* 30.

9. Easton, "A History of the Texas Lumbering Industry," 357.

10. Louise Rector interview, October 25, 1984.

11. Inez Thompson Asher interview, July 1984.

12. Croom, *When the Pines Stood Tall,* 73.

13. Easton, "A History of the Texas Lumbering Industry," 177.

14. Croom, *When the Pines Stood Tall,* 37.

15. Lee, "Growing Up in Wiergate," 324.

16. Easton, "A History of the Texas Lumbering Industry," 356.

17. Bentley, "The Dirge of the Lonesome Pine," n.p.

18. *American Lumberman,* "Timber Resources of East Texas," 126.

19. Maxwell and Baker, *Sawdust Empire,* 75.

20. Easton, "A History of the Texas Lumbering Industry," 354. This description of the Wiergate plant's operation primarily derives from Easton's detailed eyewitness account.

21. Maxwell and Baker, *Sawdust Empire,* 77.

22. *Gulf Coast Lumberman,* November 15, 1937.

23. Jake Cole interview, December 31, 1992.

24. Joe Malanders interview, July 8, 1995.

25. Memo of Conference, Silsbee, Texas, August 25, 1919, Kirby Papers, Nacogdoches, Box 358.

26. H. B. Hildreth to J. W. Link, August 28, 1922, Kirby Papers, Nacogdoches, Box 385.

27. *American Lumberman,* "Timber Resources of East Texas," 126.

28. Wilk Peters self-interview, 1984.

29. Clyde Woodward interview notes, 1957.

30. Arthur Beale interview, February 17, 1985.

31. Memo of Conference, August 25, 1919, Kirby Papers, Nacogdoches, Box 358.

32. January 16, 1912, quoted in Ferrell, "The Brotherhood of Timber Workers and the Southern Lumber Trust," 323.

33. E. T. Hickman to C. P. Myer, January 21, 1913, Kirby Papers, Nacogdoches, Box 219.

34. B. F. Bonner Memo, March 2, 1922, Kirby Papers, Nacogdoches, Box 296.

35. New Scale of Wages at Mill, 1914, Kirby Papers, Nacogdoches, Box 296.

36. E. L. Kurth to W. R. Burrow, October 11, 1916, Angelina County Lumber Company Papers, Nacogdoches, Box 412.

37. James Griner interview, May 19, 1993.

38. Joe Bob Hendrick interview, June 11, 1985.

39. Block, *East Texas Mill Towns and Ghost Towns,* 2: 124.

40. Amos Harris interview, May 22, 1985.

41. In Holland, *Mr. Claude,* 57.

42. Ibid., 98–100.

43. Ibid., 93.

44. *American Lumberman,* "The House of Thompson," 94.

45. Joe Malanders interview, July 8, 1995.

46. Edwin Nelson manuscript, n.p.; Mrs. Sidney Walters Kindley interview, 1984.

47. Edwin Nelson manuscript, n.p.

48. Haynes, *The History of Polk County,* 149.

49. Franklin Taylor interview, October 12, 1993.

50. Barlow, "Ewing—Growing Up," 12.

51. Rhoda Faye Chandler interview, September 7, 1982.

52. Myrtle Rushing interview, March 15, 1986.

53. Ibid.

54. Croom, *When the Pines Stood Tall,* 11.

55. Naomi Conner Swilley interview, April 18, 1988.

56. Gee, "The Call of Texas," 4.

57. Croom, *When the Pines Stood Tall,* 45.

58. Ibid., 46.

59. Ibid., 11.

60. Croom, "Reminiscences," *Lufkin Roundup*, June 1973, 13.

61. Croom, *When the Pines Stood Tall*, 27.

62. Ibid., 45.

63. Ibid., 41–42.

64. James Griner interview, May 19, 1994.

65. Jewel Minton interview, October 7, 1985.

66. Sadie Estes Woods interview, July 18, 1984.

67. Bowles, "The History of Trinity County, Texas," 72.

68. Rivie Vansau interview, February 20, 1985.

69. Jake Cole interview, November 7, 1993.

70. Wilburn, "Living in a Boxcar in Old Woodmeyer," 10.

71. Ervelia Jordan interview, December 10, 1985.

72. Pearl Havard interview, August 8, 1985.

73. Vina Wells interview, June 28, 1984.

74. J. W. Lewis to C. P. Myer, 1912, Kirby Papers, Nacogdoches, Box 197.

75. Vina Wells interview, June 28, 1984.

76. Holland, *Mr. Claude*, 78.

77. Pate Warner interview, June 7, 1994.

78. Croom, "Reminiscences," *Lufkin Roundup*, April 1977, 7.

79. Croom, *When the Pines Stood Tall*, 9.

80. Croom, "Reminiscences," *Lufkin Roundup*, April 1973, 20.

81. B. F. Bonner to E. C. Pope, August 24, 1904, Kirby Papers, Nacogdoches, Box 11.

82. Holland, *Mr. Claude*, 63.

83. Maxwell and Baker, *Sawdust Empire*, 150.

84. In Holland, *Mr. Claude*, 63.

85. Clyde Thompson interview, January 14, 1984.

86. *Crosscut* (First Quarter, 1992): n.p.

87. Ossie Thompson interview, September 8, 1978.

88. Ferrell, "The Brotherhood of Timber Workers and the Southern Lumber Trust," 175.

89. Ibid., 170.

90. Ibid.

91. Block, *East Texas Mill Towns and Ghost Towns*, 1: 18.

92. Ibid.

93. Arthur Beale interview, February 17, 1985.

94. In Ferrell, "The Brotherhood of Timber Workers and the Southern Lumber Trust," 172.

95. Ibid., 173–174.

96. Ibid., 178.

97. Ibid.

98. Ibid.

99. Ervelia Jordan interview, December 10, 1985.

100. *American Lumberman,* "Timber Resources of East Texas," 29, 88, 104 (respectively). Note also the images of dangerous "roll-chain" loading of logs on flatcars (p. 79) and a lodged tree at the timber front (p. 86).

101. C. P. Myer to B. F. Bonner, May 11, 1914, Kirby Papers, Nacogdoches, Box 243.

102. Jesse Parker interview, 1954.

103. J. H. McDonald to C. P. Myer, March 27, 1913, Kirby Papers, Nacogdoches, Box 215.

104. Investigation of Claim, Vastine Polk vs Kirby Lumber Company, Kirby Papers, Houston, R6 D-34, Box 72.

105. W. N. Sangster Memo, April 19, 1923, Kirby Papers, Houston, RG D-34, Box 48, File 3.

106. Report of Accidents for the Year 1925, Kirby Papers, Houston, R6 D-34, Box 48, File 2.

107. Aetna Life Insurance Co. to Receivers, August 1907, Kirby Papers, Nacogdoches, Box 115.

108. A. T. Webb to B. F. Bonner and N. W. McLeod, February 22, 1904, Kirby Papers, Nacogdoches, Box 23.

109. John G. Logge to E. J. Fountain, March 13, 1919, Kirby Papers, Nacogdoches, Box 358.

110. B. F. Bonner to T. O. Metcalfe, February 17, 1922, Kirby Papers, Nacogdoches, Box 354.

111. Manager for Receivers to Mr. Andrews, Ball, and Streetman, October 24, 1904, Kirby Papers, Nacogdoches, Box 31.

112. B. F. Bonner to Mr. Andrews, Ball, and Streetman, May 23, 1904, Kirby Papers, Nacogdoches, Box 31.

113. Case #1614, G-3 Reports, Call, August 22, 1922, Kirby Papers, Nacogdoches, Box 343.

114. Maxwell and Baker, *Sawdust Empire,* 127.

115. *American Lumberman,* "The House of Thompson," 101.

116. Maxwell and Baker, *Sawdust Empire,* 120; Easton, "A History of the Lumbering Industry in Texas," 248.

117. Easton, "A History of the Lumbering Industry in Texas," 248.

118. J. L. Payne to C. P. Myer, January 5, 1908, Kirby Papers, Nacogdoches, Box 125.

119. In Easton, "A History of the Lumbering Industry in Texas," 174.

120. Arthur Beale interview, February 17, 1985.

121. Biesele, *The Cornbread Whistle,* 36.

122. Lucille Warner interview, February 14, 1985.

123. Allen, *East Texas Lumber Workers,* 114.

124. Jake Cole interview, November 2, 1992; DeWitt Wilkerson interview, October 23, 1985; Wilk Peters self-interview, 1984.

125. Manager of Mills and Logging to W. M. Baugh, October 12, 1903, Kirby Papers, Nacogdoches, Box 31.

126. Croom, *When the Pines Stood Tall,* 11.

127. Ben Womack in Bowman, *The 35 Best Ghost Towns in East Texas,* 36.

128. Croom, *When the Pines Stood Tall,* 47.

129. Mrs. Sidney Walters Kindley interview, 1987.

Chapter Five. Dancing on the Millpond

1. Holland, *Mr. Claude,* 58.

2. Quoted in Block, *East Texas Mill Towns and Ghost Towns,* 2: 77.

3. Pate Warner interview, April 25, 1985.

4. Lee, "Growing Up In Wiergate," 325.

5. Chambers, "Life In a Southern Sawmill Community," 187.

6. Edwin Nelson manuscript, n.p.

7. Easton, "A History of the Texas Lumbering Industry," 180.

8. Dave Martinez interview, July 8, 1995.

9. Ibid., August 17, 1994.

10. Pate Warner interview, April 25, 1985.

11. Kenneth Nelson interview, August 17, 1986.

12. Ibid.

13. Martha Lee Bowers interview, January 29, 1993.

14. Croom, *When the Pines Stood Tall,* 12; James Rhone interview, April 24, 1986.

15. Vivian Warner interview, April 25, 1985.

16. L. D. Smith interview, February 13, 1986.

17. Wanda Gipson DuBose interview, July 30, 1994.

18. In Tim Spell, "Wiergate: Camelot of Mills," Houston *Chronicle,* April 17, 1988.

19. Vivian Warner interview, April 25, 1985.

20. Dred Devereaux interview, 1954.

21. L. D. Smith interview, February 13, 1986.

22. Calvin Smith interview, January 18, 1993.

23. Edwin Nelson manuscript, n.p.

24. Croom, *When the Pines Stood Tall,* 9.

25. Holland, *Mr. Claude,* 86.

26. Ibid.

27. DeWitt Wilkerson interview, October 23, 1985.

28. Dave Martinez interview, August 17, 1994.

29. Gee, "The Call of Texas," 4.

30. Calvin Smith interview, January 18, 1993; James Griner interview, May 19, 1993.

31. Holland, *Mr. Claude,* 67.

32. Poland, "Points of Interest in Manning," 27.

33. Marian Fuller interview, October 13, 1984.

34. Sadie Estes Woods interview, July 18, 1984.

35. Pate Warner interview, April 25, 1985.

36. Herbert Weeks interview, September 8, 1984; Edwin Nelson manuscript, n.p.

37. Treadaway, *Remembering Ewing,* 20.

38. Pate Warner interview, April 25, 1985.

39. Earl Hines self-interview, June 1982.

40. Burch, "The Groveton Sawmill," 29; James Griner interview, May 19, 1993.

41. Burch, "The Groveton Sawmill," 29.

42. Pate Warner interview, June 7, 1994.

43. Ibid.

44. Hines, "Prime Time," 128.

45. Jim Fuller interview, October 13, 1984.

46. Ibid.

47. In Holland, *Mr. Claude,* 74.

48. Ibid., 76.

49. Bowman, *Land of the Little Angel,* 163.

50. Bowman, *The 35 Best Ghost Towns of East Texas,* 24; Walker, *Axes, Oxen and Men,* 24; Easton, "A History of the Texas Lumbering Industry," 179.

51. Gee, "The Call of Texas," 4.

52. James Griner interview, May 19, 1993; Dave Martinez interview, August 17, 1994.

53. Easton, "A History of the Lumbering Industry in Texas," 363.

54. Horace Warren interview, January 3, 1986.

55. Wilk Peters self-interview, 1984.

56. Lester Vaughn interview, June 19, 1985; Will Jackson interview with KSPL Radio, n.d.

57. LeSassier, "I Remember," 10.

58. Marie Temple interview, October 27, 1985.

59. Edwin Nelson manuscript, n.d.

60. Metcalfe to C. E. Davidson, April 22, 1919, Kirby Papers, Nacogdoches, Box 206.

61. Poland, "Points of Interest in Manning," 28.

62. Ibid.

63. Kenneth Nelson interview, July 17, 1985.

64. Marian Fuller interview, October 13, 1984; Sadie Estes Woods interview, July 18, 1984; Herbert Weeks interview, September 8, 1984; O'Hara Chandler interview, September 8, 1984; Fenner Roth interview, September 8, 1984.

65. Grace Lee Amiott interview, January 29, 1993.

66. Dave Martinez interview, August 17, 1994.

67. Ibid.

68. Grace Lee Amiott interview, January 29, 1993.

69. Croom, *When the Pines Grew Tall*, 22; Pate Warner interview, June 7, 1994.

70. Wesley Ashworth interview, July 1984.

71. Croom, *When the Pines Grew Tall*, 22.

72. Burch, "The Mill at Groveton," 31.

73. Dolph Fillingim in Loughmiller and Loughmiller, *Big Thicket Legacy*, 184.

74. Franklin Weeks, taped address to the Diboll Historical Society, n.d.; Lexie Herndon, personal communication to James H. Conrad, 1994.

75. Sadie Estes Woods interview, July 18, 1984.

76. Croom, *When the Pines Grew Tall*, 23.

77. Horace Warren interview, January 3, 1986.

78. Oscar Allen interview, March 15, 1986.

79. Burch, "The Mill at Groveton," 26.

80. Ibid.

81. Maxwell and Baker, *Sawdust Empire*, 144.

82. Edwin Nelson manuscript, n.d.

83. Dave Martinez interview, August 17, 1994.

84. Flava Vaughn interview, June 19, 1985.

85. Quoted in Landrey, *Boardin' in the Big Thicket,* 39.

86. Ibid., 35.

87. Quoted in Easton, "A History of the East Texas Lumbering Industry," 181.

88. Manager at Call to B. F. Bonner, November 16, 1903, Kirby Papers, Nacogdoches, Box 11.

89. Ferrell, "The Brotherhood of Timber Workers and the Southern Lumber Trust," 247.

90. Block, *East Texas Mill Towns and Ghost Towns,* 2: 43–44.

91. Quoted in Ferrell, "The Brotherhood of Timber Workers and the Southern Lumber Trust," 248.

92. Ervelia Jordan interview, December 10, 1985.

93. Ferrell, "The Brotherhood of Timber Workers and the Southern Lumber Trust," 248.

94. Ibid.

95. Easton, "A History of the Texas Lumbering Industry," 181.

96. Jake Cole interview, November 2, 1992.

97. Lee, "Growing Up in Wiergate," 327.

98. Robert Conner, "Final Chapter Nears In One of the South's Big Lumber Operations," Houston *Chronicle,* December 13, 1942.

99. Inez Thompson Asher interview, July 1984; Anon., "Deweyville," 361.

100. R. F. Ford to B. F. Bonner, December 19, 1917, Kirby Papers, Nacogdoches, Box 280.

101. Metcalfe to Kirby, Bonner, Link, December 30, 1922, Kirby Papers, Nacogdoches, Box 280.

102. Anon., "Deweyville," 361.

103. James Griner interview, May 19, 1993.

104. Quoted in Loughmiller and Loughmiller, *Big Thicket Legacy,* 101.

105. Josephine Rutland Frederick interview, October 13, 1984.

106. Biesele, *The Cornbread Whistle,* 82.

107. Anon., "Deweyville," 360; Brailsford, "Artie Brailsford," 20.

108. Robert L. Weeks interview, 1954.

109. Johnson, "Baseball in the East Texas Sawmill Communities," n.p.

110. Bentley, "The Dirge of the Lonesome Pine," n.p.

111. Henry Ligon interview, April 8, 1988.

112. Edwin Nelson manuscript, n.d.

113. Croom, *When the Pines Grew Tall,* 12.

114. Franklin Taylor interview, October 12, 1993.

115. Joe Malanders interview, July 8, 1995.

116. Tinsley, "Events and Happenings in Ewing," 24.

117. Croom, *When the Pines Grew Tall*, 72.

118. Dave Martinez interview, August 17, 1994.

119. L. D. Smith interview, February 13, 1986.

120. Quoted in Loughmiller and Loughmiller, *Big Thicket Legacy*, 102.

121. Ibid., 103.

122. Ibid.

Chapter Six. Cut and Get Out

1. Chambers, "Life in a Southern Sawmill Community," 181.

2. Ibid., 181, 186.

3. Haynes, *The History of Polk County*, 147.

4. Burka, "The King of the Forest," 147.

5. Williams, *Americans and Their Forests*, 287.

6. Sitton, *Backwoodsmen*, 233–242.

7. In Maxwell and Baker, *Sawdust Empire*, 168.

8. W. Goodrich Jones, quoted in Maxwell and Martin, *A Short History of Forest Conservation in Texas*, 288.

9. Ibid.

10. Jones, quoted in Williams, *Americans and Their Forests*, 252.

11. In Easton, "A History of the Lumbering Industry in Texas," 215.

12. Clark, *The Greening of the South*, 25; Charles Dillingham and F. A. Reichart to Cecil A. Lyon and J. S. Rice, June 2, 1906, Kirby Papers, Nacogdoches, Box 75.

13. Jake Cole interview, July 9, 1992.

14. Walker, *The Southern Forest*, 134.

15. Clark, *The Greening of the South*, 34–35.

16. Block, *East Texas Mill Towns and Ghost Towns*, 2: 48.

17. Bowman, *The 35 Best Ghost Towns in East Texas*, 32.

18. Ibid.

19. Frank Ashby interview, March 19, 1992.

20. Croom, *When the Pines Stood Tall*, 79.

21. Ferrell, "The Brotherhood of Timber Workers and the Southern Lumber Trust," 199.

22. Bowman, *The 35 Best Ghost Towns of East Texas*, 74.

23. Maxwell and Baker, *Sawdust Empire,* 200.

24. In Williams, *Americans and Their Forests,* 281.

25. Chambers, "Divisions of the Pine Belt in Texas," 102.

26. Bowles, "A History of Trinity County, Texas," 125.

27. Ibid., 160.

28. Ibid., 163.

29. Ibid.

30. In Maxwell and Baker, *Sawdust Empire,* 200.

31. Ibid., 202.

32. Wesley Ashworth interview, July 1984.

33. W. N. Sangster to Stockholders, November 22, 1930, Kirby Papers, Nacogdoches, Box 455.

34. President John Henry Kirby to Board of Directors, Kirby Lumber Company, February 1, 1931, Kirby Papers, Nacogdoches, Box 455.

35. John Henry Kirby to W. N. Sangster, May 4, 1932, Kirby Papers, Nacogdoches, Box 455.

36. Unnamed correspondent to J. H. Keefe, June 20, 1932, Kirby Papers, Nacogdoches, Box 455.

37. Eddlemon, "The Depression at Call, Texas," 224.

38. Gee, "The Call of Texas," 4.

39. Eddlemon, "The Depression at Call, Texas," 224.

40. Ibid.

41. Maxwell and Baker, *Sawdust Empire,* 202.

42. In Biesele, *The Cornbread Whistle,* 66.

43. Ibid., 67.

44. Beatrice Burkhalter interview, May 25, 1982.

45. Biesele, *The Cornbread Whistle,* 68.

46. Ibid., 66.

47. Ibid., 72.

48. Aden F. Vaughn interview, June 19, 1985.

49. Rox P. Mann interview, November 17, 1987.

50. Frankie Glass interview, October 21, 1982.

51. Claude Welch interview, January 5, 1983.

52. Minutes of the Stockholders of the Wier Lumber Company, Houston, Archives, James G. Gee Library, Texas A&M University, Commerce.

53. Jake Cole interview, November 7, 1993.

54. In Bowman, *The 35 Best Ghost Towns in East Texas,* 47.

55. James Griner interview, May 19, 1993.

56. No plots of virgin longleaf survived in Texas—not even a few acres.

57. Easton, "A History of the Lumbering Industry in Texas," 360.

58. Ibid., 331.

59. Ibid., 330.

60. Ibid., 374.

61. Haynes, *A History of Polk County*, 146.

62. In Walker, *The Southern Forest*, 146. For an overview of recent operations at Diboll and Pineland of Southern Pine's successor company, Temple-Inland, see: Block, *East Texas Mill Towns and Ghost Towns*, 2: 275; Biesele, *The Cornbread Whistle*, 123–134.

63. Contract between R. W. Wier and Frances A. Lutcher and others, February 12, 1917, reprinted in Minutes of the Stockholders of the Wier Long Leaf Lumber Company, Houston, Texas, January 27, 1918.

64. Martha Lee Bowers interview, January 29, 1993.

65. Block, *East Texas Mill Towns and Ghost Towns*, 1: 225.

66. Jake Cole interview, November 7, 1993.

67. Earl Hines self-interview, 1982.

68. Hines, "Prime Time," 125.

Bibliography

Print Sources

Allen, Ruth. *East Texas Lumber Workers: An Economic and Social Picture, 1870–1930.* Austin: University of Texas Press, 1961.

American Lumberman. "The House of Thompson: Lone Star Pine, Oldest Lumber Manufacturers in the State of Texas." Chicago: 1908.

———. "Neches Valley Pine." Chicago: 1908.

———. "Timber Resources of East Texas: Their Recognition and Development by John Henry Kirby, Through the Inception and Organization of the Kirby Lumber Company of Houston Texas." Chicago: 1902.

Angelina County Lumber Company Papers, 1887–1966. Forest History Collections, Stephen F. Austin State University Library, Nacogdoches.

Anon. "Deweyville: A Ghost Town That Refused to Stay Dead." In *Newton County Nuggets,* edited by Newton County Historical Commission, pp. 358–362. Austin: Nortex Press, 1986.

Baird, W. LeRoy. "Excerpts From the Early Years of a Small Town Doctor." In *Crosscuts,* edited by Newton County Historical Commission, pp. 34–37. Austin: Eakin Press, 1984.

Barlow, Ben. "Ewing—Growing Up." In *Remembering Ewing,* edited by Lamar Tinsley, pp. 12–13. Lufkin: Pineywoods Printing, 1987.

Bentley, Max. "The Dirge of the Lonesome Pine." Published by Newton County Historical Commission, n.d., n.p.

Bevil, John Richard. "Dr. John Richard Bevil." In *Big Thicket Legacy,* edited by Campbell Loughmiller and Lynn Loughmiller, pp. 133–144. Austin: University of Texas Press, 1977.

Biesele, Megan. *The Cornbread Whistle: Oral History of a Texas Timber Company Town.* Lufkin: Diboll Historical Society, 1986.

Block, W. T. *East Texas Mill Towns and Ghost Towns,* Vols. 1–2. Lufkin: Piney-woods Foundation, 1994, 1995.

———. "Olive, Hardin County, Texas: An Extinct Sawmill Town and the Olive-Sternenberg Partnership That Built It." *The Texas Gulf Historical and Biographical Record* 26 (1990): 31–51.

———. "Tram Roads Preceded Railroads, Towns." *Big Thicket Bulletin* 65 (1980–1981): 6–7.

Boon, Effie M. "The History of Angelina County, Texas." Master's thesis, University of Texas, Austin, 1937.

Bowles, Flora G. "The History of Trinity County, Texas." Master's thesis, University of Texas, Austin, 1928.

Bowman, Bob. *The 35 Best Ghost Towns in East Texas.* Lufkin: Best of East Texas Publishers, 1988.

———, ed. *Land of the Little Angel.* Lufkin: Angelina County Historical Survey Committee, 1976.

Brailsford, Geneva. "Artie Brailsford." In *Newton County Nuggets,* edited by Newton County Historical Commission, pp. 19–21. Austin: Nortex Press, 1986.

Buber, Stanley. *Pullman: An Experiment in Industrial Order and Community Planning, 1880–1930.* New York: Oxford University Press, 1967.

Burch, Willie A. "The Groveton Sawmill." In *Journey to Jubilee: Groveton, Texas, U.S.A.,* edited by Groveton Ex-Students Association, 23–33. Groveton: 1980.

Burka, Paul. "The King of the Forest." *Texas Monthly* 10, 8 (Aug. 1982): 114–123.

Chambers, Williams. "Divisions of the Pine Forest Belt in Texas. *Economic Geography* 6 (1930): 94–103.

———. "Life in a Southern Sawmill Community." *Journal of Geography* 30 (1931): 181–188.

———. "Pine Woods Region in Southeastern Texas." *Economic Geography* 10 (1934): 302–318.

Clark, Thomas D. *The Greening of the South.* Lexington: University Press of Kentucky, 1984.

Cloud, Mrs. Josie. "My Memories About Ewing." In *Remembering Ewing,* edited by Lamar Tinsley, 10–11. Lufkin: Pineywoods Printing, 1987.

Conrad, James H. "The Invisible Empire in the Piney Woods." Paper delivered to Beaumont Historical Conference, Beaumont, 1996.

Cravens, John N. *Between Two Rivers: A History of Wells, Texas.* Wichita Falls: n.p., 1974.

———. "Kilraven: A Ghost Town in the Southern Part of Cherokee County, Texas." *East Texas Historical Journal* 9 (1971): 162–170.

———. *Three Ghost Towns of East Texas.* Abilene: Abilene Printing Company, n.d.

Creel, George. "The Feudal Towns of East Texas." *Harper's Weekly* 69 (1915): 76–78.

Crews, d'Anne McAdams. *Huntsville and Walker County, Texas.* Huntsville: Sam Houston State University Press, 1976.

Croom, Guy. "Reminiscences." *Lufkin Roundup,* April 1973, 18.

———. *When the Pines Stood Tall.* Lufkin: Red Mountain Publishing Company, 1986.

Crouch, Roscoe. "Roscoe Crouch." In *Big Thicket Legacy,* edited by Campbell Loughmiller and Lynn Loughmiller, pp. 167–174. Austin: University of Texas Press, 1977.

Curry, Vera. "The School of Manning." In *Were You at Manning?,* edited by Robert Poland, pp. 19–20. N.p., 1985.

Dickenson, Johnnie Jo. "Elmina, A Sawmill Town." In *Walker County, Texas, a History,* edited by Walker County Historical Commission, pp. 72–74. Dallas: Walker County History Book Committee, 1986.

Doak, Stella. "Interesting Places Around Manning." In *Were You at Manning?,* edited by Robert Poland, p. 17. N.p.: 1985.

Easton, Hamilton Pratt. "A History of the Texas Lumbering Industry." Ph.D dissertation, University of Texas at Austin, 1947.

Eddlemon, Mollie. "The Depression at Call, Texas." In *Crosscuts,* edited by Newton County Historical Commission, pp. 223–224. Austin: Eakin Press, 1984.

Elveston, Horace. "The Manning Church." In *Were You at Manning?,* edited by Robert Poland, pp. 18–19. N.p.: 1985.

Ferrell, Geoffrey. "The Brotherhood of Timber Workers and the Southern Lumber Trust, 1910–1914." Ph.D. dissertation, University of Texas at Austin, 1982.

Fillingim, A. Randolph. "A. Randolph Fillingim." In *Big Thicket Legacy,* edited by Campbell Loughmiller and Lynn Loughmiller, pp. 79–96. Austin: University of Texas Press, 1977.

Flournoy, M. M. "History of Manning." In *Were You at Manning?* edited by Robert Poland, pp. 3–4. N.p.: 1985.

Foley, Neil F. "The New South in the Southwest: Anglos, Blacks, and Mexicans in Central Texas, 1880–1930." Ph.D. dissertation, University of Michigan, 1990.

Forest History Collections, Stephen F. Austin State University Library, Nacogdoches.

Gee, John C., Jr. "The Call of Texas." In *Crosscuts,* edited by Newton County Historical Commission, pp. 3–5. Austin: Eakin Press, 1984.

———. "Angel of Call, Texas." In *Newton County Nuggets,* edited by Newton County Historical Commission, pp. 43–44. Austin: Nortex Press, 1986.

Gerland, Jonathan. "The Largest Sawmill in the World." *Crosscut* (1993): n.p.

Gilmer, Alexander, Lumber Company Papers. Center for American History, University of Texas at Austin.

Hahn, Steven. "Hunting, Fishing, and Foraging: Common Rights and Class Rotations in the Postbellum South." *Radical History Review* 26 (1982): 37–64.

Halliburton, Virgie. "My Marriage Started in Ewing." In *Remembering Ewing*, edited by Lamar Tinsley, p. 10. Lufkin: Pineywoods Printing, 1987.

Hart, Carter. "Carter Hart." In *Big Thicket Legacy*, edited by Campbell Loughmiller and Lynn Loughmiller, pp. 97–108. Austin: University of Texas Press, 1977.

Haynes, Emma. *The History of Polk County.* N.p.; 1937

Hines, Earl S. "Prime Time: Twenty-five Years On the Job." In *Crosscuts*, edited by Newton County Historical Commission, pp. 125–130. Austin: Eakin Press, 1984.

———. "Those Were the Days." In *Newton County Nuggets*, edited by Newton County Historical Commission, pp. 225–234. Austin: Nortex Press, 1986.

Holland, Ada Morehead. *Mr. Claude.* College Station: Texas A&M University Press, 1984.

Johnson, Melvin C. "Baseball in the East Texas Sawmill Communities. *Crosscut* (1994): n.p.

———. "Electrification of East Texas Sawmill Communities before World War I." Paper presented to the East Texas Historical Association, Nacogdoches, Texas, September 23, 1994.

———. "The Road to Possum Walk: Immigrants and the East Texas Sawmill Culture." *Crosscut* (1994): n.p.

———. "Sawmill Women: Successes in Home and in the Workplace." *Crosscut* (1994): n.p.

Johnston, Bower L. "Years in Newton County." In *Crosscuts*, edited by Newton County Historical Commission, pp. 103–105. Austin: Eakin Press, 1984.

———. "Sawmill Days." In *Newton County Nuggets*, edited by Newton County Historical Commission, pp. 366–367. Austin: Nortex Press, 1986.

Jones, Cynthia. "The Builders of Manning." In *Were You at Manning?*, edited by Robert Poland, pp. 5–7. N.p.: 1985.

Jordan, Terry G. *Trails to Texas: Southern Roots of Western Cattle Ranching.* Lincoln: University of Nebraska Press, 1981.

Jordan, Terry G., and Matti Kaup. *The American Backwoods Frontier: An Ethnic and Ecological Interpretation.* Baltimore: Johns Hopkins University Press, 1990.

Jordan, Walter. "Some Organizations of Manning." In *Were You at Manning?*, edited by Robert Poland, p. 20. N.p.: 1985.

Kilgore, Susie B. "The Business District." In *Were You at Manning?*, edited by Robert Poland, pp. 11–12. N.p.: 1985.

Kirby, Jack Temple. *Rural Worlds Lost: The American South, 1920–1960.* Baton Rouge: Louisiana State University Press, 1987.

Kirby, John Henry, Personal Papers, Houston Metropolitan Research Center, Houston.

Kirby Lumber Corporation Papers. Forest History Collections, Stephen F. Austin State University Library, Nacogdoches.

Kitchens, Alif. "General Facts About Manning." In *Were You at Manning?*, edited by Robert Poland, pp. 9–10. N.p.: 1985.

Laird, Dickie. "Important Events that Have Happened at Manning." In *Were You at Manning?*, edited by Robert Poland, pp. 10–11. N.p.: 1985.

Landrey, Wanda A. *Boardin' in the Thicket.* Denton: University of North Texas Press, 1990.

Larken, Sylvia West. "Wiergate." In *Crosscuts*, edited by Newton County Historical Commission, pp. 23–27. Austin: Eakin Press, 1984.

Lasswell, Mary. *John Henry Kirby: Prince of the Pines.* Austin: Encino Press, 1967.

LeSassier, Mrs. J. J. "I Remember." In *Remembering Ewing*, edited by Lamar Tinsley, p. 9. Lufkin: Pineywoods Printing, 1987.

Lee, James P. "Growing Up in Wiergate." In *Newton County Nuggets*, edited by Newton County Historical Commission, pp. 324–328. Austin: Nortex Press, 1986.

Maxwell, Robert S. "The Pines of Texas: A Study in Lumbering and Public Policy." *East Texas Historical Journal* 2 (1964): 77–86.

———. *Whistle in the Piney Woods: Paul Bremond and the Houston, East, and West Texas Railway.* Houston: Texas Gulf Coast Historical Association, 1963.

Maxwell, Robert S., and Robert D. Baker, *Sawdust Empire: The Texas Lumber Industry, 1830–1940.* College Station: Texas A&M University Press, 1983.

Maxwell, Robert S., and James W. Martin, *A Short History of Forest Conservation in Texas.* Nacogdoches: School of Forestry, Stephen F. Austin State University, 1970.

Montgomery, Howard. "Before and After the Birth of Wiergate, Texas." In *Newton County Nuggets*, edited by Newton County Historical Commission, pp. 331–334. Austin: Nortex Press, 1986.

Moye, James Addison. "James Addison Moye." In *Big Thicket Legacy*, edited by Campbell Loughmiller and Lynn Loughmiller, pp. 183–190. Austin: University of Texas Press, 1977.

Nelson, Edwin. Unpublished memoirs. Diboll Public Library, Diboll, Texas.

Odom, Harrell. *Over On Cochino.* Waco: Texian Press, 1980.

Owens, William A. "Big Thicket Balladry." In *Tales from the Big Thicket*, edited by Francis E. Abernethy, pp. 199–214. Austin: University of Texas Press, 1966.

Payne, Alfred B. *Captain Bill McDonald, Texas Ranger.* New York: J. J. Little and Ives, 1909.

Peoples, Mary. *Montgomery County History.* Conroe: Montgomery County Genealogical Society, 1981.

Pfleider, Audre Rudd. "J. B." In *Newton County Nuggets*, edited by Newton County Historical Commission, pp. 90–93. Austin: Nortex Press, 1986.

Platt, Lester Carroll. "Millwright Foreman." In *Newton County Nuggets*, edited by Newton County Historical Commission, pp. 148–149. Austin: Nortex Press, 1986.

Poland, Robert. "Manning In General." In *Were You at Manning?*, edited by Robert Poland, pp. 21–23. N.p.: 1985.

———. "The People of Manning." In *Were You at Manning?*, edited by Robert Poland, pp. 24–27. N.p.: 1985.

———. "Points of Interest in Manning." In *Were You at Manning?*, edited by Robert Poland, pp. 27–29. N.p.: 1985.

———. "Some Events That Happened in Manning." In *Were You at Manning?*, edited by Robert Poland, pp. 29–30. N.p.: 1985.

Raimer, Fannie. "Small Pox, Typhoid Took Toll." *Silsbee Bee,* October 9, 1969.

Rhinehart, Marilyn. "Persistence Or Change: Demographics of a Lumber Town in East Texas, 1900–1920." Paper presented to the Texas State Historical Association, 1994.

———. "Spies in the Piney Woods: John Henry Kirby's Agents Provocateurs and the Brotherhood of Timber Workers in East Texas, 1910–1912." Paper presented at the annual meeting of the Texas State Historical Association, 1995.

Richmond, Harrell. "Present Facts About Manning." In *Were You at Manning?*, edited by Robert Poland, pp. 13–14. N.p.: 1985.

Riggs, Carol. Untitled articles and notes by the editor. *Crosscut* (various issues, 1986–1995): n.p.

Roach, Hattie Joplin. *The Hills of Cherokee.* Privately published: 1952.

Roscoe, Lois. "I Was a Deweyville-ite in 1938." In *Newton County Nuggets*, edited by Newton County Historical Commission, pp. 99–103. Austin: Nortex Press, 1986.

Schaadt, Robert, ed. *Hardin County History.* Dallas: Hardin County Historical Commission, 1991.

Sitton, Thad. *Backwoodsmen: Stockmen and Hunters Along a Big Thicket River Valley.* Norman: University of Oklahoma Press, 1994.

Sitton, Thad, and Milam Rowold. *Ringing the Children In: Texas Country Schools.* College Station: Texas A&M University Press, 1987.

Smith, Calvin J., Jr. "Boyhood Memories of Wiergate." In *Newton County Nuggets*, edited by Newton County Historical Commission, pp. 335–336. Austin: Nortex Press, 1986.

Spell, Tim. "Wiergate: Camelot of Mills." *Houston Chronicle,* April 17, 1988.

Talley, W. H. "Root, Hog, Or Die!: Life in Newton County During the 1930s." In *Crosscuts,* edited by Newton County Historical Commission, pp. 217–220. Austin, Eakin Press, 1984.

Tarpley, Fred. *Jefferson: Riverport to the Southwest.* Austin: Eakin Press, 1983.

Tatum, Miriam Havard. *River Road.* Diboll: Angelina Free Press, 1979.

Taylor, Edna May. "General Description of Manning." In *Were You at Manning?*, edited by Robert Poland, pp. 8–9. N.p.: 1985.

Temple Industries Papers. Forest History Collections, Stephen F. Austin State University Library, Nacogdoches.

Texas Forestry Museum. "The Carter Sawmill Legacy in East Texas." *Crosscut* (1991): n.p.

———. "Expressions." *Crosscut* (1992): n.p.

Tinsley, Lamar. "Ewing—My Birthplace." In *Remembering Ewing*, edited by Lamar Tinsley, pp. 16–18. Lufkin: Pineywoods Printing, 1987.

———. "The Boardinghouse." In *Remembering Ewing*, edited by Lamar Tinsley, pp. 21–22. Lufkin: Pineywoods Press, 1987.

———. "Events and Happenings in Ewing." In *Remembering Ewing*, edited by Lamar Tinsley, pp. 22–24. Lufkin: Pineywoods Press, 1987.

Treadaway, Chester. "The Ewing Commissary." In *Remembering Ewing*, edited by Lamar Tinsley, pp. 18–20. Lufkin: Piney Woods Press, 1987.

Trinity County Book Committee, *Trinity County Beginnings*. Privately published, 1986.

Trinity County Historical Society. *A History of Trinity, Texas.* Crockett: Publications Development Company, 1984.

Trotti, Durward I. "Reflections of a Piney Woods Dentist." In *Newton County Nuggets*, edited by Newton County Historical Commission, pp. 114–120. Austin: Nortex Press, 1986.

Truett, Joe C., and Daniel W. Lay. *Land of Bears and Honey: A Natural History of East Texas.* Austin: University of Texas Press, 1984.

Walker, Ellen. "Ellen Walker." In *Big Thicket Legacy*, edited by Campbell Loughmiller and Lynn Loughmiller, pp. 3–13. Austin: University of Texas Press, 1977.

Walker, Laurence C. *Axes, Oxen, and Men: A Pictorial History of the Southern Pine Lumber Company.* Diboll: Angelina Free Press, 1975.

———. "His Engines Ran 'Pretty Pert' in the East Texas Forests." *Crosscut* (1988): n.p.

———. *The Southern Forest: A Chronicle.* Austin: University of Texas Press, 1991.

Weaver, Harry. "Labor Practices in the East Texas Lumber Industry." Master's thesis, Stephen F. Austin State College, Nacogdoches, 1961.

Wier Lumber Company Papers. Private collection, Houston.

Wiggins, Brown. "Brown Wiggins." In *Big Thicket Legacy*, edited by Campbell Loughmiller and Lynn Loughmiller, pp. 13–28. Austin: University of Texas Press, 1977.

Wilburn, Hazel Woods. "Living in a Boxcar in Old Woodmeyer." In *Crosscuts*, edited by Newton County Historical Commission, pp. 10–12. Austin: Eakin Press, 1984.

Williams, Michael. *Americans and Their Forests: A Historical Geography.* Cambridge: Cambridge University Press, 1989.

"With Wier at Wiergate." *Gulf Coast Lumberman*, November 15, 1937, pp. 20–24.

Wright, Solomon Alexander. *My Rambles as East Texas Cowboy, Hunter, Fisherman, Tie-cutter.* Austin: Texas Folklore Society, 1941.

Zuber, William P. *My Eighty Years in Texas.* Austin: University of Texas Press, 1971.

Oral Sources

Amiott, Grace Lee. Taped interview with James H. Conrad, 1993. East Texas State University Oral History Project, James Gee Library, Commerce, Texas (hereafter cited as ETSU).

Ashby, Frank. Taped interviews with Thad Sitton, 1992. East Texas Collection, Stephen F. Austin State University Library, Nacogdoches, Texas (hereafter cited as SFA).

Asher, Inez Thompson. Taped interview with Megan Lambert and Ann Sweeny, July 1984. Diboll Oral History Collection, Diboll Public Library, Diboll, Texas (hereafter cited as DL).

Ashworth, Wesley. Taped interview with Megan Lambert and Ann Sweeny, July 1984. DL.

Ballinger, Dewey. Taped interview with Becky Bailey, 1984. DL.

Beale, Arthur C. Taped interview with Sheila Billingsley, 1985. DL.

Bingham, J. Louis. Taped interview with Thad Sitton, 1992. SFA.

Bowers, Martha Lee. Taped interview with James H. Conrad, 1993. ETSU.

Burkhalter, Beatrice. Taped interviews with Becky Bailey, 1982, and Sherri Sheridan, 1985. DL.

Chandler, O'Hara. Taped interview with Feena Killam and Megan Lambert at Diboll Historical Society meeting, 1984. DL.

Chandler, Rhoda Faye. Taped interview with Becky Bailey, 1982. DL.

Christian, Mary Jane. Taped interview with Gayle Beene, 1985. DL.

Clement, Dr. J. C. Taped interview with Becky Bailey and Fenner Roth, 1985. DL.

Cole, Aubrey. Taped interview with Thad Sitton, 1995. Private collection.

Cole, Jake. Taped interviews with Thad Sitton, 1992, and James H. Conrad, 1993. ETSU.

Cole, Walter. Taped interview with Thad Sitton, 1992. SFA.

Currie, Ruth. Taped interview with Marie Davis, 1986. DL.

Davis, Marjory Pickle. Taped interview with Edythe Weeks and Megan Lambert, 1984. DL.

Devereaux, Dred D. Taped interview with John Larson, 1954. DL.

Davis, Elodie Miles. Taped interview with Marie Davis, 1990. DL.

DuBose, Wanda Gipson. Taped interview with Thad Sitton, 1994. Private collection.

Farley, E. A. Taped interview with Clyde Thompson, 1954. DL.

Farrington, Mrs. Frank. Taped interview with John Larson, 1953. DL.

Frederick, Josephine Rutland. Taped interview with Becky Bailey, 1984. DL.

Fuller, Jim. Taped interview with Becky Bailey, 1984. DL.

Fuller, Marian. Taped interview with Becky Bailey, 1984. DL.

Gipson, Johnnie Oliver. Taped self-interview, 1985. DL.

Glass, Frankie. Taped interview with Becky Bailey, 1982. DL.

Gossett, Laymon. Taped interview with Marie Davis, 1985. DL.

Griner, James. Taped interview with James H. Conrad, 1993. ETSU.

Harris, Amos. Taped interview with Becky Bailey, 1985. DL.

Havard, Charlie. Taped interview with Thad Sitton, 1986. SFA.

Havard, Pearl. Taped interview with Marie Davis, 1985. DL.

Hendrick, Joe Bob. Taped interview with Marie Davis, 1985. DL.

Hines, Earl. Taped self-interview, 1982. ETSU.

Jackson, Will. Taped interviews with KSPL Radio, n.d. DL.

Jordan, Ervelia. Taped interview with Marie Davis, 1985. DL.

Kindley, Mrs. Sidney Walters. Taped interview with Megan Lambert and Didney Maxey, 1984. DL.

Laing, Frank. Taped interview with Clyde Thompson, 1954. DL.

Ligon, Henry. Taped interview with Jim Ligon, 1988. DL.

Malanders, Joe. Taped interview with James H. Conrad, 1995. ETSU.

McGalin, A. L. ("Babe"). Taped interview with Thad Sitton, 1992. SFA.

Mann, Rox P. Taped interview with Tina McClenden, 1987. DL.

Martinez, Dave. Taped interviews with James H. Conrad, 1994, 1995. ETSU.

Massey, Willie. Taped interview with Marie Davis and Vivian Warner, 1986. DL.

Minton, Jewel. Taped interview with Marie Davis, 1985. DL.

Morehead, Jackie Oliver. Taped self-interview, 1985. DL.

Nash, Cora. Taped interview with Becky Bailey, 1982. DL.

Nelson, Floyd. Taped interview with Cheri Luce, 1986. DL.

Nelson, Kenneth. Taped interviews with Megan Lambert, 1985. DL.

Parker, Jesse. Taped interview with Clyde Thompson, 1954. DL.

Peters, Wilk. Taped interview with Jon Franklin, 1983, taped self-interview, 1984. DL.

Poland, Ruth. Taped interview with Martha Carswell, 1985. DL.

Rawls, R. J. Taped interview with Dan K. Utley, 1986. SFA.

Rector, Louise. Taped interview with Becky Bailey, 1984. DL.

Rhone, James. Taped interview with Marie Davis and L. D. Smith, 1986. DL.

Roth, Fenner. Taped interview with Teena Killam and Megan Lambert at meeting of Diboll Historical Society, 1984. DL.

Rushing, Jim. Taped interview with Marie Davis, 1986. DL.

Rushing, Myrtle. Taped interview with Marie Davis, 1986. DL.

Smith, Calvin. Taped interview with James H. Conrad, 1993. ETSU.

Smith, Doyle. Taped interview with James H. Conrad, 1993. ETSU.

Smith, Carey. Taped interviews with Becky Bailey, 1982, and Jim Ligon, 1988. DL.

Smith, L. D. Taped interviews with Marie Davis and Joe Smith, 1986. DL.

Smith, Roy. Taped interviews with Thad Sitton, 1986. SFA.

Spivy, Mrs. Ada. Taped interview with James H. Conrad, 1994. DL.

Sweeny, Lucille Cook. Taped interview with Franklin Weeks, 1993. DL.

Swilley, Naomi Conner. Taped interview with Marie Davis and Oneta Hendrick, 1988. DL.

Taylor, Elaine. Taped interview with Marie Davis, 1993. DL.

Taylor, Franklin. Taped interview with Marie Davis, 1993. DL.

Temple, Arthur, Jr. Taped interview with Megan Lambert, 1985; taped address to Diboll Historical Society, 1988. DL.

Temple, Latane. Taped interview with Megan Lambert, 1985. DL.

Temple, Marie H. Taped interview with Marie Davis, 1985. DL.

Thompson, Clyde. Taped interviews with Becky Bailey, 1982. DL.

Thompson, Ossie. Taped interview with Ellen Temple, 1978. DL.

Turner, Harold. Taped interview with Becky Bailey, 1982. DL.

Vaughn, Aden F. Taped interview with Marie Davis, 1985. DL.

Vaughn, Flava. Taped interview with Marie Davis, 1985. DL.

Vansau, Rivie. Taped interview with Vivian Warner and Marie Davis, 1986. DL.

Waltman, Icie. Taped interview with Marie Davis. 1986. DL.

Warner, Lucille. Taped interview with Marie Davis, 1985. DL.

Warner, Pate. Taped interviews with Marie Davis, 1985 and 1994. DL.

Warner, Vivian. Taped interviews with Marie Davis, 1985 and 1994. DL.

Warren, Horace. Taped interview with Becky Bailey, 1986. DL.

Weeks, Franklin. Taped address to Diboll Historical Society, n.d. DL.

Weeks, Robert L. Taped interview with John Larson, 1954. DL.

Weimer, Maurine. Taped interview with Becky Bailey, 1985. DL.

Welch, Claude, Sr. Taped interview with Becky Bailey, 1983. DL.

Wells, Vina. Taped interview with Becky Bailey, 1984. DL.

Wilkerson, DeWitt. Taped interview with Marie Davis and Megan Lambert, 1985. DL.

Williams, Mrs. A. Lee. Taped interview with Jim Ligon, 1988. DL.

Woods, Sadie Estes. Taped interview with Megan Lambert, Teena Killam, and Marie Davis, 1984. DL.

Woodward, Clyde J. Interview notes from interviews conducted with Robert S. Maxwell, 1957, 1960. SFA.

Index